AMERICAN LEAVES:

Familiar Notes of Thought and Life.

By SAMUEL OSGOOD

Essay Index Reprint Series

BOOKS FOR LIBRARIES PRESS
FREEPORT, NEW YORK

First Published 1866
Reprinted 1972

Library of Congress Cataloging in Publication Data

Osgood, Samuel, 1812-1880.
  American leaves.

  (Essay index reprint series)
  Reprint of the 1866 ed.
  1. U. S.--Social life and customs--19th century.
I. Title.
E166.O8 1972   917.3'03'5   72-374
ISBN 0-8369-2814-8

PRINTED IN THE UNITED STATES OF AMERICA
BY
NEW WORLD BOOK MANUFACTURING CO., INC.
HALLANDALE, FLORIDA 33009

Dedication:

THE AUTHOR DEDICATES THIS VOLUME TO THE PASTOR AND
FRIEND OF HIS YOUTH,

Rev. JAMES WALKER, D.D.,

LATE PRESIDENT OF HARVARD UNIVERSITY, WHO IN HIS
RETIREMENT ILLUSTRATES THE DIGNITY OF
THE SCHOLAR AND THE SAGE.

PREFACE.

THE papers that make up this volume were written at leisure hours, of late years, on the spur of various occasions and experiences, and, with a single exception, they have in substance appeared in *Harper's Monthly Magazine.* They of course differ widely in style and topic, and range freely into various fields of thought and observation, yet they agree in being in close sympathy with American life in treating the struggles, fears, hopes, and aspirations of our common lot. There is no attempt at the regular order of an ethical or philosophical treatise, yet there is something of interior unity in the volume, and attentive readers may perhaps own that there is more of the reality than the show of careful and consistent thinking.

Some thirteen years ago the Harper Brothers invited me to write for their Magazine, and I have done so more or less frequently since. If my humble experience is worth quoting, I will say honestly what has been the result of the effort. It seemed to me an awkward and difficult thing for a man perhaps over-scholastic in his thoughts and studies to write for the many in the most popular of American magazines, and I began with a good deal of diffidence. Now, after these years of occasional service, I can express my gratitude to the Monthly for two principal reasons—one of them expected, the other unexpected. I expected to have something of the stiffness of our too common clerical style taken out, and to learn an easier and happier diction, but I did not expect so much encouragement to the freest utterance of the most interior and sacred thoughts on the most important subjects. I have enjoyed this relation to a great circle of readers much, and have tried not to abuse their good will by crude or unworthy thinking, playful as at times may be the manner, and free and intimate the mention of personal friends and associations. It is to be hoped that the Monthly, that is a classic in American families and libraries on account of its admirable compend of current history, may not lose its hold by the liberal wish of its proprietors to add thoughtful essays from various pens to its exciting store of sketches and stories, and its instructive papers upon popular subjects.

This volume is published mainly at the request of friends, who ask for a home book that shall win the same kindly place in the family with that which was granted to previous publications in a similar vein of serious thought and kindly sympathy.

SAM'L OSGOOD.

NEW YORK, *December*, 1866.

CONTENTS.

	PAGE
Little Children	11
Our Old Pew	33
School Influences	55
American Boys	71
American Girls	93
Fortune	117
The Flag at Home	139
Learning Statesmanship	165
Off-hand Speaking	193
Art among the People	227
American Nerves	253
The Ethics of Love	281
Garden Philosophy	305
Easter Flowers	335
Toward Sunset	359

I.

Little Children.

AMERICAN LIFE.

LITTLE CHILDREN.

THE arrival of a baby in a family is a not very unusual occurrence; and without any very elaborate antiquarian investigation, we may safely believe that such events date back to the remotest ages, and are likely to continue for ages to come. Yet the coming of the little stranger is always a great circumstance; and once in our lifetime, however quiet may be our temperament or small our ambition, we make a sensation, and are the observed of all observers. The baby, who is usually awaited with anxiety, is welcomed with open arms; and in spite of the present formidable aspect of the bread question, and the frequent reason for calculating the proportion between the size of the bread-basket and the number of mouths waiting to be fed, the new claimnant contrives to find a home with a hospitality perhaps quite as cordial in lowly as in stately households. Immediately the new-comer begins to show that marked characteristic of every new age, the revolutionary spirit; and the first shrill cry that announces his advent heralds his assault upon all the settled habitudes of the family. Every thing must yield not so much to his whims as to his dependence, and the whole family, from the old grandfather — if such venerable head there be — down to the least pet of the nursery who has just graduated from babyhood, is enlisted by a resistless sympathy in the service of the little pensioner. The baby rules in the majesty of his weakness; and while other thrones are perhaps becoming a little shaky, this majesty keeps its seat and stands among the established institutions of our race.

We are writing perhaps somewhat pleasantly upon so grave a theme as childhood; but we trust that our cheery tone, like the laugh of childhood itself, will be found to win tenderness, as well as to express joy. We confess to being lovers of little children, not only in the abstract but in the concrete; and while well aware that the stern lessons of political economy may hint a certain limit of moderation in the philoprogenitive ambition, we know of no reasonable limit to the affection, and have no fears that good Jean Paul's creed will become too popular — that creed which all catechisms might admit, "I love God and little children." In fact, the affection that little children win from us interprets God's love to us. God loves us not because we can help Him, but because He helps us; and the best that he asks of us is that we should be willing to let Him help us by his providence and grace. He is glorified not by rising above Himself — for the All-mighty and All-perfect can not rise above Himself — but by his condescension; and the anthem "Glory to God in the highest," was heard on earth when the Eternal Being descended to our humanity and dwelt with the Holy Child at Bethlehem. As we in our poor way repeat that condescension, we have a nearer sense of God's love; and as we befriend those whose helplessness claims our care, we rise to new wisdom and new joy. We may not, indeed, entertain any such philosophy of loving-kindness, yet may none the less have its fruits; and undoubtedly the new peace that comes into a family with the little child's coming is proof that the hearts that reach down in such tenderness to that little one are not only opened by parental affections, but also by filial faith, and the soul, like the seed-corn, as it presses its roots into the earth, opens its leaves toward heaven to drink in the rain and the sunshine of God. Whatever may be the reason, God's blessing goes with babies, and we do not care to say what kind of a world this would be without their presence. The monk and nun share in the benediction, and if nowhere else, they find something to pet even in the hour of their devotion, and there is to them something human as well as divine in the holy mother and child over the altar. The priest is no priest of God unless he leads little children to the good Shepherd; and as to the celibates not under ghostly vows, the bachelors and maids among us, we can promise them little true peace unless they continue — as they generally do — to care for some brother or sister's children in the absence of any of their own.

We are the more ready to say our word for children because, in spite of the manifest tenderness of our American people toward their offspring, there are symptoms of a national conspiracy against childhood, and Herod is out-Heroded — not by any wholesale slaughter of innocents, for such an assassin would be torn into inch pieces by our mothers before he put his hand upon the second victim, but by the prevalent impatience of the slow march of nature, and the rage for crowding the early bud forward into premature flower and fruit. If many people could have their way there would cease to be any more little children, and the babies in long clothes would stride forth in pantaloons or petticoats to astonish beholders with precocious feats, as marvelous as the duties of the learned fleas, and quite as honorable to our humanity. We, of course, protest, as we have done before, against this whole forcing process in every stage of its development, and most of all in the early stage when the plant is so tender that fatal violence may be done to its delicate organism.

We say then, first of all, let us secure to our little children their proper naturalness, or their just place and development under that system of natural law to which in their physical constitution they belong. Their own mother's bosom should be the first guaranty of this natural right, and we are quite willing to be voted very stupid and old-fashioned in insisting that every mother should nurse her own child if she possibly can. We have no words to express our condemnation of the idea, becoming in quarters of somewhat equivocal fashion not uncommon, that the mother's natural office should be made over to some hireling, and that it is better to trust the hope of the family to some strange breast — perhaps to some half ogress with blood tainted with rum or what is worse — than break the mother's rest, or keep her from midnight routs, by care of her child. If a mother is stinted by nature in the fountains of aliment, she must submit to her privation and do the best in her power to supply her loss by other aid, but even then she ought not to think her care abated, but rather increased, by the transfer; and no wealth nor service can dismiss the mother's eye from its providential watch over her offspring. We believe in refinement, and are lovers of elegance; but we hold the refinement and elegance to be empty pretension that undertake to slight honest human instincts, and try to be wiser than God and nature. We are not, indeed, ambitious of playing the physiologist, and entering into the particulars of the nursery, diet, bathing, clothing, and exercise of children. It is clear that immense errors prevail in each of these respects; and the bills of mortality, that show so large a portion of our race to be cut off in infancy, prove that all the mistakes are not to be charged to the doctors, and that so costly and precious a product as human life is most lavishly and recklessly squandered. The old system of overdosing has been matched by the new system of overpetting or overtraining; and perhaps as many children have been destroyed by being daintily kept from the fresh air and free muscular activity as of old were destroyed by the laudanum bottle and its attendant abominations. We can not rejoice too much in the comparative emancipation of the nursery from the apothecary's shop, and are quite sure that the regular medical practice is not surrendering all the honors of this emancipation to the votaries of infinitesimals, but is disposed to give even less medicine to children than anxious parents often desire. Let this negative reform be carried out into a more positive policy, and all the blessed agencies of light, air, and water, and motion will win new honors in the field so long occupied by drugs, and often make grassy play-grounds a better herbarium than gardens of balm and poppies, saffron and senna and rhubarb.

We are well aware that the idea of entire naturalness may be carried so far as to be run into the ground; and some of our own champions of nature so glorify instinct at the expense of discipline as to remind us of what Voltaire said of some of the extravagances of poor Rousseau — they made him feel like getting down and going on all fours. Yet it will be found that they are poor students of Nature who find any follies in her teachings; and the freest physical development will be helped instead of being harmed by due regard to the superior moral and intellectual laws. Thus the proper check upon indolence and the sensual passions is found in the just development of the higher muscular and nervous faculties, and the child who is physically well educated is by this very fact raised above the merely animal life by being made physically as well as morally a truly human creature. That we too often miss the due method of physical discipline appears not only from the frequent sickness of children, but from the stiffness and want of ease that seem to possess them as soon as they come under our training hand, and to present them to the world as the only young creatures that are not free and graceful in their movements. We have made some improvements in the dress of boys and girls, that give nature fairer play; yet much remains to be done to complete the emancipation, by putting off all cramping encumbrances and allowing every limb and muscle full sweep. Instead of leaving the fashions of dress to a set of *modistes*, we would submit them to a council of artists and physicians, and so strike a brave blow at once for beauty and health in the nursery, with the hope that the offspring of God's noblest creature might not always surrender the palm of grace and freedom to kittens and lambs.

The question of the intellectual discipline of children is closely connected with their physical training, and many are the victims of the book and the school-room. The old method was to consider the school as a kind of prison-house for the scions of our perverse humanity, where learning was to be forced down reluctant throats by terror, in the absence of any intrinsic charms in the medicinal draught. The staple of study was in the main the work of the memory, and improvement was measured, like bricklaying, by the foot, the quantity laid being final proof of the work done. Rules of grammar and arithmetic that had no sort of lodgment in the juvenile understanding were laboriously committed to memory, and verses of Scripture and poetry were learned without stint. This old-fashioned system is exploded, to the infinite relief of millions of otherwise cramped muscles and aching heads. It will be well if the new system does not fall into another kind of narrowness by dismissing the memory from its rightful office, and forcing little children to be philosophers before their time. Childhood loves variety, and the alternation of activities that is so essential to the comfort and energy of us all is imperiously necessary to the development and even to the sanity of children. They soon weary of one thing, and judicious training will seek to study the laws of mental alternation so as to secure unity in variety, and by the interchange of exercises lead out the faculties in due order and force. Nothing is clearer than that little children are soon tired of one attitude of body, and a careful observer will note the same weariness of one attitude of the mind. The little fellow who has been sitting an hour aches to stand or walk or run; and so, too, when he has been receiving impressions from his book or teacher, he aches to change his mental attitude, and give expression to his feelings or ideas by some positive act. If we scrutinize this necessity of change, we shall find a remarkable illustration of it in the senses most essential to education, which are created as if it were in couples, as if to relieve guard with each other. The nerves of sensibility exchange labors with the nerves of motion, so that when we receive a sensation we long to make some corresponding muscular movement, and our condition is intolerable when our nerves are constantly excited and our muscles are kept in rest. The ear and the eye, each in its way, illustrate this law by alternating with their natural allies the voice and the hand. When we have listened, we long to speak; and when we have seen, we long to touch. So, on the other hand, when we have spoken we are ready to listen, and when we have touched we are the more ready to see. The same interchange of functions may be traced throughout all the faculties of the mind, and it will be a new day in the education both of young and old when the vast significance of this law is discerned, and by a wisely-adjusted alternation of exercises variety and unity of culture may be secured, and monotony and fickleness may be alike set aside. It will be then found that the just discipline of children is not the dull, unwholesome thing which it is often supposed to be, and that the work of the school-room may gain not a little life and force from the sports of the play-ground. We do not, indeed, propose to do away with all hard work in school; for if there were no hard work there could be none of the happy feeling of relief when it is done, and play would lose its zest if all the hours were pastime. What we ask is that study should be in accordance with and not against the nature of the mind, and so the terrible habit be shunned that makes study so false and spectral, and shuts the world of books out of the free air and bright sunshine of nature and of God. The very tones which children, even bright children, often fall into the moment they open a book tell the whole story; and the transition from the free, ringing voice of the play-ground to that formal drawl or whine, proves that the mistake of separating words from things has begun thus early, and the blight of pedantry has fallen upon these fresh and opening buds of our hope and joy.

We suppose that the root of most mistakes in the education of little children comes from overlooking the important distinction between the lessons that are to be put into them and the mental life that is to be brought out of them; or, in other words, from forgetting that the mind is not a sheet of blank paper to be written upon, but a leaf whose vital organism is to be developed. Children are thus not only to be taught, but they are to be animated; and the proof of their proficiency is not so much in what they *know* as in what they *are*. Sometimes the contrast between the child's own mind and his learning is most striking; and if frequently the lesson is in advance of the little student's thought, the thought is not seldom in advance of the lesson—as in the case of those startling questions and marvelous fancies with which the pets of the nursery sometimes confound the wiseacres of the parlor and library. Probably these questions and fancies take the child quite as much by surprise as they do the parent, and they come not from any theory or purpose, but from some spontaneous impulse, which shows that, in childhood as in maturity, the mind within us, God's generous and mysterious gift, is greater and more fruitful than our own will or calculation. Whether we think of it or not, a large part of the archness of little children which so delights us comes from this contrast between their mind and their acquirements. There is a charm in the lisp of their words, as in the stumbling of their steps, that presents to us in playful contrast their great aspirations and their small achievements. There is something in them very young, and something very old, and the jumble of bright intuitions and funny mistakes in their expressions reminds us of the odd figure which some urchin of the nursery cuts when he buries his head under his father's ponderous hat, or nestles in his grandfather's roomy arm-chair, with spectacles gravely mounted upon the minature nose. The old element in children comes from the rational principle which is not the creature of the schools but the gift of God; and it is the flashes from this true light that so often startle us with signs of intelligence in children quite as incongruous with their years as father's hat or grandfather's arm-chair.

It is important that this distinction should be carefully noted both in school education and at home; for ill fares the training that counts the mind as naught but a passive tablet, and the lesson as the only vital power. Even the faculty that holds the humblest place in the scale, and is usually thought to be the mere drudge or baggage-master of the intellect—the memory—is not a passive tablet, but a vital force, and holds no truth firmly without taking it as a truth to be assimilated with some measure of vital sense, instead of a dead tradition to be buried. A little child's memory is surely a living force, and any thoughtful observer who watches its spontaneous play, as it produces and reproduces its vivid impressions of scenes and characters in such marvelous round, will not wonder that the ancients called Mnemosyne the Mother of the Muses, since the fancies of the nursery, as well as the inventions of the drama and the epic, come from the mysterious power that receives all impressions of nature and life, and recombines or remembers them in such vivid and novel combinations. We who have children of our own know well that the degrading theory of the materialist as to the native powers of our children is far less reasonable than the poet's beautiful picture of the exuberance of these powers in their spontaneous play, and that the faculty of memory thus presented by Wordsworth deserves more respect, and claims more inspiration, than dull pedants believe:

> " Behold the child among his new-born blisses—
> A six years' darling of a pigmy size !
> See where, 'mid work of his own hand, he lies,
> Fretted by sallies of his mother's kisses,
> With light upon him from his father's eyes !
> See at his feet some little plan or chart,
> Some fragment from his dream of human life,
> Shaped by himself with newly learned art ;
> A wedding or a festival,
> A mourning or a funeral !
>
> " And this hath now his heart,
> And unto this he frames his song :
> Then will he fit his tongue
> To dialogues of business, love, or strife ;
> But it will not be long
> Ere this be thrown aside.
>
> And with new joy and pride
> The little actor cons another part,
> Filling from time to time his 'humorous stage'
> With all the persons down to palsied age
> That life brings with her in her equipage ;
> As if his whole vocation
> Were endless imitation."

Happy will it be for us when such true and cheerful

philosophy is carried out in our schools and households; and, while all wholesome instruction is given and firm discipline is applied, all care shall be used to quicken the intellectual faculties without cramming them with crude verbiage, and, to bring out the active will without breaking its buoyant spring under arbitary appliances. There is something in the free and healthful development of a child's mind that acts upon his whole future, and justifies us in applying to it one of the sacred words of religion, or in calling the child mentally regenerate who is thus newly and well born into the atmosphere of truth and resolution. Too many of us bear the marks of the cramping process from our childhood, as of an imperfect birth; and it is not only in crooked spines and round shoulders that we have reason to remember the twists and stoop that set their mark upon us in our tender years.

What we have said of physical and intellectual training applies with equal force to the heart, or to the whole range of our affections and desires. It is by the heart that little children mainly rule us, and by this that we should rule them. In fact it is impossible to separate their affections from their senses and thoughts, or to run through their mental processes any thing like the sharp line of demarcation which metaphysicians run between ideas and emotions. Even the bodily senses of a bright child are full of affection, and a red apple or a downy peach is grasped and devoured, not in gluttonous sensualism, but in rapturous enthusiasm, as if the palate were connected with the highest sensibilities, and a sweet taste, like a delicious fragrance, could waft the fancy into the land of the blessed. We profess to know children pretty well, and we have seen too much of the old Adam in their moods and freaks to allow us to call them angels; yet we do sacredly recognize in them a wealth of ready affection which it is treason against God and humanity to deny or to neglect. Their very weakness is ready to open into a precious grace if we will only guide it wisely, and the child's natural dependence soon rises into a filial faith. This trusting temper in them is a great comfort to us, by rewarding our protection, and when wisely guided it is a great blessing to them, by leading them to the true rock of reliance. There is something in the perfect trust in which a little child comes to our arms that opens all the springs of loving-kindness; and if the lion passions within us are ever near the golden age when they are to lie down with lamb-like gentleness, it is when a little child leads them. This ready confidence goes naturally with a spontaneous good-will, and nothing pleases the little one more than to be employed in some affectionate service, so that often the best cure for a freak of petulance is a call to some small mission of love. A bright boy of one of our friends took on bitterly and would not be comforted when he heard that his father was going to Europe, but immediately dried his tears when told by his father that he was expected to look after the family, and especially to look after mother's comfort. Although just out of his petticoats he was delighted with the idea of doing some thing, and so proved the wisdom of that philosophy which prescribes active kindness to others as the medicine for our own complaints.

LITTLE CHILDREN. 27

The young heart that so easily trusts and loves has quite as ready a spring of joy, and it is marvelous upon how small a capital unspoiled children can be happy. Too soon we allow them to unlearn this blessed alchemy, and, instead of turning all things into gold by the sunshine of their native glee, they are perversely led to wish to turn gold into all things by the dazzling glare and feverish heat of false fashions. Any one may see the two methods at a glance who will take an exact account of what a healthy child in the country needs to set him up in the full play of his joy, and compare it with the huge and never-ending inventory of novelties and dainties which are essential, we will not say to the happiness, but to the decent quiet of one of the pet specimens of our too artificial city manners. A half dollar will buy the marbles, top, and hoop that will insure the delight that is rarely won by the uncounted gold that is lavished on costly toys and trashy confectionary. It is well to keep this native fountain of joy open and flowing, for whether wealth or limitation be the lot of our children, they can have from us no better heritage than the habit of enjoying simple pleasures, and thriving on "human nature's daily food"—the common gifts of good Providence. A child in the family with this spirit is a well-spring of comfort that refreshes the whole house with living water; and the care-worn father, as he comes home from his business and takes such a little piece of blessedness to his heart, needs no metaphysics of optimism to make him believe that God is good, nor any brandy or billiard table to give his spirits a reaction from the yoke of labor.

How to secure a child's heart in its proper trust, affection and joy, is, of course, a great question, and we do not aim to have any new theory of moral and religious training. Of one thing, however, we are quite sure — the superiority of practical example over all speculative teaching. A child may have morality and religion, yet can not easily be a theoretical moralist or theologian, and must learn of God and humanity in the school of actual life and genuine experience. The true way to teach little children moral and spiritual realities is by presenting these as realities, and allowing the facts to precede and suggest the interpretation, just as, in the study of nature, the things go before the definitions, and the flowers and the stars are seen with the eye before botany and astronomy are read with the understanding. On this principle a true and genial home-life is better discipline for the child than any lectures on domestic economy, and a broad and earnest church-life is far better than bodies of divinity or libraries of ecclesiastical history. In this conviction thoughtful and practical persons of all religious creeds seem to be agreeing; and there is something quite emphatic and encouraging in the universality and warmth of the desire to open the fold of the Good Shepherd to the young lambs, and nurture children in the faith that the Christian Church is their true home, and they go from their own Providential mother in renouncing or slighting her watch and care. Nothing is more marked in the religious history of our own country than the growing disposition to secure to childhood its spiritual birthright, and to confirm a holy faith by the charms of early association, as well as by the light of timely instruction. If the strength of our national attachment to Christianity were to be put to the test, it would be found to have quite as strong a hold upon us by its little tendrils as its stout branches, and that many a strong will is fastened to the Rock of Ages by the loving faith of little children, those tendrils of the human vine.

We could write on to any length upon a topic so winning; but we must not indulge our own humor at the expense of the reader's patience, nor forget that little children are not in every home, and that time, that pushes them on toward maturity, as well as death, which so often cuts them down in their blossom, is calling them away. Yet they never do go away; and childhood, whether it ripens into manhood or is stricken by death, lives transfigured, not blighted, in every loving heart. This view of the subject should not be slighted; and it is important to have an eye upon the future influence of this spring time, when it becomes a cherished remembrance or may become a disheartening regret. We do not believe indeed in keeping such anxious watch for the future as to forget the present, nor in thinking so much of our way of living as to lose the zest of life itself. We can be happy, however, in our own or our children's early years without any premature care or precocious ingenuity. The method that best serves the present need best secures the future heritage, and the young life that opens most genially and healthfully under vernal skies and breezes has best hope of summer blooms and autumn fruits. It will be found that the most pleasing amusements, like spring buds, have a prospective utility, and the memory of a truly happy childhood is a treasure of manly strength and joy. It would be well if parents and kindred would bear in mind this charm of early association in their holiday gifts and festivities, and thus lay up for the little ones a store of enduring memorials and satisfactions, instead of wasting so much time and money upon flashy trifles that last but for a day or a month, and have no prospective worth or meaning. We need all such ministries to keep our own hearts fresh and young by the remembrance of our early days; that time, instead of being the sepulchre, may be the garden of our youth, where the seeds of our young joys may spring up and bear blossom and fruit an hundred fold; making us thus younger in feeling as we are older in years, and bidding us, in the words of the blessed Master, "enter the kingdom of heaven like a little child."

It is not wise to forget, moreover, that, if children are taken away, there is comfort in other and nearer memorials than the marble and the grassy mound of the cemetery; and our home associations should be sacred with their memory, not only by our frequent regrets and constant love, but by all the hallowed festivals and keepsakes that keep the absent one from being lost to us, and so secure to the family all its treasures. We need not draw upon any art of rhetoric to tell the grief of a true parent over the coffin of a little child, for it seems like the drying up of the very fountain of life in which age renews its youth, and the charm and freshness of childhood return to us in our hardness and care. Yesterday a smile from that little face took fifty years from our shoulders, and we were merry as the little smiler, and ready to live over with glee the most youthful antics as if they were the play of our own spirits. Now that face is changed, and the burden of years falls back upon us with added weight. Who will wonder at the parents' grief when it is remembered how wonderfully the little sleeper blended the powers of memory and hope, and at once revived the old days and cheered on the new. The torch thus extinguished leaves to darkness the field of remembrance and expectation, and no wonder that anguish at the bereavement sometimes verges upon despair. But good Providence brings the balm out of the ground watered with tears; and of all human sorrows none are so blessed and uplifting as that which draws parents upward toward the little ones whose angels do behold the face of our Father in heaven. Do the best that we can for them while they are with us, and whether they go or stay their blessing is still ours, and their trust, and affection, and joy are treasures evermore.

Play on, then, little friends, and be loving and true while you play. We work the more bravely at sight of your joy, and your work will be better if your play opens your hearts, and braces your limbs, and quickens your spirit for the trials and the joys to come. We were little boys ourselves once, and with all our grave lessons we mean to be old boys still.

II.

Our Old Pew.

OUR OLD PEW.

WE are quite well aware that there is nothing especially attractive to this fast and not very reverential generation in the title of this article; and while the merits of "The Old Arm-chair," and "The Old Oaken Bucket," "The Old Mill," "The Old School-house," and almost every ancient thing on earth, have been said or sung to not indifferent ears, so far as our observation goes, we are the first to say a word for the Old Pew. If our saying may turn out to be as much a sermon as a song, we hope to win a friendly ear from the large and growing class of our readers who cherish time-hallowed remembrances sacredly, and believe that home-life gains in geniality as well as in elevation by coming under wholesome church influence.

I have had it (here a while we use the first person) in mind for some time to write an essay upon the Church view of the Family, and my thoughts take the present shape from a visit to my native home and the old church of our childhood. I always go home in mid-summer, and it is pleasant to make a double use of the college holidays by taking the old homestead on the way to the Cambridge Commencement. I have just returned from that annual visit, and I found the workmen busy with dismantling the interior of our church, or "meeting-house," as the people there usually style their places of worship. I was glad to be in time to see the building before the work of destruction had gone far, and sit a moment in the old pew before its homely pine and mahogany were torn away to make room for more modern accommodations. The moment spoke for a whole lifetime, and recalled vividly the forty years that have passed since I first took my seat there, and looked up with childish reverence to the lofty ceiling and the solemn preacher. The ceiling does not, indeed, seem to me very lofty now, yet it lifts my thoughts higher than any vaulted cathedral; and the preacher, although he now wears the square cap of an academic president and rules over the oldest university in the land, is not as awful as he was then; and it was very pleasant as I sat, last week, at his table, and enjoyed his sparkling wit and sententious wisdom, to be assured that the familarity which abates awe need not bring contempt, and that true reverence may grow with friendly fellowship. I can honestly say that the best influence over my boyish days came from that pulpit; and although the preacher was a deep thinker, and I could not understand all of his sermons, there was something in every sermon that came home to me, and even when I could not understand the thought, I understood the manner, being perfectly convinced by the tone and gesture that he meant to do us good, and the spirit and the trust were with him. Like other men, I, of course have had my temptations, and I can truly say that, whenever enticed to venture upon any wrong course, no power has been stronger with me for the right than the remembrance of those wholesome counsels of our old minister, and that searching question, "How shall I look him in the face if I waste my time and opportunities and make a fool or reprobate of myself?" He is now no longer in that pulpit, except on some occasional visit, and the forty years that have gone over his head since I first saw him there have changed him from a somewhat fiery young polemic to a calm and almost judicial sage, yet no man has better kept the promise of his prime, and his ripe autumn fruit is the fitting harvest of his green and vigorous springtime. One thing it is very cheerful to note in him as the sear and yellow leaf comes on; he is merrier as well as wiser, and perhaps his genial temper is as good a moral now as was his close and vehement preaching forty years ago.

The aspect of the empty pews, as they waited the blow, of the hammer (not the auctioneer's), was not as cheering as that of the pulpit; for forty years make sad havoc in a congregation, and as memory called the roll of the old familiar faces no answer came, in many cases, except from the tombstones that record their names. Death had made especial ravages among the solid men who sat in the middle alley, or what in New England is called the "Broad Aisle." I used to look at them with wonder not unmixed with reverence, for they were mostly the rich men of the town whose stately houses stood in decided contrast with our simpler homes. They have passed away, and for the most part their wealth has gone with them, and strangers live in their houses and occupy their pews. An instructive essay might be written upon the lives and fortunes of some twenty of those solid men, and the lesson might throw some light upon the nature and permanence of our American prosperity. Other faces, however, than theirs dwell most pleasantly in my remembrance, and our old church had its notable persons who have made their mark upon the thought and business of our day. The navy officers worshiped usually with us, and many a weather-beaten head bowed down there in reverence that had braved the battle and the breeze in perils that have become part of our national history. There, too, for years, sat the noted orator and statesman of our vicinity, since more than ever a national name, probably the most regular worshiper in the whole congregation, present morning and afternoon, and at the usual services and communion, the most successful man of his time, yet always bearing the mark of care upon his brow, and apparently needing no grave warnings of the altar to convince him that no crown is without its cross, and he who wins fame and fortune can not have them without paying a high price. Edward Everett has died an honored patriot, and as an old neighbor, I was glad to say my humble word in New York in his memory. Other men sat there, too, who have won a good name of the public in literature, science, and the learned professions. I will confess, however, that there are some associations with the worshipers that impressed me quite as much as the view of captains and senators and their peers. The school-boy and collegian, as he sat in the family pew, joined none the less fervently in the worship from being aware that gentler eyes than his were turned toward the pulpit, although sometimes, perhaps, an occasional glance toward this or that fair school-mate might have mingled with the love that is divine some little alloy of earthly feeling. He remembers to this day two faces that strongly impressed his boyhood, and gave a tinge of romance to the old sanctuary. Not far in front of his pew sat a child, a little girl with a rivulet of brown ringlets falling down her shoulders, and as she grew in stature, she became, even before he made her acquaintance, a kind of fairy of the boy's day-dreams. Another lassie, of smaller stature and more merry laugh, and with a hand small and dimpled enough to win a sculptor's eye, sometimes entered into his Sunday thoughts and made it pleasanter to go to church. Those two children, the picturesque Laura and the statuesque Hebe, are matrons now, each with her due share of offspring. Was it a merciful Providence that their various attractions so kept the student oscillating between them as to save him from so falling in love as to spoil his studies, or from venturing upon some juvenile declaration that might have brought a disheartening refusal from grave parents, and made him a laughing-stock among the young people? These, perhaps, may seem to be frivolous associations with a sacred place; yet there is a spirit of chivalry natural to boyhood which readily connects womanly grace with religion, and does not prevent a romantic nature from saying the prayers heartily with a little lovely companionship in the sanctuary. Our Puritan churches are so barren in ornament, without a picture or inscription to vary their blank walls, that the human heart is compelled to be its own artist, and set up a Madonna or two of its own from pictured fancies if not upon glass or canvas.

After all these somewhat playful reminiscences, we confess that the old edifice abounds in serious suggestions; and before we surrendered the old pew to destruction, we were compelled to note a few thoughts upon the welfare of the family as connected with the church and its ministry. The first thought that forces itself upon us comes from the importance of duly considering the *individual characteristics* of the members of the family in religious education, and of not forgetting, in our wholesale methods of training the young, that each girl or boy is an original from the hand of God, and, as such, demands, in some respects, a peculiar nurture. The whole family, indeed, is fenced up within that boarded enclosure, as within the partitions of a sheep-pen, in a way that tends to hide all marked characteristics in a prosaic uniformity. Yet even the Sunday seat with the Sunday face in the gravest sanctuary does not wholly tone down to one dead level every salient point of character. The soberest members of the family, who are intent upon prayer and Bible and sermon with all their hearts and eyes, will, by their way of sitting or holding their head or book, or their cast of countenance, betray their idiosyncrasy; and the imperious shake of the solemn father's head, or the anxious glance of the careful mother's eye, will be, to a shrewd observer, a great revelation of character. Then the children, with their volatile spirits, can not fail to show what is in them, and any man who has a keen eye to human nature need not take his Shakspeare or Lord Bacon to church with him to open to him the secrets of the human breast and prove the force of nature over circumstances. A half dozen girls and boys are a compend of the world's history, and in the hints of pride or vanity, sensitiveness or resolution, quietude or restlessness, listlessness or anxiety, a sagacious looker-on may detect qualities that have made the earth's leading characters and their subjects or disciples.

We must confess that this fact of individuality of nature and experience is not sufficiently considered in our churches, and too often the whole congregation is preached to as if all were exactly alike, and were to be turned to religion upon a kind of turning-lathe very much after the same pattern. Not only in the tone and direction of the services, but in the very order of the services, there is too little regard to individual dispositions and faculties. As a general rule, we are convinced that young people are surfeited with mere preaching, and that the ear and understanding are tasked to an extent wholly out of proportion with the eye, the fancy, and the affections. Our churches run too much to sermons, and to prayers that are often but sermons aimed toward heaven. There is too little to see and feel — too little cheering music, social fellowship, and ritual symbol. We remember what a godsend it was to us in our boyhood when a baby was baptized, and the minister, after the singing of a hymn, came down from the pulpit, and, in the gaze of the great company who stood on tip-toe to be spectators as well as listeners, named the child, after the Divine commission, in a way that made us feel, better than we could then explain, that a little baby is a sacred and mysterious gift, and under that frail mantle of clay rests that royal humanity which the Father made, and the Son redeemed, and the Spirit sanctified. There was very little else in our church to vary the usual tenor of worship. Never a marriage, with its festive sanctity, nor a funeral, with its solemn shadow — never a Christmas wreath nor an Easter flower, to bring into the sanctuary some sacred sense of the rich fullness of human life and the wide range of God's providence. What poetry we had in connection with religion came to us in spite of the church, and even our noble minister, with all his gifts of wisdom, his iron logic and pointed moral and often eloquent appeal, seldom dealt in pathos or ideality, seldom presented church seasons in a way to attract young hearts. We needed some direct appeal from him to bring us to ourselves and to God. The old catechising in a manner filled the want, and a few words from his revered lips to each of us as we met in the church on Wednesday afternoons were treasured up for years, and are riches to us now. Yet there was generally little contact between the pastor and the children of the flock — little of that personal counsel which, in our Protestant faith, may have all the unction and point of the old confessional without its tyranny. Many a youth suffers sadly from not having his own religious difficulties fitly met, and his own religious sensibilities and powers brought out. He finds himself sternly questioned by his own reason, and strongly tempted by his own heart and the world. He finds himself unable to think and feel as others seem to do, and often is in danger of giving over his soul to despair as an utter reprobate, simply because he is made in a peculiar mould, and must take to religion, if at all, as to every thing else, in his own way, and not in another person's way. He is, perhaps, of a sober, ethical disposition like St. James, and wonders that he has not Peter's fiery zeal or Paul's impassioned faith. A true and timely word might set him right, and instead of vainly trying to make of him somebody else, it might help him be himself among the other children of God. There is no end to the illustrations of the principle in question, and a new day will come to our churches when it is duly remembered that in the same pew vast diversity of gifts exists, and we show reverence for the Creator by giving fair play and full nurture to every soul that He has called into being. Perhaps every thoughtful reader can remember cases of promising youths who have been allowed to drift loose from all serious convictions, if not from good morals, in the absence of such personal care for their welfare. Surely it is a somewhat startling thought, as we look upon the tenants of a church-pew, to reflect how many various dispositions are there represented, and what care is needed to give each nature its true development.

Study any family group, moreover, not only as made up of separate persons, but as forming one household. Generally, a looker-on may discern a family likeness in the whole company of children; and even the father and mother, without any unity of blood, assimilate somewhat in appearance by constant association. The intention of Providence evidently is that the family shall be one, not only by living under the same roof, but by breathing the same spirit and furthering the same plans of life. It is equally evident that mere blood is not enough to make them one, and many of the most terrible quarrels that stain history and convulse society have been between blood relations. Mere unity of blood may sometimes create discord; for where, for example, a certain high temper runs in the veins, the inmates of a household may be tempted to quarrel even because they are so much alike. But without such high tempers, and in a family with good average dispositions, there is sure to be sufficient variety of traits to excite uncomfortable feelings, if all are not induced to agree upon some principle of harmony above personal notions and caprices. Hence the blessing of a strong and wholesome religious influence over the household, and the need of enlarging and elevating home life by church devotion and fellowship. It is by no means easy for relatives, even for brothers and sisters, to agree when they wish to do so by mere good nature, much less by a descent etiquette that disguises chagrin, or by a compromise of manner that tolerates failings for the sake of having its own failings tolerated in turn. It is a great art to solder different metals together; and without the proper amalgam, the more they are brought together the more they clatter and chafe. The higher the materials to be united, the higher must be the element of union; and human souls can come together only in the atmosphere of love, that is the soul's true life and Heaven's best gift. Hence the blessing of a sound, hearty religion in drawing the family together; and the pew, whose door opens to welcome them from the household, should dismiss them to their homes all the warmer in domestic affection from being more fervent as children of God. It would be well, it seems to us, if preaching had an eye more to this end, and our clergy would remember that every Sunday, in the hundred or two families present in the pews, there must be not a few cases where the first principles of brotherly and filial and parental love need to be inculcated. Sometimes the tenderest appeals to home feeling touch the very natures that seem least open to gentle emotions; and we believe that generally, whenever the preacher says a cordial and unaffected word, especially for good mothers, the sternest looking men in the audience, with not a few of the more refractory boys, will be found inclining to the melting mood.

It may startle sentimental ears to be told that respectable families are not always by mere force of nature harmonious, and need the benefit of church and clergy to bring them into tune. But we are ready to go even further, and to maintain that the very families that have within themselves the largest elements of happiness are very apt to disagree unless they are harmonized by a spirit above their own self-wills. True harmony is the agreement of differences, and where the differences seem at first to be the greatest, as in a concert of various voices and instruments, the harmony may be the most complete. What a fearful din arises when first the drum and trumpet the flute and fife, the harp and horn lift up their miscellaneous voices; and the novice might well think that Bedlam had broke loose or Babel had come again. But listen again, and the performers no longer following a chance caprice follow the notes of the great master, and the full burst of harmony speaks the triumphant reconciliation of that host of differences, the very best passages in the whole piece harmonizing the most opposite instruments and perhaps making the silver flute keep friendly company with the brazen drum, or the quivering harp give grateful relief to the sonorous trumpet. Human characters are more various than metal or strings or reed, and require a finer touch and higher mastery to bring them into tune. We are not, of course, speaking now of positive quarrels in a family; for hard words imply low breeding, and rude blows degrade households below the level of those for whom we write. Yet there may be a whole world of discomfort without sinking into such degradation, and family jars may rob life of its best charm, even when they do not break the visible order of the family, or go beyond hard thoughts and moody tempers. The trouble may come from the over-sensitive who feel acutely every cold look or harsh word, or from the strong will that resents every restraint as an imposition; and often these two traits of character are found to organize a standing disagreement in a family, when delicate nerves on one side, and hot blood on the other, live in a state of chronic warfare, like the tearful rain and flashing lightning of a thunder-shower. We do not believe, indeed, that temperaments can be changed; but we do know that they can be regulated, and at the very point where disagreement most readily commences there the true harmony should begin; for just at that point the necessity of self-control and self-sacrifice most clearly appears, and when these set up their cross of self-consecration the crown of peace will not long be withheld. We suppose that the happiest couple need in some way to find out this secret for themselves and their chilren, and that no families have so deep and enduring enjoyment as those who learn in due season that human tempers and impulses are very mutable and erring, and must be brought under the influence of a superior authority and spirit. We believe that the simplest lessons of the Gospel, if heeded in due time, might prevent many a family quarrel; and that, instead of an angry divorce, a deeper harmony would unite many a sensitive wife and irritable husband, if the sense of infirmity or wrong had only brought humility before God's mercy-seat instead of multiplying scandal in the world's mischievous ear.

Generally the feminine part of the household is more under the influence of the pew than the masculine part, and is especially better for the influence, when true wisdom guides the pulpit and good sense goes with the sentiment of the ministrations. Sometimes this very subject divides the household, and the husband and wife differ decidedly as to the merits of the preacher or the worth of the sanctuary. Most frequently the skeptical element in the family is on the masculine side; and where actual skepticism does not exist, a certain reserve, or indifference, almost as much nullifies the influence of the Church. How to interest the men and boys is a great question of our time, and one which is answered in various ways, and most conspicuously by two classes of preachers — the sensation orators, who thin the theatre and caucus by their more inebriating appeals, and the rough-and-ready school of divines, who seem to carry the boxing-gloves and foils into the pulpit, and preach bodily exercise as well as godliness, and recommend a very literal style of knock-down arguments. These may do well in their place; and it takes all sorts of people to make up a church as a world. But, for ourselves, we have far more hope of interesting indifferent men, and even reclaiming refractory boys, by a consistent, calm, and resolute ministry, that urges a Divine authority with devout grace, and aims to nurture the people within God's kingdom in the atmosphere of love, and upon the living bread and waters of the Father's household, than by any sensation rhetoric or rough-and-ready pugnacity. The great question to be settled is, whether life is to be under a divine law or not; and if under a divine law, whether under the divine love also. Now, surely the ministry that mingles true dignity with sympathy and unction is most likely to secure this end, and urge an authority that is gracious and a grace that is authoritative. If a good share of solid sense and clear logic is united with such a ministry, all the better for its power over the masculine part of the family in bringing them to true reverence for sacred things, and into wholesome harmony with the generally devout temper of the women of the household.

There is a great deal of undeveloped talent in the family; and it is a startling question to ask on Sunday, as we look about upon the congregation, what would be the career of these girls and boys if their destinies were to chime exactly with their powers, and they were to become the most and the best that they can become? But talent is not by any means confined to the taste, intellect, or imagination, but embraces every capacity and faculty of usefulness and enjoyment, or of receiving and imparting good. How much more startling becomes the question when extended to all those varieties of sensibility and affection and conscience and thought and purpose in which life has its highest worth and peace! Every Sunday how various and many are the keys touched by the preacher's word, and what power has a true master in bringing out the true tones from that many-voiced humanity! Hence the need — which we urge as our final leading thought — the need of cherishing a true catholicity in church, and of thus making the family feel not only that they are individuals and also one household, but that they belong to a universal empire, a spiritual kingdom, and are to cherish its divine citizenship in the due use of their powers and capacities. They will be all the more a family by recognizing their true union with the universal family; just as each city is more a city by knowing its due relation to the State and nation. Without going into any ambitious discussions of the true breadth of human culture, and the value of a cosmopolitan spirit in society and the world, we are content now with maintaining that each household needs a personal sense of the place of each member under the Divine government to give to each character its just charm and power. The round of a single Sunday's service, more than any week-day's schooling or any ball-room's elegances, should teach a true humanity and test a true grace and dignity. In fact, what great aspect of History, Providence, or Human Life is there which is not, in some way, presented or suggested by the Scriptures, hymns, prayers, and meditations of a well-conducted season of worship? The good old Bible itself is a great text-book of humanity as well as of God, and gathers within its lids the thoughts and experiences not only of famous saints and sages but of nations and ages. It unites with the acts of worship and instruction to win the assembly to a sense of citizenship beyond that of any one cast or family, and to ennoble daily life by the dignity of a divine birthright. The household needs this influence; for when left to itself it tends to a narrow clannishness, or belittling familism, that impoverishes the home, by making it the all-in-all, as much as he impoverishes his estate who persists in shutting himself up within its bounds by walls that shut out the steps of men, and the range of mountain and river, and the light of heaven itself. The true influence, when fitly used, not only enlarges the views of the family, by due knowledge of the broad sweep of the Divine plans and the rich diversity of Providential characters, but it brings each mind to its true bearings by presenting the essential ideas and motives which every human soul must accept if it would be loyal to its birthright. Thus comes that sacred filial sense and purpose which give the true aim and power, and guide and strenghten all human relations by the master-spirit of a truly filial heart. The human father is a better father from looking to the Divine Parent; and the son is a better son by leaning upon that infinite love; and the friend and the brother can give a richer sympathy by exalting personal affection into a spiritual fellowship, and ennobling private feeling by universal charity. So great is the grace and power of such a high standard over the family that camps and courts imitate its loftiness, and in a certain way — imperfect, indeed — the tone of military honor and social gentility is always bearing witness of the claims of the higher worth over the lower interest, and measuring life more by the quality of its spirit than by the quantity of its goods. The highest quality attaches to the family that is most loyal to the highest good, or has the clearest sense and the bravest service of the divine kingdom. Every true home must have something of this quality; and the lowliest cottage need ask no honors from courts or camps, fame or fashion, when its sons and daughters know and serve the Supreme Power and the Eternal Love. That family may fill a humble seat in the visible church, but it is higher than any dome or spire that pierces the sky; for God's true children are as high as his own mercy-seat, and their Sunday faces, in their reverence and joy, show forth something of the glory and blessedness there enthroned.

It may seem to some that we are dealing in overstrained

phrases, and that we have mounted from the old pew to the pulpit, and caught a little of the cant and exaggeration sometimes found there. But we are, we trust, quite in a common-sense vein, and can say in all soberness that every man who can remember a single true Sunday's devotion in church will verify what has been said, and allow that, in our best hours there, we have a certain sense of belonging to the great spiritual family, and being cheered by the Universal Light and animated by the Universal Will. It is most touching and impressive to look upon the assembly where all feel this experience, and men and women of all callings, conditions, and culture are drawn together not only by the common reverence for the sanctuary shown in their common carefulness of garb and manner, but by the great and blessed conviction that they meet together in one Father, and hear His voice and feel his breath in the One Word and Spirit.

We have written in a somewhat old-fashioned strain, although by no means belonging to the class of croakers and fogies. We believe in the old Gospel as the best news, and hold to every good institution that dispenses its living waters. By this time we suppose that our old pew has been made into fire-wood, and thus returned some of the light and warmth which it has been receiving for forty years from the altar. We doubt not that the new and more graceful structure that is taking its place will, in due time, have a story of its own to tell, and we trust that it may have a better story-teller than we. What forty years to come will bring to pass in that or in any sanctuary no sober man will venture to predict; and nothing would better illustrate the mutability of human life and fortune than an exact picture of the old church, with its people, when first opened for worship, in 1818, and now when it is to be transformed. In many of those pews then sat young couples just beginning the world together, more than one fair wife bringing a bride's garment and hopes to the sanctuary. Those intervening years have brought with the new and able preacher new cares as well as new blessings to those seats, and the space between the young husband and wife has been occupied by new faces, with eyes brightening and opening with growing intelligence; and sometimes saddened by vacant spaces that speak of eyes that have been closed in death. How instructive and impressive would be a series of photographs of the family groups in any of those pews at intervals of every five or ten years, and showing the occupants in their various stages of life and culture! A keen eye must see in the boy of forty years ago the features and character of the man now fifty; yet the keenest eye must allow its inability to play the prophet of the next forty years, and turn with grateful heart from the old pew to the old pulpit and the old Bible, happy to be assured that we are in better hands than our own, and we are governed by One whose ways are not as our ways, and whose thoughts not as our thoughts.

Farewell, old Church! We can not forget your seats and walls without forgetting the best gifts that we have ever had from God and man.

III.

School Influences.

SCHOOL INFLUENCES.

WE have but begun to see the power of our public schools. Much as we are in the habit of glorifying them, even at the expense of household nurture and church life. We have looked upon them chiefly as sources of knowledge and have some times forgotten their power over manners and morals, associations and habits. I will not here enter into any discipline of the excellencies and defects of our American Public School system, but will be content to bear cheerful testimony to its vast and in the main, good influences. The school books of America are a noble fruit of the institutions of our age and undeniable proof of the hand of God in history; our thousands and tens of thousands of teachers are as estimable and effective a body of men and women as have ever given themselves to the task of popular education, and to them in no small measure we are to ascribe the flaming patriotism and loyal enthusiasm that has made of our school houses mighty fortresses, and trained the girls and boys of the nation in devotion to the life of the nation, and the birthright of the soul as the gift of God to us and our fathers, as well as to the new generations.

I have known our schools in all their phases, and seen their defects and virtues for over forty years, first as a school-boy, then as a committee man, and of late years as friend and visitor. Here in New York city, our professional men, especially our clergy, are not so closely connected with our schools, as is usual in New England. There the clergy are generally the leading members of the committees, whilst here political preferences are apt to decide the choice, and our school officers are drawn largely from the dominant class of politicians. The result is that some times the visiting officer knows less than the scholars he examines, and finds himself put down by the bright boys that he undertakes to question and correct. Perhaps more frequently the incompetent officials are more modest and entrust their charge to abler hands than their own, and generally invite men of culture to do the speaking. Generally, however, the exhibitions and receptions, which in many respects are most charming, lack the oversight of an experienced and sagacious head, and are defective in unity and point, and often long and wearisome in the extreme to the heated and crowded assembly.

In point of discipline, my impression is that our New York schools are excellent, and great good feeling cheers and elevates the deference of scholar to teacher. In some cases even the worship that tends to be formal becomes affectionate, gentle and even beautiful, and some of our teachers carry with them a really pastoral unction into their work. It is pleasant to see that so many of them stand the wear and tear of their calling so well, and live

SCHOOL INFLUENCES.

and thrive in every way in its round. I have known no more cheering occasion than the quarter century festival given in one of our girls' schools last year to one of our best and most experienced instructors, a lady whose worth as a friend and parishoner, I had known for years. It was a perfect ovation of music and flowers, congratulation and love. Handsome gifts were presented in behalf of her pupils of the whole twenty-five years, who were there in person from playful little school girls up to blooming matrons. God's blessing on her and her calling. If our rich parishoners had been as liberal as she and her sainted sister to appeals from the pulpit, our pastoral characters would have been at least tenfold increased. Instead of dwelling further upon our schools here, I will take the liberty to lay before our readers some hearty words that were said after ending a long term of years as a school committee man in New England, and on speaking for the first time at a festive assembly in the great and genial metropolis.

These remarks are published the less reluctantly as copies of them have been asked for and were not to be had, and they have some little historical interest that is not limited to the future of the sons of New England.

It was one of the facetious sayings of Sidney Smith, that if a man were about to review a book, he had better not read it, for fear of prejudicing his mind as to its merits, and because, moreover, a reviewer may write down many brilliant generalities that might be at once extinguished by the author's prosaic facts. Now, Mr. President, I am unfortunate that I cannot respond to your call from so favorable a point of view, for I have read the common schools of New England again and again. What can a plodding worker, who has been these twelve years a Yankee school committee man, say, in this brilliant assembly, from an experience so prosaic and upon a topic so familiar? I have been less than three months released from that long campaign of service among the young infantry of New England, and the words of your excellent sentiment seem to send me back to the committee room, or upon the old round of visitation from district to district.

Shall I quote from my reminisences of school administration? The whole evening would be quite as little adequate for the task as would your patience. How vividly those years come back now, with their remembrances of hundreds of teachers examined and found capable or incapable; of thousands of scholars at their lessons, visited now at a venture, as they happened to be in their every day dress and demeanor, and now, at the great exhibition, with their faces so bright, and their dress so nice; little boys, great boys, little girls, great girls, all looking like a garden bed of pleasant flowers after a June shower. I could tell you of the oceans of school books submitted to our sage inspection, all warranted to be the best ever written and promising to work all kinds of wonders, from the teaching a new way to unlock the mystery of A B C, to the condensing all physics or metaphysics, nay, to packing the whole cyclopedia of knowledge within two pretty covers. I could tell you of regular meetings of the committee for ordinary business, and extra meetings for extraordinary occasions; such occasions, for example, as presented by the inhabitants of some district, who have been so ignorant of the treatise of Malthus, on population, as to demand an enlargement of the school house, or by the complaints of some injured mother who declares that her son, who has a perfect disposition, has been whipped black and blue for nothing; or, again, the summons comes to us to consider what we shall do to supply the place of our best high school master, who has accepted a professorship in a western college, or to find successors to three of our most interesting school mistresses, who, (alas, most frequent cause of defection!) have decided to accept the degree of M. R. S., and transfer their gift of teaching to another sphere.

But, Mr. President, I will spare your patience and keep to myself the chronicles of those years of various, and, I may add, pleasant service — merely adding, that I know the schools of New England well, and that they are in all respects improving under the faithful labors of zealous friends, faithful teachers, and the guardianship of an elevated public opinion, which identifies their interest with the public honor, I will say a few words of more serious bearing.

Sir, from my soul, I honor the common school. I honor it in its humble origin, and in its majestic triumph. Do we look for its origin; look to the common sense of our fathers, and you find it at once. The common school, as we understand it — the school not maintained by charity, but established and supported by the people themselves, for the good of their own children — is the growth of the common sentiment of the Pilgrims in their peculiar position.

To one judging of the future with a superficial mind, it might have seemed as if, to the cavaliers of Virginia rather than to the puritans of Massachusetts, this palm of honor would have been given. As early as 1621, a free school was established in the Old Dominion, and priestly prerogative and chartered wealth presided over its beginning. But this plant struck no root into the soil. It was only an exotic, and soon languished away. It was not the growth of the colonists themselves, but a charity institution imported from abroad. The master and usher were endowed with one thousand acres of land and the privilege of five servants. Yet all was in vain. Not such was the case with the Puritan educational movement, whose first public expression seems to have been embodied in the vote of a Boston town meeting in 1635, to the effect that "our brother Philemon Pormont shall be entreated to become school master for the teaching and nurturing of youth among us." Soon the town vote became the colonial law of 1647; every fifty householders were to support a school for teaching and writing, whilst every hundred householders were to provide a master capable of preparing youth for college.

There is no mystery about this noble movement. It was the most obvious expression of the mind of the forefathers. They believed in the God of the Bible, and wished their children to learn his attributes and will from his own word. They had sacrificed every thing for civil and religious liberty, and were determined that their children should be able to understand their duties to the state. They were dependent upon their own labor, and were resolved that their children should be taught the best way to earn an honest living. So the school-house arose. Religion and liberty gave the rude edifice a consecration beyond that of pontiffs and pageants. Hard handed industry stood by and gave its blessing. New England with her stern face as of stone looked into the windows of the school-room, and followed with her gaze the groups of boys and girls to their humble homes. Translated into words, her expression was this: "Learn, children, learn to know and to do the right, learn to work well, and my hard face shall smile upon you as sweetly as the Blessed Mother of old smiled upon her child in his manger-cradle." Sons of New England, has not our mother fulfilled her promise? Has she not smiled upon all industry? Who will not say that her vernal villages and thriving towns are fairer to our eye than rich prairies that ask no toil, or tropical islands that know no winter's cold? Mighty this great stimulus necessity, this need of earning our bread. How it gives an appetite for knowledge and an aim to life! Nay, what is there in the world that will drive the nonsense out of a boy or man sooner than the being obliged to get his own living for himself? Marvellous the power that industry has found in the common school.

See this power in its actual results. Consider the

triumphs of the school. My eloquent friend has spoken of the triumph of our arms, and of the present commanding attitude of our nation before the world. I will not gainsay his strong words nor deny altogether, the need and the worth of our brave armies and navies. But, surely, theirs are not the best triumphs — theirs are not the mightiest weapons. The school-master and school-mistress command a stronger host than were ever led by the stout-hearted Taylor or the brave and unflinching Scott. The school-boy's satchel has better ammunition than the soldier's cartridge box. The glance of the school-girl's eye has more to do with the progress of civilization than the gleam of the bayonet, or the flash of the musket.

I am making no empty rhetorical flourish in celebrating the power of the common school. Who shall set a limit to its triumphs? Already it has gone to the extreme borders of our nation, and invaded regions that are to add new grandeur to our peaceful empire. The ring of the back-woodsman's axe is more than the sound of bugle and drum, the reveille of our advancing hosts, and the chimney of the distant school, wherever its smoke is seen, tells that the best of forts has been planted on our borders. The principle of popular education goes with the New Englander wherever he goes. It has doubled Cape Horn with him in his tempestuous voyage; it has climbed the Rocky Mountains with him in his perilous march; it has stood by his side as he has cast his vote as a legislator, in giving law to the New El Dorado of the west.

O sir, my Yankee blood was stirred within me, as I read

that constitution of California. Hear it, eulogists of the Pizarros — hear it, admirers of conquerers whose greed for gold makes them reckless of blood and mindful only of gain and lust. The cursed passion has not blinded the eyes of our people even amid the dangers and distractions of their unsettled home, to the worth of that which is better than silver or gold. Education is made a corner stone of the new state, and broad lands are secured for ever for its support. The day will be when new triumphs shall confirm and consolidate this peaceful agency — nay, when a cordon of these forts of knowledge shall connect Eastport with San Francisco, Wisconsin with Cape Sable.

But triumph is not measured by extension so much as by elevation. The school has elevated its standard as well as extended its domain. If the trumpet of the Archangel could recall the dead, and some particles of the dust that lie buried on old Copp's Hill, or in the Granary Burying Ground, could be re-animated with intelligence, and the spirit of Philemon Pormont, the famous Boston school-master of two centuries since, could look around upon us, there would be some things in his own line that would be well worth his inspection. I care not what place we choose for the supposed visit, whether it be the noble institutions of New York, or Providence, or Boston.

But to carry out the idea better, let it be his own Boston. Enter now this handsome building, a primary schoolhouse. Its architecture is something of an improvement on this model before us, (pointing to the red school-house in sugar upon the table,) as much care being taken to admit fresh air now, as was of old taken to keep out the rude winds of winter. Yet all honor be given to the old architecture of our fathers — honor beyond that rendered to any of the structures in which the Pugins or Barrys of our day servilely imitate and pretend to revive the edifices of an extinct age. The Puritans did their best for the school house; and following them, we ought to do ours. Go into the school, mark the cheerfulness and order of the scholars, the means of educating at once the senses and the intellect, the round of lessons, anon enlivened by music that makes the hours pass with a smile. Go through the various steps of the system. Visit the High School, and there hear Sherwin's boys solve problems in the higher mathematics in a manner that would have made the eyes of Oaks, the marvel of ancient provincial calculation, start out of his head with wonder at what the world has come to. Look into the Latin School, and hear Diswell and Gardner's scholars say their Latin and Greek in a way that would have made the man who was christened in that blanket, the learned and pious John Cotton, believe that Oxford and Cambridge had crossed the ocean, and learning was not indeed to be buried in the graves of our fathers.

There are some things, perhaps, at which Philemon would shake his head. He used to think that almost all of science was in two books — the Bible and the arithmetic: first the Bible, second the arithmetic. He might think that we had changed the order, put the arithmetic first, and made the rule of three more prominent than the golden rule in our system of education. How is it? Are we secularizing education, and giving our immediate temporal interests supremacy over spiritual things? I will not undertake to say that New England feels none of the prevalent disposition to worship the dollar, and to study out ways to its shrine. The old Puritan may have a stern account in the matter with his children, yet they are not, by any means, wholly unworthy their ancestry, and while to him they may look somewhat irreverently in view of his ghostly austerity, they have no apologies to make to any men of other sections of the country who accuse New England of being moved by a grovelling utilitarianism.

Our southern and western brothers sometimes say, that the Yankees are cold and calculating; without passion or enthusiasm, without poetry or romance; that for eloquence you must cross Mason and Dixon's line or the Alleghanies. Now, we do not believe a word of this stuff. New England has heart, great heart too. Her utility is the expression of noble ideas. Her uses embody manly energies and Christian sentiments. Her common expediencies tend towards the beautiful in taste, and the human in feeling. Behold her fair villages, her valleys and hills, telling at once of thrift and of thought. Look to her schools, colleges, her homes for the blind and mute, her retreats for the widow and the orphan, her churches. With her, utility in her best efforts is but the expression of her best faith, the application of the highest truth to practical life. Her spiritual teachers are practical, her practical leaders have not been unspiritual.

Think of Edwards, that dweller in the upper air of metaphysical divinity. If he reasoned of the affections and the will, it was to bring the truth of God to act directly on the lives of men. His mind, like the stately mountains, between which he lived and labored, lifted its summit to the clouds, and sent down into the fields and homes of men streams of living water. Think of Channing, so spiritual and so practical, writing of the workingman's culture, and of the Sunday school, as earnestly as of the glory of God and dignity of the soul which God has made. His mind was like the ocean on whose shore he was cradled, and whose waves sparkling in beauty and swelling in grandeur, bear goodly ships upon their bosom and roll the treasures of the world towards the peaceful marts of industry.

Our practical men are not unspiritual. Our great utilitarian, Franklin, penned, with his own hand, a manual of prayer to the God of nature, and the mind that drew lightning from the heavens, believed in a descending light far beyond the brightness of the electric spark. Bowditch, under his hand does not dull mathematical science beam with a divine radiance, and give the universe a more spiritual expression? Because of him the sailor guides his vessel more securely, and has sweeter visions of home, as with open book he watches the chart, and stars, and the compass. Nay, has he not shown the relation between exact science and the divine intellect? and does not cold calculas become even a ministry of faith, as he applies the law of numbers and figures to the heavens, and shows us that mathematics can note with the precision of musical notation, the harmony which the heavenly orbs follow in their rythmic and eternal marches? Sir, our Yankee utility is no foe of the ideal or the spiritual. It has been the handmaid of humanity and faith.

Such may it ever be; and when society wins better order, and the marvellous development of industrial art and material wealth shall be guided by a truer philosophy of accommodation, doubt not that, among the agencies in this more Christian civilization, the New England school house will do its part.

Mr. President, the hours trip on now with merry step. But you will not say that, in mentioning the name of a good man who has lately gone from the world, I am twining cypress with your festive myrtle. Nay, do I not rather add an amaranth to the chaplet that crowns our feast?

Twelve years ago, a great educational movement begun in Massachusetts, which has had vast influence throughout the whole union, and which has done wonders in raising up a noble band of teachers by means of normal schools. If I understand the case, three men were chief in this work — Edmund Dwight, Edward Everett, Horace Mann — neither of them more efficient than the first, the noble Boston merchant, who gave his wealth and heart to the cause. He has died within the year past. An enterprising merchant, his gains were large and his charity kept pace with their advance. A philanthropist, his benevolence was as unostentatious as it was unwearied. A Christian, he had much of the strict virtue of the old Puritan day, and all of the courtesy and refinement that give grace to the modern gentleman. This word of appreciation and gratitude I am moved to say now in memory of Edmund Dwight of Massachusetts.

IV.

American Boys.

AMERICAN BOYS.

PROBABLY in every age, since the time of poor Adam and Eve's trouble with their willful son, the world has been supposed to be near its end on account of the naughtiness of boys. We confess that, for ourselves, in moments of wrath at the impish perversity, or of sorrow at the precocious wickedness of noted specimens of American boyhood, we have sometimes been tempted to that supposition, and certainly we could not much wonder if Young America furnished more food for the Prophet's avenging bears than Young Israel supplied. Yet the world has continued to be and generation after generation has risen from petticoats to jackets and trowsers, and jackets and trowsers to coats and pantaloons, without any utter extinction of the line of masculine succession. That succession will probably be kept up in this hemisphere, and here, as of old, the folly of youth will in due time be subdued by the wisdom of age. All the more earnestly, because of our good hope for the ultimate welfare of our country, we are disposed to look carefully and seriously at the tendencies of our sons, desirous at once of discovering their peculiar temptations and advantages.

Our daughters are constitutionally more marked by sensibility, and our sons are more marked by willfulness. The conseqnence is that we are more anxious what will happen *to* our daughters, and what will happen *from* our sons — the daughter's sensitiveness exposing her to receive harm, and the son's willfulness exposing him to do harm. We are not wise to quarrel with Nature, and we must expect that boys will be more noisy and mischievous than girls; nay, we may count it a good sign of a lad's force of character if there is a good share of aggressive, fun-loving pluck in his composition. Well managed, his animal spirits will give him all the more manly loyalty, and, when true to the right cause, he will be all the more true because so much living sap has gone up into the fruit of his obedience. Yet what is more sad than force of will perverted to base uses, and the strength of manhood sunk into the service of base lusts or fiendish passions? What is more sad than the sight presented every day in our streets — the scores of precocious manikins with the worst vices of men written over features almost infantile in their mould — boys who are hardly old enough to be beyond their mothers' watch, now swaggering with all the airs of experienced bloods, and polluting the air of God's heaven with the vocabulary of hell? Where such monstrous excesses are not found, how frequent is the utter repudiation of the proper reverence to age and authority! How many a stripling among us seems to think it the very first proof of manly spirit to break the Divine law which gives the home its blessedness and the state its security, and to be proud to show that he is above all such obselete notions as giving honor to father or mother.

We shall be sorry to believe that American boys are worse than others; yet it is very clear to us that they are exposed to some temptations peculiar to themselves, and that the natural willfulness of boyhood is here much exaggerated by our social habits and institutions. The American boy partakes by nature, of course, of the temper of his English cousins, whose blood, in the main, he has in his veins; yet how different are the habits of the two parties! The English boy is encouraged, — nay, compelled — to remain a boy; and his place at home, at school, at play, and at church, is such as to foster the proper spirit of boyhood. He is made constantly to feel that he is under discipline; and when apparently most free from constraint, and let out to play, upon the play-ground he is still bound by the laws of the game, and there is something in the rough sport that at once gives wholesome vent to his exuberant spirit and subdues his dogged individuality into something like loyal allegiance. The American boy, on the other hand, is accustomed to hear all authority challenged, not only by reprobate outlaws but by speculative theorists; and very often, before the training of the nursery is complete or the lessons of the school are half mastered, he is either in fancy or in fact put upon some form of money-getting that tempts him, if it does not force him, to be his own master. He is not encouraged to be a boy either in play or in earnest. At school every trait of morbid precocity is hailed too often as proof of genius, and the wholesome mirth of the play-ground is sometimes proscribed as childish and useless. The more manly sports have been in many quarters neglected for exciting books and shows, and in some cases the novel and the theatre have carried the day over the good old cricket and foot-ball. The restless will, that ought to be calmed and consolidated into manly force by brave exercise, is allowed to wear and fret itself into a petulant willfulness; and thus the natural delicacy of the American constitution is exaggerated by a perverse training. The normal check for nervous sensitiveness is muscular exercise, and by an hour's stout motion in the open air the nerves calm their fever, and the healthful balance of life is restored. Our school-boys are too often strangers to this grand secret of nature, and many of those most overtasked with study try to balance the weariness of the desk by in-door excitements quite as exhausting. It would delight us to see a serious and determined movement sweep through the country in favor of the revival of the old-fashioned manly sports, and we anticipate more good from them than from any efforts in behalf of balls and theatres, with their suffocating atmosphere, glaring lights, and wasting excitement. We have sometimes been led into very grave apprehensions for the moral purity as well as the physical health of our boys, on account of the neglect of the robust sports that at once occupy the time and vent the animal spirits. The moment the constitution becomes nervous and excitable — a morbid sensitiveness taking the place of a wholesome muscular activity — there is a fearful exposure to prurient enticements, and monstrous abuses are, we fear, the frequent and fatal consequence. We are confident that early rising, cold water. and the brave old playgrounds are quite as much needed as more faithful schools and churches to better the future of our sons. For our own part, we like far better the natural rudeness of boyhood than an unnatural delicacy; and it offends us far less to see a youth a little rough in manners, with a slight tendency to use his fists too freely, than to see him over sedentary, with a paleness and excitability that may indicate overstudy and may tempt morbid indulgences. The best cure for boyish rudeness is to give due play to boyish strength, and the outdoor cure, under heaven's own air and sunshine, is more likely to rid the exuberant plant of its rank juices than any hothouse training. Our schools and colleges are ruled too much upon the hot-bed principle, and the pale faces in the halls and recitation-rooms are, to shrewd observers, signs of destroyers of health far less noble than the classic page or the midnight lamp. Few persons, we believe, study too much, but most scholars study unwisely; and with more of the right sort of play there would be more of the right sort of work, and far less of the vices that haunt languid muscles and overwrought nerves.

This tendency among our youth is much exaggerated by their too frequent habits of diet, especially by the use of tobacco. Personally we abominate the use of that weed in any shape, and it seems to us the filthiest of all habits for men to stuff their mouths, and stain their teeth, and swell their expectorations to the nausea of beholders with this yellow narcotic; and although a little of the aroma of a good cigar may not be offensive even to delicate nostrils, the whole atmosphere of a regular smoker is a nuisance, and his clothes are steeped in a fetid exhalation that, to sensitive olfactories, dismally announces his arrival before he enters the room. But for boy smokers and chewers we have no vestige of patience or toleration; and the sight beyond all others most ridiculous, were it not so painful, is that of a little juvenile, hardly old enough to go out without his mother, puffing huge volumes of smoke from a monstrous cigar, and, in his pale face and affected swagger, presenting in himself those two fearful traits of our Young America — the union of puny health with braggart insolence. We had a strong specimen of this union at an academic assembly in this city not long since, where the exercises were often rudely interrupted by a score or two of precocious striplings, who solaced themselves in the intervals of their stampedes by stimulating their courage with plugs of tobacco, in the absence of other stimulus. The worthy President rebuked them; and a sound flogging would have been no more than their due.

The first crisis in the career of our sons is probably at school, where they must run the gauntlet between two ranks of tempers — the pattern good boys, who slave themselves, mind and body, to the reigning spirit of emulation; and, on the other hand, the great company of idlers, whose truancy and mischief-making sometimes have a chivalrous fascination to young blood beyond the attractions of the more demure book-worms. He may consider himself a favored father whose son escapes the ordeal with health unbroken and principles intact, and who bids adieu to his school-days with good scholarship not purchased by feebleness of limb, and a good constitution, indebted for its robustness to better sport than robbing hen-roosts or giving bloody noses.

We need not enter into the private history of college life, or say what hosts of trials and temptations every collegian must conquer or subdue, for comparatively a small class of our youth enter college; and, moreover, it is the lot of the great multitude of our sons who are in stores and counting-rooms to be exposed to many of the same dangers as beset such students, so that it is best to say a word especially of those who are in training for business. The life of clerks and young salesmen in our cities is a curious and unwritten chapter of our American life, and few volumes would be more instructive than a catalogue of the hundred thousand youth in this city who are under some form of business training, and looking forward to a time of independence and competence. It would be sometimes pathetically and sometimes repulsively interesting to know how much compensation these young men receive for their labor or attendance, and how much money they spend yearly, and for what purposes. The account would vary from touching instances of self-sacrificing frugality to monstrous cases of prodigality, fraud, and dissipation. How poor boys live, and how rich boys live, it would be well for us to know — well for us also to see that poor boys, or so regarded, mysteriously spend sometimes more money than the sons of our merchant princes. It would be important to ascertain whether it is not true that, as a general rule, the young men of our cities are very exacting in their expenses, and if the cost of keeping a dashing youth in dress, amusements, etc., would not be amply sufficient to maintain an old-fashioned family in comfortable frugality. We have been told, on good authority, that our merchants object to take the sons of their own associates in gentility into their counting-rooms, on account of their self-indulgence and prodigality; and that something of the same preference for foreign service is appearing in merchandise which is already an established fact in our housekeeping. Some leading firms give the preference decidedly to English, French, or German assistants in their counting-houses, and are weary in trying to teach dainty young gentlemen the importance of learning how to take care of themselves, as a more important accomplishment than to drive a fast horse or parade the newest fashions of a coat or hat. The whole field of dissipation here opens upon us, and grave questions arise as to the obvious disposition to provide pleasures beyond the domestic circle, especially to separate young men from their fitting feminine associates, and gather them together by themselves in clubs, where man only rules, or else drive them to dens of infamy, where woman is seen only in her degradation. The whole subject of club-life, in its various forms, needs to be studied seriously, and we shall probably be startled at the vastness of the arrangements for keeping young men by themselves, too often to their disadvantage. Not only the establishments known as clubs, and some of which are wholly reputable, but many establishments not thus known, and bearing very innocent names, would swell the list. The engine-houses sometimes fan worse fires than those which their brave champions extinguish ; and we have heard of little coteries of youth in cities and villages hiring rooms (each coterie for its own uses) in order to have free access to the games and liquors that parental rule and feminine delicacy do not allow under the household roof. The examination of such errors would bring new blessings upon the Mercantile Library, and other like associations, that band young men together for their good, and call them from their homes for a season, only to send them back better sons, brothers, and lovers. We are in advance of our subject, we are aware, in these remarks, since we have been dealing more with the schooling and apprenticeship of our sons than with their direct business career.

At school however, and often long before the youth enters his teens, the second crisis of his career casts its ominous shadow before, and the American boy is called to think, perhaps to decide, upon the business he shall pursue. Here is a great and fearful question, and one that, in some respects, is becoming more embarrassing in the changes of fortune and the revolutions in social ideas. The old idea was that a boy should, if there were no reason for the contrary course, follow his father's calling, and be a farmer, mechanic, merchant, lawyer, or what not, according to the paternal precedent. But now the tendency is quite otherwise, and it is the general disposition of our young people to press *upward* (as they consider it) into the occupations that demand the least manual labor, and seem to offer the greatest prestige of what is called gentility. The consequence is, that farming and the mechanic arts have lost much of their old attractiveness to the sons of farmers and mechanics and the ranks of trade and the professions are overstocked with aspirants. The number of youth in our cities who are seeking some kind of employment that allows them to have a delicate hand, and wear kid gloves and polished boots is enormous, and furnishes a fearful number of recruits to the army of vice and crime. What the cause of the disinclination to the manual arts is, it is not always easy to say; and certainly, in the nature of things, there is far more demand for intellect, and far more exercise of manly power, in tilling the soil or building houses and ships, than in selling silks or calicoes behind the counter. It would be a great gain if ten thousand clerks could at once go into the fields and work-shops, where they are wanted, and leave their places to ten thousand young women, who have nothing to do but to make their poor fingers the hopeless rivals of the sewing machine, and to anticipate the uncertain time when some young man, not yet able to pay for his own board and clothes, shall venture upon the enterprise of taking a wife less thrifty than himself. It is partly from the false feminine notions of gentility that much of the rising aversion to manual labor springs, and much harm comes from the frequent preference of the dainty swain of the counter over the far abler worker at the plow or plane by sentimental maidens, who have studied out their ideas of the gentleman from trashy novels and not from the good old Bible and its noble standard of the gentle heart.

It would be very interesting and instructive if we could have a census of the boys who annually leave the public schools, with a full statement of their purposes for the future. It would be found, we think, far more illustrative of vain ambition than of republican industry and simplicity. It might appear that, with all our theoretic assertion of the dignity of labor, nowhere on earth are the sons of the laboring classes so desirous of escaping their father's lot as here, and nowhere are there so many aspirants for dainty gentility as here. Undoubtedly the changes that have lately taken place in the position of labor have had much to do with the tendency to overcrowd trade and the professions. Hosts of foreigners now throng our work-shops, and underbid natives in prices, and often scandalize them by profligacy. But the same inundation threatens many forms of trade. In many towns and cities the retail business is fast falling into the hands of foreigners, and the number of Irish and German grocers is becoming enormous, while many branches of dry-goods traffic are in the hands of Jews. We believe that any practical man who will compare the promise of trade now with its promise thirty or forty years ago, can give a picture as startling as true of the present trials of our young aspirants to fortune as compared to the trials of the old times. There is always, of course, an opening for sagacity and energy, but with the increase of facilities the difficulties of success have also increased; and the young American who starts in the race of fortune with the fond dream of a golden goal, finds himself between two sets of rivals, one of whom snatch after the small prizes and the other after the high prizes. He finds the retail business crowded with a host of foreigners, who can live on next to nothing and undersell fair competitors; and, on the other hand the strong-holds of wholesale traffic are held by mighty monopolists, who are as formidable from their marble and iron warehouses, to aspirants without friends or fortune, as the Malakoff, with its guns and soldiery, would be to a squad of assailants without guns or intrenchments to back them in their advance.

With the increase in the difficulties of doing a successful business there is no corresponding diminution in the demands of living — surely no corresponding increase in the social alleviations of ill success. Society is constantly becoming more exacting, and he is a bold man who dares to begin a moderate business with the habits of household simplicity that were thought fifty years ago not unworthy the family of a prosperous merchant and a distinguished lawyer. Here comes in a potent element in the welfare of our sons — the present condition of household life, and the standard of expectation among those who are to be their wives, if any wives they are to have. It is a very serious question whom our son shall marry, and it is a serious question to him even if he never marries at all; for, as our nature is constituted, a young man thinks too much of pleasing his female friends, and his standard of manly conduct and independent position is largely decided by the reigning feminine code of expectation. Now there are certainly very grave difficulties in reconciling the average promise of any moderate business with the average standard of household expenditure; and the question which Mr. Punch jocularly discusses, "Can a man marry on three hundred pounds a year?" is with many of our young men far from a joking matter. Many families, indeed, do live on less than three hundred pounds a year in America, and many must live on three hundred dollars a year, if they live at all. But the cases of frugal living most frequently adduced among people of comfortable homes are from country life where many articles that cost high in the city are regarded as costing no more than air and water, being treated almost as much like gifts of nature. Let a fair money price be set to the potatoes, corn, milk, eggs, apples, pork, etc., consumed by the plain farmer, and his outlay thus estimated rises into figures somewhat formidable. But take the most modest standard of city gentility as our guide, and Mr. Punch's three hundred pounds sink into insignificance. No man ought to pay more than one quarter of his income for rent; and what kind of a house will one quarter of fifteen hundred dollars procure in a city like ours? Nay, how hard it is to procure, for thrice three hundred dollars, a house with what are called the modern conveniences, and now a desirable house costs two thousand a year! Then there is the matter of servants; and the most moderate standard of gentility in our towns insists upon having at least one servant, while our city habits prescribe from two to five or six servants, the standard number being three in well-to-do families. We are willing to astonish the more luxurious portion of our readers by confessing at once that we write more for the common lot than for the favored few, and that the boys for whose future we are most solicitous are those who are in our public schools, and who represent the average condition of the American people. Of our millions of school-boys, thousands are destined to fame or fortune; but such is not the general lot, and not only the largest but the most important class can not be expected to rise above the necessity of frugal living, while in the outset the greater proportion of the few who rise to wealth are obliged to practice great frugality. We may consider it, then, the almost universal condition of our sons that they ought to begin life in a very modest way, and if they marry as early as the best wisdom and morality dictate they must at once put down their foot against the prevalent social ostentation. The first years of married life do much to decide the whole future of the family; and if a man finds himself committed to a style of expenditure beyond his means he is embarrassed, and enfeebled, and dispirited at the very time when he ought to be gaining courage, health, and means for the sober years that are coming. Here, surely, is a most vital point in the welfare of our sons — the need of such an adjustment of our household habits as to bring a reasonably early marriage within the mark of moderate expenditure. The boarding-house and the hotel are the too ready resort in this need; but while their frugality to the purse is more than doubtful, their waste of heart and mind is beyond all question, and our American life is often wounded to the vitals by the consequent breaking down of domestic quietude, privacy, and industry. The true antidote must be found in simpler and more republican methods of housekeeping, that shall secure due comfort and refinement without wreck of health and competence. Neat homes for small families are the very first want in our towns and cities; and with their rise we need the growth, especially on the part of our young women, more reasonable notions of social respectability. As society now is, our young women form their standard of expectation upon exceptional cases; and even if they do not expect to have decidedly rich husbands, they are not content to look forward to the moderate income that most kinds of regular industry bring. A little plain figuring might, perhaps, be of great use to the thousands of tapered-fingered, narrow-chested, lily-cheeked girls who have selected their husbands from the pages of trashy novels, and resigned — at least, in their dreams — their maiden liberty to some dashing Alphonso for a villa, a carriage, and all the attendant elegances.

Perhaps those who are themselves penniless are sometimes most exacting of fortune, and least disposed to prolong the hard livelihood which they by experience know too well. Plain figures from the arithmetic might be more suggestive than the tropes of romance. The simplest statements of the average yield of industrious labor and enterprise would astonish many of our ambitious republican maidens, and their often more ambitious mammas, more than the trumpet of judgment, and it would be seen that the standard of dependence is generally based upon exceptional luck, and not upon regular industry. Begin with the returns of common labor, which gives the unit from which calculation should start. A hard-working man, not master of a regular trade, is highly favored, either in city or country, if he earns, on an average of working days, a dollar a day, in gold, or three hundred dollars a year; while an accomplished mechanic, not master of a shop, is favored if he gains a dollar a day more, or four hundred and fifty dollars a year, throughout all times and all weather. A capable clerk can not expect during his first years of service much more; and probably an offer of five hundred dollars salary would bring at this time more candidates for a tolerable clerkship, demanding considerable gifts of address and penmanship, than the advertiser could examine in a week. The smaller kinds of retail business yield very scanty incomes — and these, too, are very precarious, especially in the dry-goods trade; so that while they tempt showy tastes they impose very close limitations of expense. The professions that require scholastic education offer a few pecuniary prizes, but present a very low average reward. A good teacher is highly favored who is sure of Mr. Punch's three hundred pounds a year, or fifteen hundred dollars in gold; and in the country towns half that sum is often eagerly welcomed. Lawyers and doctors do not generally at first earn their bread and rent, and must trust to some collateral resources from parents or wives, or teaching or writing, to keep soul and body together. Our clergy in the country towns do not average in gold six hundred dollars a year; and the few who, in cities, have salaries of four, five, or even six thousand dollars, in gold, are burdened by a rate of conventional expenditure that keeps them often without a dollar of surplus. Leaving out of account a very few lawyers, and still fewer physicians, the only class of men who can expect large incomes from their business are successful merchants; and it is to them that we may justly ascribe the origin of the prevalent standard of social ostentation. Our successful merchants are our millionaires, or else those who expend the income of millions of dollars without any corresponding capital. The latter, probably, have done more than any other class to corrupt our republican principles, and our most frequent and dangerous prodigality may be ascribed to the great number of merchants who are doing a large business mainly on credit, and who regulate their expenses upon the standard of their most lucrative years. They do not not mean to be extravagant or dishonest — for we regard our merchants as generally quite honorable in their purposes — but they are too often under a fatal hallucination by mistaking the exception for the rule, and learning their sad error in the fatal years of revulsion and shipwreck. The great majority of businesses can claim but very moderate gains in the average balances of a twenty years' operation; and he may be set down as a very fortunate man, in any ordinary business, who for twenty years supports his family modestly, educates his children well, pays his debts, and lays up a thousand dollars yearly. Such a moderate accumulation may, to many, seem contemptible, but there are thousands who have called it contemptible who would think themselves vastly favored now if they could pay their debts and call a single thousand dollars their own.

The sober truth is that we are wrong in our whole standard

of social expectation, and that we ought to open our eyes to the simple facts, and train our sons to adjust their methods by the rule and not by the exception. We are well aware that young blood does not relish restraint, and that it is far harder to stop a fast youth from running the wrong way than it is to push him forward in the right way. It is precisely for this very reason that we hope for a better day for our Young America, whether it walks in petticoats or pantaloons. We do not believe much in mere negations, and young people are not much bettered by being scolded and kept down. The way to improve them is to carry a war into the enemy's country, and enlist the warmth of young blood in the bold and aggressive affirmation of the true republican principles in their sober sense, honest frugality, stout industry, and manly independence. We hope to see the true Young America rising from our schools, homes and churches, and supplanting the hideous carricatures that now so often pass for the real likeness. We hope to see hosts of young men among us who are more proud of frugal habits sustained by honest and intelligent labor, than of prodigality pampered by gambling, adventure or enslaving debt. We hope to see hosts of young women who are more eager to be wives of worthy young fellows whom they can love and help on in the world by good economy and womanly affectionateness than to sell themselves to churlishness or decrepitude, and sacrifice heart and soul to luxury and pretension. The education that shall train such young men and young women will be quite startling to our regiments of street and parlor gentry who pride themselves on their elegance and uselessness; but it will be found in the end that the best refinement, as well as the best sense, is with the new movement, and true taste will rise as vulgar ostentation and laziness fall. We look anxiously for the coming of this better time — and its coming will inaugerate a new day for our sons, by giving them the true motive for their work and the true companionship for their household. Our America has many questions to settle, but none is more important than this: When shall our sons seek the true honor in the best usefulness, and when shall the power of woman help them in the seeking? We might choose many samples of American skill and enterprise to prove our progress in civilization, but the best proof must be the best specimen of our standard American life. The fastest ship, the best reaping-machine, the most perfect photograph, the most deadly revolver, or the most voluble Congressman, would be poor trifles to send to some great World's Fair compared with the model republican home in which a worthy youth and maiden from our public schools have mated hearts and hands, and found all the substantial blessings of life, with Heaven's smile, in the reward of patient and honorable industry, whether more or less than three hundred pounds a year.

V.

American Girls.

AMERICAN GIRLS.

OUR daughters — what is to be their lot in life? This is a question that thousands of parents are now asking with peculiar solicitude. In one respect we are far more anxious for them than for our sons; for, while our sons are likely to be so tempted by their passions and position as to be guilty of misconduct, our daughters, from their sensitiveness and dependence, are more exposed to misfortune. Our misgivings as to the future of our sons is mainly on account of what they may be tempted to do, while our misgivings as to the future of our daughters is mainly on account of what may happen to them. By nature and association a girl is, in respectable society, far more effectually guarded from immorality than a boy, yet by no means more effectually guarded from suffering. Her delicate organization, that feels so much more quickly the play of heat and cold, feels quite as quickly the smiles and frowns, the warmth and chills, in the social sphere. A woman, as such, is more in the passive tone than man, and however gifted may be her intellect, she rather waits on fortune than commands it. The great event in her social lot is a type of her whole destiny. In marriage she is the party to be sought, and loses her prestige the moment she seems to be the party seeking. In the Court of Fortune, too, her position is much the same, and they are few, and by no means the most winning of their sex, who can lay aside the usual feminine delicacy and reserve, and march with bold stride up the heights of fame and fortune, without allowing the sweeping petticoat to interfere with the freedom of their step. We may lament that it is so, and that so many noble women wait, and wait apparently in vain, for a lot worthy of their mind and heart; yet so it has been, and so it is likely to be until some signal changes are made in our social order. There is a great deal of permanent truth in what Martin Luther said to his wife Catharine when she was weeping convulsively over the body of their dear daughter: "Do not take on so, dear wife; remember that this is a very hard world for girls, and say, 'God's will be done.'" For girls who have their own way to make this is a hard world in the most obvious sense, for it is far from easy for them to win a proper living. For girls, too, whose way is made for them by the wealth and care of parents, this is not always an easy world, for the heart may be more exacting as means more abound, and the affections may be starved or tortured in a home overflowing with luxuries.

In our American life the natural dependence of woman upon circumstances is increased by a variety of causes. Here woman has a peculiar delicacy of physical constitution that makes her especially sensitive to external influences, even when in tolerable health, and renders it very difficult for her to keep herself in full health. Whether it is the climate, or our way of living, or whatever may be the cause, the fact is certain that the American girl is a very delicate plant; beautiful, indeed, in comparison with others; more exquisitely organized than the English and German girl, and more self-relying than the Italian or French, yet not generally strong in nerve and muscle, and too ready to fade before her true mid-summer has come. The statistics given us by such alarmists as Miss Catharine Beecher, in her memorable and important book on the health of American women, may be too partial in their character, and deal too exclusively with the dark side of the subject, yet the facts stated can not be questioned, and if there be a brighter side the dark side must still be recognized. We have heard persons who might be expected to know what they say, declare that they can hardly name a single instance of perfect health among the young women of their acquaintance, and the physicians whom we hear speaking of the subject not seldom lose their patience in setting forth the miseries of feminine invalidism, with its shattered nerves and morbid circulations. If half of what is said is true, it is one half too much; and if our mothers had not been better gifted with maternal faculties than the candidates now ready for the bridal ring, the present number of the native American population could be accounted for only by miracle, not by natural descent. If the ill were confined to the over-luxurious and the affluent, the marvel would be less; but the truth is, that

E

the daughters of the farmer and the mechanic, who are not exposed to such excesses of indulgence, are not exempt from the same lot; and perhaps the most melancholy portion of the statistics of female health in America is furnished by the medical annals of some of our country towns. It may be, and probably is the case, that in such towns the laws of diet, dress, air, and exercise are more ignored and neglected than in families of tolerable intelligence in the city; and we are quite certain that sometimes the daughters of hard-working farmers eat, dress, sleep, and idle in a way very rare even among city fashionists.

In affluent families in the city the cookery is usually tolerable, and hot cakes green with saleratus, and pastry heavy as lead, are monstrosities never seen, while the sleep-rooms are ample and well-ventilated, wholly unlike the stinted bed-rooms in which some country people shut themselves up, and even in the heat of summer persist in shutting down the windows, from fear of the damp or the pestilence in the night-air. We believe that, on the whole, our city people take as much exercise — certainly as much out-door exercise — as is habitual with a large class of country girls. We have known a farmer's daughter look upon a walk of a mile to church as an intolerable grievance, and we have been amazed to find the idea current in some country families that walking is hardly a desirable process, and that a stroll through the pleasant green lanes to as great a distance as a city belle often condescends to sweep with her dainty crinoline in Broadway or the Avenue, is a thing not to be thought of. Such cases may be exceptions, yet it is strange that they exist at all, and we must regard it as one of the causes of the ill-health of American girls in the medium ranks of society that notions of inactivity and unnatural living that are wholly exploded in the most favored quarters, still keep their foothold in more lowly homes, and perhaps are cherished as proofs of superior gentility. On the whole, it may be true that the country is quite on the level with the city in its exposure of the health of daughters, and that quite as much mischief is done by neglect of the common laws of diet, air, and exercise in the farm-house as is done by the late hours and exciting pleasures of city mansions. Better ideas are indeed making progress, yet far too tardily, and in many cases the jewel of health is lost before the secret of its preservation is found. For our own part, we could rejoice in the rise of a new order of missionaries, whose mission it should be to preach the law and gospel of health, as a part of the doctrine of salvation by the water of baptism and the bread of life. The water and the bread that signify spiritual purification and nurture have also their physical significance, and the time may be near for bringing health of soul and body into nearer than the usual connection. Certainly, if the two are ever so near as to be identical, it is in the education of those who are to be mothers, and whose health or sickness may be the blessing or bane to the mind and body of their offspring.

Very likely the climate of America gives to our women something of the delicacy to their constitution, yet our habits of living and our stimulating social system contribute quite as much toward the result. Our social system, in one respect, is more stimulating to the nerves of women than the social systems of the Old World with its hereditary rank and fixed conventions. Here all the paths of fame and fortune are nominally open to all aspirants, and our young people, in most communities, are brought up in schools and churches where a feeling of social equality prevails. Our sons begin life quite ready to contest the highest rewards of business and politics with their richer school-fellows, and our daughters have very nearly the same tastes and expectations, whatever may be the differences of rank or fortune. The boy is trained to rough it in the fight, and if he can not reach his first aim, he persists till he finds some work or place worth possessing. But the girl, far more sensitive, with tastes more exacting and gifts less obtrusive, is left far more at the mercy of circumstance, and may find herself at once set wholly apart from the society of the schoolmate who was next her in the class, perhaps her confidante in play-hours without being her equal in study. A limited purse, an uncongenial home, objectionable relatives, or one of a thousand causes may separate the sensitive and aspiring school-girl from her cherished associates, and may make her whole life seem a disappointment because it falls below the standard of girlish aspiration. So true is it that our American society gives to most of our well-educated girls the same ideal of what is desirable, and makes them very sensitive to the charms of that ideal without by any means equalizing proportionately the means of attaining the mark. Very soon that arbiter of social distinction that is nowhere more powerful than here — wealth with its heraldry of dress — begins to show its sceptre and proclaim its sway, and the girls who before played together merrily in the plain gowns of the school-room, find themselves parted widely asunder by the costumes of the drawing-room; and pretty Fanny, in her muslin and ribbon, may seem even to herself a creature of coarser mould than stately Georgiana with her brocade and diamonds. We may call this sensitiveness to externals in the young women of America ludicrous or contemptible, yet it is a great and melancholy fact — a fact to be estimated not only by the tears and heart-burnings which it causes, but by the petulant tempers, the pretentious and unjustifiable extravagance, the ill-assorted marriages, which are the not infrequent result. There are probably few parents in moderate circumstances in our cities and towns who are not troubled by the painful dependence of their daughters upon externals, and the mortifying comparisons which are apt to be instituted by the prevalent scale of external distinctions. In our cities, the differences that are very soon instituted between girls who were equals at school by differences of dress and style of living may seem to be more conspicuous, yet it must be remembered that in cities the schools themselves in a measure forestall the more extreme comparisons, by bringing together into the more costly seminaries scholars of a certain average amount of privilege, while in the large towns or secondary cities it is no unusual thing for all the young people to be brought together as companions in the same schools, and we know high schools in which (we are glad that it is so) the daughters of the blacksmith and drayman sit side by side with the daughters of the judge and the banker. Now, this republicanism in education stands in marvelous contrast with the non-republicanism of society; and the contrast is becoming greater, instead of less, by the growing expensiveness of social habits. They who were equals and perhaps fond companions at school, find that mutual embarrassments spring from continuing the intimacy, and that each is becoming more marked by style of dress or entertaining than by intellectual endowments. The blacksmith's daughter tasks her father's purse too much by arraying herself in attire fitting for the banker's party or ball, and even the successful professional man finds it difficult to keep his daughters on tolerably equal terms in society with his richer neighbors. Brilliant gifts, of talent or beauty, may, indeed, set at naught more superficial distinctions; but these are very rare, and with young women of average endowments it must be allowed that the rising ostentation is having more and more power, and working against the equalizing tendency of American education. The simple cost of dressing moderately within the requirements of what is called good society in our cities and large towns, is a very formidable item in the calculation of families of moderate means, and to a young woman of refined tastes, who is dependent upon her own exertion for support, the sum is often quite disheartening. A girl of superior gifts and education may, indeed, by teaching, maintain herself handsomely, and even assist her infirm relatives; but the usual compensation of a teacher is generally a meagre support; for what will two or three or four hundred dollars a year even in gold do toward boarding and clothing a person of delicate tastes and fastidious associations? When a young woman depends upon more arduous and less lucrative labors, such as those of the needle, she must burn the lamp of sacrifice as well as toil, and not only abandon her time but also her cherished love of ornament to the inexorable necessity. Certainly the great tragedy of American life is writing itself now in the fortunes of the hosts of women dependent upon precarious means of support. In one respect the tragedy is sometimes deeper with the young than the mature, for to the young it brings greater temptation to couple shame with sorrow, and sacrifice virtue for bread and costume. We know very well how powerful a safeguard the American girl has in her pure instincts and Christian breeding; yet the safeguard is not always effectual, and the streets of our city too often bring to light the shame that has been hiding itself in our quiet towns and rural villages. Not sensuality, we believe, but the desire, so universal in America, of appearing well dressed, causes the downfall of the greater number of American girls who lapse from purity. Fearful stories have come to our ears of cases quite near to the rightful sympathies of Christian people, and they that study the subject most thoroughly are very sure to mingle pity with their condemnation. To most parents, the mere supposition of a daughter's disgrace is an utter monstrosity not to be thought of for a moment. May it always continue to be so considered! and that it may be so, the causes that sometimes tempt innocence to shame must be studied and guarded against.

In our solicitude for the lot of American daughters, we confess that we think more anxiously of the general average than of exceptional cases, whether above or below the average. We think more frequently of the girls in our public schools, who are to share the common welfare and decide the general character of the nation, than of the few rich who are petted in our palaces, or the few poor who are left to starve in our streets. Our standard American woman ought to be a fair representative of the common lot and we look for her in the pleasant array of intelligent faces that cheer the visitor at our public school examinations, from year to year. Go into one of our best schools on such a day, and meditate upon the probable destiny of that great company. Listen to the recitation of that first class of some fifty girls, and try in their faces to read the horoscope of their destiny. At first sight they may seem almost as much alike as if all of one circle of relatives, yet a closer scrutiny reveals the widest differences of fortune, position, and even of nationality. Of most of them, however, we may predicate one fact — the fact that they are, in the main, to depend upon themselves, and meet the trials incident to American society with a temperament peculiarly ambitious and sensitive. Most of them have been educated by some sacrifice on the part of their parents, and will have no dowry except a good education, and a little help in setting up their household gods, whenever they have a household of their own. Most of them are evidently not robust, and even their prettiness is purchased by fragility of frame, and in too many of them the paleness or the delicate bloom of the cheek, and the fine lines of the lip and the nostrils, are offset by a stoop of the shoulders, and a narrowness of the chest. We are not disposed to croak over their future, but we can not promise them, on the whole, a very easy lot, whether they marry or remain single. Some high prizes are to be distributed among them in the lottery of life, but the blanks are to be more numerous unless a high purpose shall elevate to its own level a mediocre or a lowly lot. They may be spared the ills that haunt the more ambitious heads of the procession from the fashionable boarding-school that marches by them in their promenade, yet they will not escape all the evils of social ostentation — and some of them, perhaps, may chase the gilded toy more eagerly because they see it only in the enchantment of distance. Ten or fifteen years will make marvelous revelations to those fifty maidens, and will call not a few of them away from the world. Those of the company whose lot is most to be cherished as an example are those of them who bless some honest man's home as wife and mother, and adorn and enlarge with a true woman's grace the moderate share of wordly good bestowed. Two or three of them may be called to preside over splendid mansions, with husbands of large wealth, more probably acquired than inherited; and at least quite as many will lure perplexed husbands into reckless extravagance, and sacrifice the household to the frequent American folly of trying to seem what we are not, and destroying the reality of peace to keep up the appearance of pride.

A considerable number of the fifty will never marry—

for it is evident that the proportion of marriages does not increase among the educated class in America, especially among those who are trained to study actions in their consequences, and to temper impulse by discretion; and the moment the mercantile habit of counting the cost prevails, the list of marriages signally falls. In the year 1850 the number of marriages in the United States, according to the census, was 197,029, while the number of deaths was 324,394 including 52,504 slaves. In England and Wales, the year before, the number of marriages was 141,599, and the number of deaths was 219,052 — the ratio of marriages to deaths there being somewhat greater than with us. Part of the high ratio in Great Britain is to be accounted for by the improvidence of the poor, who marry as readily as animals mate, without reckoning consequences, and part of it may be more hopefully accounted for by the less exacting standard of common life there, and the willingness of people in moderate circumstances to live according to their means, as their fathers and mothers did before them. Our observation in this country — which has been pretty wide and various — leads us to believe that, in proportion to the male population, a larger number of marriages takes place in country towns, where farm life makes a wife an economy as well as a comfort, and in manufacturing places, where young people of simple habits and quick sensibilities are brought much into each other's company. Our impression is, that in American cities the ratio of marriage in proportion to the male population, is on the decrease; a fact which we ascribe in part to the increase of the expenses of living incident to the inflation, not only of the prices of provisions, but of the demands of social ambition; and in part to the growth of European habits among us, and the facilities for licentious pleasures. As to this latter point — the facilities for licentiousness — we have been lately startled by statistics of European states on this subject, in a pamphlet from the pen of an English clergyman — Rev. R. Everest — who has given a comparative view of the proportion of marriages to population in Europe, and shown the remarkable coincidence between the existence of extravagant habits and general licentiousness, especially in the contrast between the small ratio of marriages and the large ratio of the illegitimate births in the imperial cities and the court districts, and the ratio between the two in the more plebeian cities and districts. Wherever two castes prevail, and a certain class are bound to a certain rate of expense and style, marriage is invariably much restricted, and the titled class tend to corrupt the poor and untitled. In this country, where no hereditary rank exists, social ambition is creating castes almost as offensive, and often quite as corrupting; and in our great cities the number of men constantly increases, whose tastes, or ambition, or selfishness preclude them from marriage under their average opportunities; and hence the very obvious result of an increasing proportion of persons who live by pandering to their licentiousness.

Whatever may be the cause, marriage is on the decrease among the more wary, thoughtful classes; and we can not but be impressed by the authoritative statistics of Massachusetts, which state that, there is a greater proportion of marriages among the foreign residents, most of whom are comparatively poor and unthrifty. We are quite certain that, taking any considerable number of years in the aggregate, the ratio of marriages to population decreases with the increase of habits of extravagance, and the necessity of keeping up a costly establishment. We believe that marriages will decrease until the times or manners change, and that among the facts that are to shape the destiny of the daughters of America, especially in the older and more luxurious cities, we must number the relatively fewer chances to be offered in the matrimonial lottery, and the moral necessity of there being a larger proportion of unmarried women. We do not say that marriage is of itself a blessing, irrespective of character and circumstance — and are quite ready to allow that to marry ill is worse by far than not to marry at all — yet we quite as firmly believe that a good marriage is the best condition for woman as for man; and we can not but regret the tendency that must keep so many of our daughters single, so long as they abide by the tastes in which they have been educated. A father whose heart is in the right place, and who loves his daughters as a true father always will, can not, indeed, be accused of wishing to be rid of his daughters, and so far as his own personal feelings are concerned he would rejoice to have them always with him; but this may not be, since time and change are always at work, and the daughter's welfare is better secured by a new home that may continue after the old home is broken up, and father and mother are no more.

We confess that we are advocates for marriage, and for marriages as early as the laws of health and the dictates of prudence allow. Young people are saved from many evils by identifying their whole destiny with each other's, and the wife's affections and the husband's purity are then in the best possible keeping, under God's law and Christ's grace. We know very well that theorists of extreme classes who have noted the decrease in the number of marriages in high life, are inclined to rejoice at it, and for opposite reasons — the one class because they think celibacy to be the higher condition, the other class because they think the old relation of the wife to the husband wholly wrong, and any change is to be welcomed that obliges woman to make herself independent of man, and cease to wait in any way upon his favor. Without arguing with the ascetic the question whether, to certain persons of peculiar position and temperament, celibacy may not be a duty, we are content to say, that, on the whole, monastic life, in its best estate, has little charm to a large and thoughtful observer of man's nature and God's providence; and if, in certain cases, the cowl and vail have fallen upon men and women who were virgins for the kingdom of heaven's sake, the cowl and the vail do not of themselves imply virginal affections, and when not assumed voluntarily they are apt to imply or create quite the opposite state of mind. A community in a large proportion nominally celibate is not usually conspicuous for the contentment of the women or the purity of the men, and we do not believe that Heaven is like to be any nearer the hosts of celibates, who are now made such, not by any monastic rules, nor in any Libyan deserts, but by the artificial exactions of fashion, and in the hotels and monster boarding-houses of our cities. We believe that a true Christian wife has a purity that angels may not scorn, and many a nun might covet, and that the man who keeps his marriage-vows need not ask of any ghostly monk for lessons in manly virtue. The longer we live the more we reverence God's obvious law, and the less admire the devices of men who forbid marriage, and so undertake to be wiser than God.

We quite as little incline to follow those alleged reformers who promise to bring on a new future of women by making her the rival of man. We already acquiesce in all reasonable efforts to rid her of legal and social burdens — to secure to her due rights of person, property and employment. We believe that a much wider field should be opened for her gifts, and that many branches of art both useful and ornamental have been wrongly closed against her. At the same time she is herself and not man, and she is made less effective then instead of more so by training her to imitate man either in speech, manner, or costume. We believe in the petticoat as an institution older and more sacred than the Magna Charta; and although in these days of boundless skirts we can not exactly say that we hope its shadow may never be less, we do honestly believe that its dominion is coeval with that of true civilization, and that man loses the only authority that can effectually tame him when woman loses the delicacy of mind and costume that marks her as his counterpart and not as his rival. The masculine school of woman's rights reformers have hurt the sex whom they profess to befriend, by disparaging the traits most characteristic of their nature, and giving them a certain boldness and hardness that fail of being manly and are ashamed of being womanly. For our part, we are willing to own honestly the mutual dependence of the sexes, and their duty to bless each other by being what God has made them. We men can have no true heart or home without a good woman's blessing, and no gift of fortune or favor seems blessed until a wife, or daughter or mother smiles upon it as woman only can smile. Why may not she honestly return the sentiment, and say that a woman never finds her true sphere until, in some relation of life, and chief of all in her own home, a true man's wisdom and strength harmonize with her trusting affection and quick perception! She will own this truth, and she is too sagacious not to see that she loses her hold on man the moment that she begins to rival him by stentorian speech or by pantalooned strides. But God's providence is a better teacher than we can hope to be, and His wisdom is proved by the lot of the most obstreperous champions of womans rights. The mother silences the Amazon, and the female agitators and orators of the pulpit and the rostrum appear at the cradle very much as other women; and the closed pulpit and the silent rostrum are signs not of mob violence but of Nature's gentle law.

Although not agreeing with the ascetic or the radical as to the means of emancipating woman from the yoke of marriage, we do believe that much may and should be done to secure to her a larger self-reliance and usefulness, to train her to be energetic without being masculine, and so to rule her education as to give her truer dignity and freedom, whether married or single. The same social progress that will make marriage more practicable and hopeful will make single life more dignified, and without believing in any social nostrums that shall at once cure all domestic ills, we are convinced that due thought on the part of earnest parents and teachers, preachers and authors, can work out a better day for the destiny of our daughters. We need to apply the first principles of good sense to the current modes of living, and demand some other sanction than mere fashion for the style of expense which we think authoritative. The matter of dress, furniture, house building, servants, entertainments, and all the household economies, that have so much to do with the destiny of woman, need to be thoroughly revised, and a substantial check put to the extravagance that is putting the yoke of nominal poverty upon young women of moderate means, and shutting them out from the comforts of a true home, while it burdens the nominally rich with constantly increasing competitions and discontents. Good taste may do much toward checking extravagance, and we seriously believe that a more artistic eye would often lessen by one-half the cost of dress and furniture, and save our daughters from the barbarous folly that sacrifices true beauty to mere expensiveness. It may cost something too much to dress handsomely, yet it is clear that the best-dressed women do not spend the most money on their clothes, and that they who are most likely to ruin their husbands by their monstrous bills at the jewelers or silk and lace stores, generally succeed more in imitating the fashion-plate of our magazines and the windows of our fancy stores, than in presenting a fairer image of feminine humanity decked with the pearl of greatest price. It will be a day worth noting in the calendar when woman emancipates herself from the yoke of vulgar fashion, and when good taste and true beauty, not the scale of mere expensiveness and rarity, preside over her wardrobe and drawing-room.

The basis of all true reform, however, must be deeper than taste or sentiment. It must be in character, that finds its best treasure not in the accidents but in the substance of being, and believes with the Master that life does not consist in the abundance of things possessed. The good old Christianity that has stood by the daughters of the Church through so many struggles is to stand by them still in the peculiar crisis of our new ages. The problem once was to save woman from the hand of barbaric lust and place her under the protection of the sanctuary, and the problem was solved. The problem now is, how to save her from the yoke of modern materialism, and to secure to pure character and spiritual faith a respect and influence that the world is now eager to monopolize for wealth and ostentation. This problem, too, will be solved, and they who solve it under God's law, and with Christ's grace, will be the best benefactors of our daughters.

VI.

Fortune.

FORTUNE.

THE old idolatries have passed away, and their statues and temples are little now but dust. The few shrines that remain show the defeat of paganism more signally than the shrines that have vanished. The crumbling walls of the empty Parthenon record the downfall of Minerva on the Acropolis of Athens, and the rejuvenated Parthenon, now crowned with the cross, celebrates daily at Rome the triumph of Christianity over the heathen gods. Yet on one point the world is about as idolatrous as ever, and invokes one mysterious name about as superstitiously as when temples were built to the goddess Fortuna and her various symbols, the rudder, the wheel, the globe, the horn of plenty, and the wings — indicated her fitful temper and her various gifts. Now, as of old, the multitude crowd every place where Fortune divides her frowns and favors. No matter what the place or the auspices, however mean or majestic — whether a raffle in a grog-shop, among greasy tipplers, or a card-table in a gamester's brilliant pandemonium, with dainty gentlemen and perhaps jeweled ladies for players; whether a dog-fight for pennies in a filthy cellar, or a horse-race, with thousands of pounds at stake, on grounds famous as the haunts of the beauty and chivalry of centuries — wherever Fortune holds her court, she is sure to find ready suitors. In peace and war she still keeps her prestige; and when no battle compels combatants to watch for her fitful signals, she hangs up her banner in the busy streets of trade, and solid men, who are not to be caught by the shining wheel at the lottery-office, may be entrapped at once by the specious bulletins of the stock-board, and give their money for that which is not bread.

But apart from all tropes and figures, do we not all seriously recognize the fact, which was of old so superstitiously regarded by the idolaters of Fortune — the fact that there is in human destiny a wide margin of apparent chance, and that, in all our enterprises, there is another party quite as powerful as human will — a mighty and mysterious power, which decrees that the battle is not always to the strong, nor the race to the swift, neither yet bread to the wise, nor yet riches to men of understanding, nor yet favor to men of skill, but time and chance happen to all! Never more than now have our people been impressed with the power of time and chance; for no man among us can live a year without decided proofs that his welfare is not wholly in his own keeping, and that changes have come upon the most sagacious from causes alike beyond their foresight and control. With our life for our text, let us then consider the turns of Fortune, and their lesson. It will be best to speak first of the field in which Fortune plays her part, that we may the more clearly see how men bocome her dupes, and how they may become her masters.

I. The field of fortune — where and what is it? Surely it is every where, all about us and within us; in every sphere of nature, society, and business. This field, however, has an impassable limit on either side — a limit beyond which chance has no power. The one boundary is the Impossible, the other is the Inevitable. Whatever in the very nature of things can not be, and whatever in the very nature of things must be, is of course beyond the sphere of contingency, and, as absolutely fixed, is dismissed from our hopes and fears. Thus, it is certain that we must die, certain that we can not stop the motion of the globe, and no man in his senses tries to escape either form of necessity — the necessity that is expressed by the words "inevitable" and "impossible." But how wide is the margin between the two — that broad field of possibility and probability in which most of the work of our life is done, and our loss and gain, joy and grief, are decided! As soon as any prize seems within our possible reach, it engages our attention; and as soon as the possibility becomes probability, the prize is sought as an object of reasonable enterprise. It interests us most when the issue between hope and fear is nearest the crisis, or when it is about half-way between the limit of impossibility and the limit of certainty, and the interest flags the moment we see that it can not be ours, or that it must be ours. So true is it that complete success has something of the nonchalence of utter defeat, and the fox who has all the grapes to himself is apt to think as little of them as the fox who thinks them sour because he can not get them. So true is it that with most of Fortune's favors,

> " The lovely toy, so fiercely sought
> Hath lost its charm by being caught; "

so true it is that whatever ceases to excite our anxiety ceases to have the highest zest. Therefore it is that so much of our life is at the mercy of what is called chance, and in the field of fortune we find our work as well as our play.

Strictly speaking, of course there is no such thing as chance; for with the Almighty Mind there can be nothing casual or fortuitous, and all things are known to the All-seeing One. But to us all things are casual that are unknown; and whatever can be, or may probably be, is to our mind somewhat a matter of chance. In the region of uncertainty chance ranges, and the region of uncertainty covers the great portion of our actions, hopes, and fears. The boundaries of the unknown are, indeed, in some respects, lessened by the progress of science, art, travel, and observation; yet, when one mystery is explored another rises in the distance, and there probably never was an age when thinking men so felt and acknowledged the mystery of the universe and its life as in this age of boasted illumination. We sometimes boast of understanding Nature, and so mastering her laws as to predict, if not to control, her phenomena; but how signally nature baffles us still, and in winds, waters, heat, cold, calms, storms, earthquakes, lightnings, health, disease, the mighty mother is taking us knowing ones by surprise very much as of old when her colossal image was set up in the sands by the great pyramids, and that face of stone, the Sphinx, propounded to all passers-by the great riddle of time. Knowing as we boast of being, every day is a surprise from the elements in some respects, and last winter's cold, and this summer's heat, come to us from a power that all our philosophy can as little predict as control. Our whole life bears witness of the uncertainties of nature, and the elements constantly make their mark upon us, now in the vexation of an influenza, and now in the terrors of the cholera, now in a fire and now in a shipwreck.

Our human nature surely is not exempt from the uncertainties of the material world. If winds and waters, vegetation and animals, have moods and changes that we can not predict, is it easier to predict the moods of man or of woman? It was well that Fortune was represented in the human form; for all chances gather around and within our poor humanity, and there is no contingency of nature or events that does not in some way act upon or from our human life. We have something of the whole universe within us — from the earth in our bones to the electric and magnetic force that flashes along our nerves; while to the mysteries of nature we add the mystery of our own mind, which surprises us sometimes more than it does our neighbors. Certainly there is a large region of the unknown in human thoughts, feelings, and actions; so that when we forecast our destiny, we think, perhaps, above all things, more anxiously of the issues of our own dispositions and the conduct and character of other men. Others may harm us or help us much, and our fortunes and happiness depend much upon what our associates in business or friendship shall do or fail to do for us. Fortune was represented human, and also as a woman; not, indeed, as a giddy girl but as a matron, her statue implying, not perhaps what our modern life so often shows, that married women are the fastest of their sex, but the deeper fact, that sensibility and experience, like a woman's and a mother's, have much to do with deciding and appreciating the turns of human welfare. The in-door as well as the out-door side of life thus comes in for its share of notice, and Mother Fortune speaks to us of all changes in the heart and the home as well as in the market and the state. Who like a mother can feel the good and ill that come from or to our mutable humanity? The mother, if a worldling, fosters and shares the false ambition of the whole family; and if a true woman, she is the heart of all their goodness, and shares all their joy and grief. This year's experience in the Old World and the New, in peace and war, in business enterprises and in household changes, is full of lessons in this world's chances — full of proofs that not only in nature but also in mankind there is a great margin of contingency. Strange developements of character have been more startling than any changes of the elements, and unexpected heroism and unexpected treachery have made more mark upon the year than the plenty of the harvests or the outbreak of earthquakes and tornadoes. Nay, the moods of men have been at the bottom of the most astounding events; and the war in Germany and the panic throughout Europe and America, come from fits of thought and feeling, which in the world of mind, are quite as mysterious as the tides and storms, of electricity and magnetism in nature.

So nature and man combine their uncertainties to give Fortune her field, and what we call the times is the record of her movements. The times! Who shall undertake to enumerate the host of contingencies that form and swell that marvelous tide upon which we are all floating? Who, least of all, shall presume to foretell what the times shall be? Let us contrast the opening of 1857 with the opening of 1858, and acknowledge the vanity of human expectations in that great financial revolution. It is hard to read the year backward, and explain the causes of events, now that the consequences have developed them in a measure. Who can say that he could read the year forward or tell its results in advance? The most sagacious practical men saw no great crisis near at hand, and the business community had all sail set as for pleasant weather when the storm broke upon them in a general wreck. Some, indeed, foreboded evil, and are always foreboding it. But who predicted any thing like the state of things now realized? Perhaps most thoughtful men expected a degree of financial pressure, but who expected such a crash? Who could tell what contingency would check the rising expansion of trade, and like a chill wind bring down the air-castles that the sunshine has been building upon the rarefied summer vapors? The turn of the financial times depends upon the adjustment of balances in trade, and when the balance is doubtful a slight cause may destroy the equilibrium, as the leap of a chamois or the wing of an eagle may unsettle the nicely-poised mountain boulder, and carry ruin and death into the peaceful Alpine valley. Who shall tell when the balance of trade passes the line of safety, or when the foot of the chamois or the wing of the eagle shall throw it from its poise? There are always prophets enough after the event has happened; but they who most sagaciously read the signs of things to come, most modestly own the short-sightedness of man and the vanity of human expectations. If any wiseacre claims prophetic honors, let him test his inspiration by telling what will be the price of money, or merchandise, or lands in one year; or let him tell us the news of the next steamer, or the issue of the next Presidential election. We commend to our prophets the wisdom of the new Spiritualist seers, who confine their foresight to events that have happened — predict to the believing neophyte who his father was, and what his own name is — and as to future events or distant occurrances are as wise as the wooden tables that rap out their mystical communications. Who could foretell the issue of our great warfare, or predict the long disappointment and the final victory, the downfall of so many commanders and the rise of Sherman and Grant? No, we are not prophets; and we must all own that in the times there is a region of contingency that baffles the keenest scrutiny, and that though there is, as Kossuth said, a logic of events which the wise man reasons out, wise men, like Kossuth himself, have invariably failed to reason them out fully, and are constantly surprised, like common men, by unexpected ill and good. Open the last newspaper, and the eye, by the merest glance at the names and topics treated, needs little moralizing to note the constant chances of time and the short-sightedness of human expectation. The atlantic cable has brought us revelations as strange as romantic, and we stand amazed at the new aspect which Bismark's pluck and genius have given to the map of Europe. Nay, the mere record of marriages and deaths is of itself lesson enough, and tells as much of the vicissitudes of human life as the price-current tells the vicissitudes of trade. Over each cradle and over each grave the Fates keep their watch; and when we ask what shall be this new life, or what has been that departed life, we know full well that the time and chance that write so much of the epitaph on the grave will write quite as much of the career of the little sleeper in the cradle.

II. So powerful is the combination of chances that men call Fortune; and it is a serious question how we shall meet its force. Deny its existence or importance we may not, for all history and life are witness that, mighty as human will may be, it is not the only arbiter of our destiny, and that circumstance is a mighty element in our lot. Meet it we must, either wisely or foolishly; and a glance at the freaks of Fortune with human folly may help us to the wisdom that is a match for her caprices. Observe her dupes, that we may better know her masters. Her dupes are of two chief classes, who differ from each other partly by native temperament and partly by diversity of experience, according as hope or fear predominates, and they become madcaps or cowards under her smiles or frowns.

They who are won by her smiles are not the less her dupes, and more victims have been made by her favor than her frowns. First among her madcaps comes the gamester, who loves hazard for its own sake, and leaves care and toil to plodding drudges while he waits on Fortune's golden wheel. No matter what may be the gamester's implements, whether cards or dice, the cock-pit or the race-ground, the election returns or stock market, he is always the same perverse character. His error is in regarding chance, not as the incident, but the main element, if not the whole of welfare, and risking all upon the issue of his game. His mischief is that he produces no value, and moreover fosters a spirit that discourages industry and unsettles moral principle. If there is an element of chance in all business, the distinction is, that in legitimate business chance is the incident, and, not as in gambling, the issue turns upon substantial probabilities, and not upon fitful possibilities. Every gambling hell, therefore, stands apart from legitimate trade, and has affinity only with those forms of traffic that create no value, and give market to no value, but merely feed the fire of an unwholesome and, in the end, ruinous gaming. Arithmetic shows the gambler's folly, and experience proves that his game is, in the end, as ruinous to fortune and character as to sobriety.

Let the gamester pass, yet not without leaving with us some wholesome hints for a type of character not less dangerous, if far less repulsive than he. The schemer, or speculator, is a more decent and plausible character; and although not inviting us to the card-table or the horse-race, he offers to show us the road to fortune or fame without the old-fashioned process of thought and labor. We suffer much from this race, and many who are wise enough to escape their enticements, and not to stake all upon their visions, share in the general ruin which their counsels bring. If all who have lost their property within a year, by consequence of schemes that have offered boundless wealth without careful toil or persistent enterprise could be gathered together, no edifice would hold the multitude; and no man among us is so merry as not to mingle a tear of pity with his censure of their folly. An element of scheming indeed, belongs to our nature; but woe to the man whose schemes turn upon fitful chances, not upon well-studied probabilities and well-adjusted plans of action. There is an element of imagination, indeed, in every sound man, and invention belongs to sober business as well as to poetical creation or mechanical ingenuity. But the sound man's visions turn upon facts and principles, not upon games and hazards. His inventions come to him under the clear ray of experience and insight as by light from above, and he does not run after every will-o'-the-wisp that shapes its morbid gases into the guise of a star, and shines to beguile and bewilder, not to enlighten its followers. There are few subjects upon which the world needs more light than upon the distinction between wild scheming and practical invention and discovery in the fields of enterprise. There is more false fancy in many a bank or counting house than in most poets' garrets; and Wall Street might sometimes dispute with Bloomingdale the palm of being the haunt of moon-struck dreamers. We all, perhaps, share in the schemer's visions, and, in our own way, cherish our pet castles in the clouds. Look well to it that they do not cost us our firm footing upon the earth, and our firm seat in our solid homes!

If scheming, like gaming implies a certain fever of the fancy and sensibility, adventure adds to these a certain element of daring, and the adventurer has about him something of the romance that always attaches to a daring will. What a charm always attaches to the soldier of fortune, and something of the same charm attaches to those who carry the same spirit into business, statesmanship, and even religion. Adventurers have had more than their fair share in governing the world, and, from the days of Nimrod to those of William Walker, from Mohammed's time to Brigham Young's, filibusterism has been a power in the State and the Church. In our day it appears in every path of trade, and the sobriety of business is constantly disturbed by courage enlisted in the service of folly or fanaticism. We need a new Cervantes to give a quietus to the mad knight-errantry of money-making and land-stealing; and, if the truth were known, we might see all around us rueful Don Quixotes, whose daring had begun the wild adventure, and coarse Sancho Panzas, whose longing stomachs had enlisted in the knight's hopeful service, and found but poor fare and beatings as their part of the booty. Such adventure differs from fair enterprise in its spirit and object; in its spirit which mistakes audacity for true courage; and its object, which dares danger for the sake and not in spite of the risk. There is adventure, indeed, in all enterprise; but true enterprise seeks the well-known good through paths of peril, sure of the reward of fidelity if not of success. Enterprise is willing sometimes, to lead the forlorn hope in face of death itself; and death itself, that defeats the end, does not defeat the spirit or break the power of the deed. Mere adventure belongs to the madcaps who are giddy under Fortune's smiles; true enterprise counts well her chances, and braves them for a prevailing hope from a sober purpose.

Such are Fortune's madcaps — the gamester, the schemer, the adventurer — who are so crazy for Fortune's favor as to lose sight of the blanks in her lottery, and to risk all for her prizes. A sanguine temperament may combine with certain successes to fever their blood; and we confess to a certain liking to the whole class in comparison with the opposite extreme; so much more amiable to us is too much hope than too little, and we could forgive these madmen easily, if their only failing was looking too much on the bright side. But we must remember that nothing is in the end so disheartening as false hope; and the madcap, when beaten, may be the most arrant of cowards; and the spendthrift, when beggared, may be the meanest of churls. Glance now at Fortune's cowards, and they swarm before us a motley yet mighty procession. There is the lounger bolstering up his natural laziness by fear of the risks of labor, and doing nothing because he is not sure of gaining every thing. In his basest form he is the sluggard, sinking into an idiocy of the will quite as abject as the fool's idiocy of the wits, and losing all the prerogatives of humanity except the genius for sitting and attaining such proficiency in this as to tire out the everlasting hills in sedentary talent. The sluggard may be stupid, but not innocent; and some of the worst curses of humanity come from his stagnant blood. Little removed above him is the lounger of a daintier class, the idler about town, whose finances are as much a problem as the quadrature of the circle, the philosopher's stone, or perpetual motion; for no man can tell how he lives, always spending and never earning. Sometimes the lounger is a youth of fortune, and the interest of the problem changes, and the only solution of his aimless conduct may be the theory that his filial affection does not allow him to be engrossed with any useful occupation, lest he might not be ready at the proper time to put on mourning for his deceased parent, and to open with filial promptness the good father's grave and last will and testament.

With more sensibility, and less sloth, the croaker follows the lounger, and is as slow in good works, but not in words, as he. The croaker's talk is constantly of mischances; and if he speaks of the horn of plenty, he says nothing of the fruits and flowers in its capacious depth, but points out its little end. Whatever his theme — be it health, property, society, pleasure, humanity, religion — he is forever groaning over the miseries of men; and if his predictions are sometimes right, it is because he is generally wrong, just as a clock that always points at the midnight hour is sure to be right when midnight comes round again. Let the croaker go, for the air is heavy and stifling with his presence. True indeed it is that our life is often troubled, and our burdens are heavy; but why be forever groaning over the sad fact? If we would march well through ill to good, we must march by music, not by groans; and the harder the road the braver and cheerier should the music be.

We like better that highest specimen of the cowards of fortune, the recluse — although we are very far from liking him altogether; for he makes the sad mistake of trying to get out of the world because it is not perfect, and of risking nothing that he may lose nothing. In one of his forms he is the recluse from business, determined not to run its risks, and forgetting that he may be risking the best of his goods, his usefulness, and his mental health. Or he may be the recluse from domestic ties, resolved not to marry because women are not angels, children are plagues, and marriage is a lottery full of blanks, forgetting that he may be by himself and not have an angel for a companion; that moody selfishness is more a plague than roguish little boys and girls; and that he may not take a chance in Hymen's lottery, and yet have a miserable blank in his own loneliness. In his highest form, that of the meditative student, the recluse is not blameless; and he who quits the world to find wisdom in solitude, shuts out the best light when he shuts the door upon actual life and our poor struggling humanity. He meditates best who has felt the touch of reality and moved among men and things, and the world's great thinkers have been workers among the world's great facts. If care and the world bring some annoyance, this is better than visionary dreaming; and a little discomfort is necessary to keep a man awake, and feel duly for the pinch in other men's fortunes. We always admired the sagacity of the pilgrim who vowed with his companion to travel on foot to Jerusalem with peas in his shoes, but who took the precaution to boil his peas, and thereby display an ease of motion quite unaccountable to his limping companion. It is foolish to borrow trouble, and equally foolish to shun the trouble that fairly belongs to us in our own time and place in the world. We are wiser and better for some anxiety and trial, and all the true sages and saints have needed a little spurring from some thorn in the flesh or fortune, to keep them awake to the highest light and up to the highest mark. The great poets have been heroes, and the last resort, if we seek any of their inspiration, is the coward's part, or running away from our own post among men. The coward, whether lounger, croaker, or recluse, is like the madcap, the dupe of Fortune, and not master of her chances nor a match for her freaks.

III. The only master of her chances is the truly practical man, who is neither madcap nor coward, and proof alike against her smiles and her frowns. Consider in what manner it is that the practical man is a match for fortune, and able to meet and master her on her own ground.

He first of all brings to his aid the force of a sound judgment, and in its light he notes calmly and keenly the goods and ills at stake, and studies carefully the best way to shun the ill and seize the good. He is strong at once from this very point of view, and because forewarned he is forearmed. His judgment, observant of substantial good, is wisdom; and as studious of the best means to win that good, it is prudence. With wisdom and prudence for his counselors, he judges Fortune's threats and promises by a scale of substantial values, and measures the way to the true value by a scale of reasonable probabilities. So he escapes a world of follies and tricks. Not in the gambler's madness nor the lounger's alarms, but with firm, yet cautious eye, he scans the prizes to be gained or lost, and chooses prudent means to wise ends. The great wilderness of uncertain chances is no longer a wilderness to him; for he knows to what point he is to travel, with wisdom for his star and compass, and with prudence for his pathfinder and guide. To him, thus wise and prudent, there is a gradual opening of the fact that there is over all chances a prevailing law, and over the combinations of events, as over the revolutions of the globe, there is a presiding purpose. Probabilities become to him clearer and clearer; and in his own vocation, as well as in the great mission of life, a light shines upon the road that he is to tread, until its dim shadows vanish into day. He is not, indeed, infallible; for to err is human: but he has studied chances till he has found the main chance, and in his ruling policy the element of certainty is so combined with the element of risk, that the risk serves to quicken and vitalize the whole combination — as the oxygen in the atmosphere, in itself so inebriating and consuming, gives spirit and life when mingled in moderate proportion with the more solid and nutritious nitrogen. To change the figure, he aims to live and work in the temperate zone of sound sense and solid strength, and he is not in danger of running off into tropical fevers or polar icebergs, for he is content to be warm without being burned, and to be cool without being frozen.

To judgment the practical man adds fortitude, which is the heart's master of the ups and downs of fortune as judgment is the head's mastery. Fortitude, we suppose, in its derivation, carries this idea; and a man of fortitude is he who is equal to either fortune. Fortitude can suffer and can dare, appearing as patience under the ills that must be borne, and as courage against the ills that must be surmounted. By patience and by courage the practical man is mightily armed as with shield and sword — with the one receiving the blows that he can not shun, and with the other pressing on against his foe. Patience and courage, the one teaching us what we must calmly bear, and so ridding us of a host of vain and wasting repinings — the other calling out our best powers, and cheering us bravely on to our work. He is conqueror of ills inevitable who calmly bears them, and he is conqueror of ills not inevitable who boldly braves them. In all spheres of life we need both, for we must all bear defeats and ought all to win victories. Rome indeed boasted, that when Fortune entered the Eternal City she laid aside her wings; but surely, if Rome took from Fortune her fickle wings, it was only by teaching the patience and courage that conquer by endurance as by daring, and the true Roman fortitude won back the fitful goddess by daring to do without her smiles.

To judgment and fortitude add fidelity, and our list of the forces of the practical man is complete. Fidelity, with single eye and persistent purpose, presses on to its aim, and wins the best success, not only because in the end it secures the largest amount of good, but because it is in itself success. He who does the best that he can, according to his measure of wisdom and prudence, patience and courage, is a successful man. In the long-run the most substantial goods are his. When he succeeds, his success is not shame, and when he is shipwrecked — as the best masters sometimes are — his wreck is better trophy than the pirate cruiser's flaunting flag, that ows its safety to its inhumanity; and all true men say of fidelity defeated, what even the worldling Napoleon said of the convoy of brave prisoners after a battle: "Honor to the brave in misfortune." Fidelity defeated is on the way to success, and in all ventures that are worthy, character is the best part of capital.

Judgment, fortitude, fidelity — by these the practical man masters Fortune in spite of her changing chances. He will succeed, and can not be put down. His success will be the best, although it may not be what the world calls the largest. In business he may not have the largest, but he will have the best, fortune, from his gains, though limited, he will win the best good. In the professions he may not gain the largest honors, but he will win the truest usefulness and peace. When the sod is put on his grave, men shall say, "Well done, good and faithful servant;" and the voice from heaven shall not refuse its Amen. His success will have height as well as breadth, and every good that comes to him will lift up his faith and affections toward the throne of God, while it widens his earthly domain.

In our public halls and libraries we may meditate upon the struggle with Fortune, as if in the Temple of History and of Human Life. The statues of true men in those halls, and the thoughts and deeds of so many generations recorded upon those shelves, press the subject home upon our thoughts, and bid us meet our chances as they met theirs. May we not take a wholesome hint from the solemn past for the better education of our children and the method of our living?

In our too-easy kindness to our children are we not sometimes more cruel than kind, and do we not educate them as if there were nothing but prosperity on earth, and Fortune had all smiles and no frowns? Would not our daughters be nobler women if more of the household utilities were united with the showy graces of their culture, and they were taught to think it a better destiny to share and lighten a true man's hardships than to be pampered by a churl's abundance? Do we not, Americans, sometimes so magnify the term Lady as to forget the better word Woman, and so pet this world's dainty Ladyhood as to slight the true Womanhood that God hath made in his own image? Our sons, too, we belittle and enfeeble by over-indulgence; and even when we devote them to study, we forget that there are two alphabets and two ways of reading. There is an A B C of the spelling book, and an A B C of nature and life; and he who would read the great book of facts, must read it with a ready hand as well as open eyes. We surely weaken and degrade our sons if we do not bring them from the beginning to be wise and brave and faithful amidst all the changes of fortune — all the ups and downs of life.

And the reigning standard of living, how false to the best lessons of experience and the true philosophy of our being! We spread so broad the surface of ease and display as to make it hard to rise to manly independence and peace, and sacrifice life itself to the shows of living. Less show and more substance, less worldliness and more manliness, less luxury and more peace, less vanity and more worth, and our lives would rise above the chances of fortune, and our homes rest upon the Rock unchangeable, with living water in its clefts. Even then time and chance might touch us sometimes rudely; but it would be under God's control, and no longer dupes of Fortune, we become children of Providence.

VII.

The Flag at Home.

VII

The Trilogy of Desire

THE FLAG AT HOME.

WE have been for years so accustomed to see our flag upon our houses and hanging from our windows, that we have almost forgotten how startling a sight it at first was, and how deep a lesson it ought to teach us as it floats over our home, and thus connects the peace of the family with the power of the nation. Before we were, perhaps, proud enough of our country and our flag; but our pride of late years was reserved too much for certain state occasions — as for a military parade, the arrival of a fleet, the anniversary of a victory, or the return of the national holiday. Even then we must confess to being sometimes a little surfeited with the show of patriotic enthusiasm, and the Stars and Stripes, though well enough in their place on our national ships and forts, were regarded by dainty eyes as a little vulgar when brought too near, very much as Fourth of July fire-crackers are regarded by sensitive ears. There was indeed some reason for our distaste at the frequent obtrusion of the symbol of our nationality; for it was too often made under the auspices of persons more intent on displaying themselves than on serving the country; and too many of militia musters have been more alarming to quiet citizens than to public enemies; and the hereditary bunting that perpetuates the virtue of our fathers sometimes has been disgraced by the inebriety of the sons, being exhibited upon tents whose inmates beat each other instead of the invader, and fell more frequently by liquor than by bullets.

Even when our martial enthusiasm has been truly stirred by imposing military displays, as so often by the excellent citizen soldiery of our great city, it has been very much as at some grand scenic effect upon the stage. We did not, indeed, doubt that our men were brave, and our nation powerful, and our arms invincible, yet we had little thought of those troops being part of an actual army, or of claiming the flag as part of our own household, after that it had been borne so gayly past our window.

How changed is our feeling now! The first blow that was struck at our national life moved us all to lift up the flag upon our houses and churches, as the Crusaders of old lifted up the insulted cross. We can remember what a thrill went through the heart of the nation when the flag was first unfurled upon our church spires; but the precursors of this signal appeared upon many a roof below, and the fire that blazed aloft upon the towers was kindled from the hearths of the people. The feeling that came over the nation took us all by surprise, and, like every great experience, it neither came by calculation nor can it be analyzed by cold criticism, nor comprehended by mere prudence. Our life is greater than we know, and whenever its interior fountains are stirred, we are reverently to await a revelation instead of prescribing an opinion or conceit. We have awaited now many years the developments of our national life, and from time to time we have tried to give our views of their import. We propose now to extend our observations into a somewhat new direction, and speak of the lesson of the flag at the window, or the relation between our homes and our country, or the life of the family and the nation.

We remark at the outset, that the signs of the times show that we are taking the nation *home* with us as never before, and making our public interests a part of our private welfare. The change is greater than we are at first prepared to admit; for while private welfare tends to become too much a very narrow, engrossing, and even selfish object, public interest, on the other hand, is too apt to be left in the vagueness of remote distance, or to the abstractions and the round numbers that are to be found in our tables of statistics. It is very easy to say "our country," or to repeat the statistics of our population, domain, wealth, and lines of communication. But how much more vivid and stirring is the word "home," and with the sound of the word the eye rests upon or recalls the cherished object itself. We see it, the whole of it, just as it is, precisely so large or so small, with exactly so many inmates, of such years, features, and voices, with furniture and garden, as distinct as in a picture. Perhaps the most distinct and engrossing object of all is she who is generally the ruling spirit of the house, the wife and mother. We call our country our mother; and so she ought to be, and to some extent so she is; but she does not stand before us so distinctly as our mother in blood — as she who bore us, and is always bearing with us and forbearing. The mother in the house is a very private and somewhat exclusive person, and is apt to impart to us something of her own clannishness, and to shut us up within the circle of her own affections, when she is too generous to tie us to the apron strings of her will. Great is the gain, then, when she brings the nation within her own charmed circle, and gives the country a hearty place in the household. Sometimes this adoption is not merely an interior feeling but a visible act; and no sight is to us more expressive than that so often seen for a few years — the good mother seated at the window from which floats the household flag, and watching intently the passing regiment, and waving her handkerchief to some friend or kinsman, perhaps to her own sons or brothers, as they are marching, not on a holiday pageant, but to the war, in defence of the life of the nation. The sight of her and her daughters brings the whole country nearer to us, and the great continent seems to rise before us in living personality, and to speak with her voice, and to glow with our affections. The nation seems to live in the person of its queen, and here every patriotic woman does a great deal to animate and impersonate the whole government.

We undoubtedly suffer something from the absence of the traditional symbols and titled personages which embody and concentrate the laws and customs of the old nationalities. As yet no person moves us as the Queen moves the English when she visits the army, or as the Czar stirs the Russians, when, as autocrat and pontiff at once, he rides among the battalions that welcome him with hymns as well as cannon. Yet we are gaining in national symbolism, and never, since Washington's time, has a President been greeted as our last martyred chief; and never, since time was, has more enthusiasm been rising toward any queen than that which is rising in our camps toward the noble women who made such sacrifices for the health and comfort of our soldiers. She who looks out from the window to give the soldiers her blessing as they march to the war, should receive that blessing with increase when they return. The whole nation should and will join in the blessing; for she, the true woman, it is who enables the soldier more than any thing else to keep his country in his heart as part of his home. Surely we are governed far more than we think by tangible objects and personal associations; so that it is very hard to love our country, and even our religion, apart from congenial places and persons. The flag is something tangible, and it seems sometimes to have a supernatural virtue in rousing patriotism. There is a reverence for our flag amounting almost to worship; yet without some human face or word to go with it, the flag is a very insufficient incentive, and the good soldier feels its power far more when he receives the silken banner at the hands of some fair woman, and sees her cheering face wherever he marches, and hears her encouraging voice above all other music. In some way every soldier is enabled to interpret his country by some such personal association, and so give it a place in his fancy and affections, as well as in his reason and conscience. The more we do to cherish such associations so much the better for the nation, and so much greater is the safeguard against the narrow individualism and private thrift that are so apt to be in the ascendant among us.

As a people we are much given to arithmetic, and nowhere on earth is the multiplication-table so widely taught and applied as with us. Far be it from us to disparage this important document, or to bring down upon our heads the wrath of its significant figures, which can gather at a word in such ratios that roll up volumes sometimes more startling than the thunder-clouds. Yet we must modestly suggest that the multiplication-table can not do every thing, nor even the most important thing. It can multiply the unit into thousands and millions, but it can not give us the unit itself to start with. It may figure up the number of houses in the country, or of men in the army, but it can not give us an adequate idea of a single house or a single man. In fact, no kind of knowledge is so deceptive and unsatisfactory as that which is merely numerical. We learn something, but not the chief thing, when we learn that we are a nation of thirty millions of inhabitants. We learn the great thing only when we are told what kind of people they are, and especially what kind of a man is to be regarded as the average specimen or representative character of the whole. Whatever tends to translate the abstractions of statistics into personal form and feature corrects their insufficiency and makes their facts vital. Now, certainly, all household images and associations have this tendency, and the muster-roll of a regiment begins to mean something to us the moment we recognize some familiar name, and remember, perhaps some old neighbor or schoolmate whose home we have passed, and whose parents, and brothers, and sisters we know. The whole army starts into life as it is thus estimated by a standard that the heart can recognize, and there is something very near to degradation in being known merely as one of a certain number, without local habitation or name. How repulsive it is, not only to our pride but to our affections, to be called number one or number ten instead of our own name; and the prison has no indignity greater than that of labeling its inmates numerically, and knowing them only by their number, like so many hack horses. Women are especially averse to such computation; and we can not imagine any greater affront put upon a circle of stately dames or blooming damsels than by omitting their characteristic names, and slighting their characteristic costume, and telling them off by number, as so many hats or umbrellas left in care of the porter. Womanly affection is altogether private and personal, and carries its personality into public affairs, and helps us, harder and more abstracted men, to carry it there also.

Tell a woman, for example, that a thousand men were slain in the last battle, and she receives the news with amazement, perhaps with horror, yet does not lose her composure nearly so much as when she hears that one of her own acquaintance was among the number; and as she thinks of him in the agonies of death, she sees the whole thousand who suffered with him, and the *many* appear before her in the *one*. This is the way, indeed, with the human heart, but it comes largely from its home training; and but for this personal and affectionate view of affairs public life would lose its personal interest, the country would evaporate into an airy abstraction, or sink down into a coarse trading copartnership, and the flag would be shorn of its best power in being torn away from its allies in the household.

Let us not be narrow in either direction; and we are to shun the extreme of sentimental emotion as the extreme of cold calculation. Let us be willing to read the census all the more because we look into the house, and the aggregate numbers will mean all the more to us as we study the contents of the separate units that swell into hundreds and thousands. We need to take the household and personal view of our nation all the more from the fact that we not only lack the central court and permanent head that tend to bring national life home to the popular fancy, but we also share peculiarly in the habit of calculation that is so characteristic of our time, and sometimes come near displacing enthusiasm by prudence, and living personality by scientific abstractions. Without going over in theory to the Positivist School of Comte, and while retaining our nominal spiritual faith, we often virtually adopt his principles, and regard our country too much in its mere statistics; not as our benign mother, whom we know and love by heart, but as the great farm and storehouse, which we are to estimate by tables of agriculture, commerce, and manufactures. The French Positivist himself found out his mistake before he died, and in a measure corrected it by that same method that we are recommending; and Comte, who boasted of having reduced every study to an exact science, and of being able to read the future as the past by his sociological theory, confessed that he learned from a single friend more than from all his figures and laws, and that without the friendship of a noble woman, with the light of her home, he must have been without religion, if not a stranger to true humanity. His case is more or less our own; and all public generalities are unmeaning until we interpret them by personal affections and bring them home to our own hearts. It matters little over how many square miles or millions of people our flag waves, if we do not connect it with our own household, and feel its protection while we are under our own roof. The flag at the window thus teaches a great truth; as well as presents a glowing symbol; for it teaches us to study our nation in its personal relations, and breathe human life into numerical abstractions.

Not only do we thus interpret round numbers by a definite point, by the unit that makes all the figures significant, but we have the means of taking an interior view of the whole nation, or looking into the life of the people. Regarding the nation only in the *mass*, the view is alike *indefinite* and *superficial*. If we think of the *many*, we fail to see them *definitely*, unless we see them *one* by *one*; and we fail to see them *profoundly*, unless we judge them one by one, with *insight* as well as *sight*. The home view of the nation ought to combine these two characteristics, and at once give point in our indefiniteness and depth in our superficiality. Our army, for example. when thus interpreted, presents itself before us in a wholly new light. That we have had a million men in the field is a great fact, but of itself it may excite no more emotion than any other large numerical statement. Indeed, the largeness of the number rather overwhelms than impresses us, and it is impossible to conceive of such a multitude. But put the subject in another light. See that regiment marching through our streets, and remember that a mother is looking from her window to catch the last glimpse of her own son; and as he marches past and makes the salute that mingles filial love with chivalry and patriotism, he gives us a new measure of our army. He gives us the unit, not only of *sight*, but of *insight* — not only of number, but of character. Then remember that there are a thousand such regiments under our flag, and the ruling motive that led them to the field is in great part the same that animates that young soldier, and surely we have a most significant and instructive view of the whole force at our command. The whole host immediately becomes personal and pictorial to our eye, and graphic to our fancy and affections. Our loyalty takes a more interior character as we connect the purposes of the individual with the institutions and men that we are to serve. We ask anxiously how our soldier is to be treated alike by friends and foes. We see a good officer with other eyes and affections the moment we look upon him as having charge of our personal friends. The great battles, discussions, dangers and enterprises of the nation thus come home to us, and we are all enlisted by heart in the public service, and made spectators of national scenes. We really pine for more of such personal associations with the destiny of our country, and our statistics of products and returns of popular majorities are most dreary until centralized and vivified by some commanding personality. We yearn for some hero whom we may honor and love, not only for our own sake, but for the sake of our mothers, wives, and children. Knowing so many characters in the national group, and having one or more there who bears our own name or hope, we crave the presence of some ruling spirit who shall animate all by his own eloquence or courage, and ennoble us and our children and homes by his own high humanity. Thus the advent of a great man does not throw contempt on the mass of the people, but puts a soul into the whole; and the *all* whom we do not and can not know live for the first time for us in the *one* whom we know and do honor.

In monarchical countries the people are made to take a personal interest in common public affairs, and especially in great national emergencies, by loyalty to the princes who lead them; and in sober and utilitarian England the sons of the Royal family are put into the army and navy expressly to bring the public service nearer to the life of the people, and to connect the throne with their business and homes. Surely a republic ought not to have less enthusiasm, and effort should be made to win favor to every branch of national interest by identifying it with persons near to the popular heart. As we watch the career of the leading men among us now, we care for them all the more by our care for those whose welfare is committed to their charge; and we rejoice in every victory and mourn at every defeat most heartily as we think of the homes gladdened or saddened by the issue. We read with different eyes of the deeds of Foote, Farragut, Sherman, or Grant, when we think that our own or our neighbor's son is in that command; and should the army return with its trophies what bounds could be put to our enthusiasm, when love for the soldier in the ranks combines with pride in the commander to bring out our plaudits, and perhaps our tears? In some way this principle of sympathy is acting upon our whole community as probably never before in the history of nations, for never before was so large an army gathered on the globe of materials that so unite officers and men in the same companionship, and embody the affections and interests of the whole people. Our troops went forth from our homes as no other army ever went; and the bayonet, as well as the sword, was borne by men of gentle nurture, who love, and are loved by gentle mothers and wives and sisters and daughters and friends. He who wins laurels wins them therefore, in a peculiar sense, for others as well as himself; and we hardly venture to predict the honors and rewards in store for our brave leaders when they return from the conflict and are welcomed to the homes whose sons have been partners in their heroism, even at the cost of wounds or life itself. Surely, then, our public life is closely allying itself with our private life, and the two factors of our national power — the elements of command and of obedience — are meeting together as never before.

We are, undoubtedly, in this way bringing a new method of observation and judgment to bear upon our rulers and officers. We are looking at them not only from the caucus, the exchange, the Senate, but from the household; and from our windows we are scrutinizing men, manners and institutions. The morals of our officers, in the camp and the field, are to be canvassed with new closeness, and stern judgment is to be passed upon usages and institutions that are now especially in question. North and South, East and West are looking out of the window with very sharp eyes at each other; and not only in every newspaper-office, but in thousands of private houses, correspondence is going on between the people and our soldiers of a degree and kind that must tell on public opinion, and even shape the materials for history. Our campaigns have annalists such as were never before known; and the flag at the window is the eloquent symbol of a new element in our nationality — that mighty power that has every postal conveyance at its command, and enables every man and woman in the land to write dispatches to friends every where within our lines, and to stamp the dispatch with the head of Washington, and give it the sanctity of the great nationality that he founded. Letters have always been written since the human fingers knew their cunning; but never till now have they so united the home and the nation, and made a nation's history out of its household affections. Each section of the country must share in this illustration; and we are ready to believe that the result must be such as to give us all a more humane view of each other's dispositions and relations — to feel that at heart we may be once more one people, and that in some respects the very men who were in arms against us are cherishing the very affections and purposes that we hold most dear. We have no fondness for the rebel chiefs, and find it very hard, sometimes, to keep from cursing them before God and man. Yet we may so far enlarge our view as to discern some elements in their motives that are not utterly depraved; and we surely, in the fullness of our solicitude for our own kindred, may remember that the human heart is not bound by any political or geographical lines; and our enemy may love and be loved very much as we are, and on that very account may be worthy of better usages and laws than those which he insists upon maintaining, to the harm of the nation and the scandal of the world. His life, too, has its household side, and one, moreover, enough like our own to win our sympathy, and enough unlike our own to enlist our service in the hope of bettering his lot in spite of himself. The flag from our window has thirty-four stars on its folds, and shall have we trust and pray, no less a number. Our window, therefore, waves a blessing to his, and offers him protection under the light of one — nay, of all — of those stars, and gives him warning as stern as the protection is merciful.

We have been speaking thus far of the importance of taking the *nation home* with us, or of giving definiteness and depth to our public life by looking at it from our domestic point of view. But we must not forget the other aspect of the subject, nor fail to see the need of *taking* the *home abroad* with us, and enlarging private feeling and interest by large public associations and ideas. If we look out of the window to see who are in the street, we must expect those in the street to look up to us, and to have some control over our thoughts. It will not do to interpret every thing from our own personal view, or insist upon giving the whole country the tone of our household or the color of our spectacles. We certainly have been too much imprisoned in our private interests, and we need to enlarge our horizon by generous patriotism as well as humanity. If the home view of public life is instructive, the public view of home life is no less so; and we do a great deal to cure our prejudices and repinings by seeing clearly that our lot is bound up with the common lot. If home-life teaches the worth of the unit, and enables us to see number *one* with distinctness, and indeed compels us not only to say number two in connubial fondness, and number three, or four, or a dozen, in parental tenderness, public life enables us to count thousands and millions, and see that we personally are, after all, but one soul in thirty millions. Now it is a great thing really to enter into this thought; for we are prone to a monstrous egotism, and are tempted to take it for granted that the nation, if not the universe turns upon our personal will or welfare as its centre. What a lesson for us it is to remember that this great country at once measures our greatness and insignificance, and that we belong to it as but one among the millions, and instead of being sure of wealth or luxury under its flag, we must share in its trials, and may be compelled to lay down our life in its defense! Look upon the troops in the street or camp and consider that each man there has body and soul like ourselves, and when wounded or injured he suffers as we must do in like circumstances. It may let down our pride somewhat, but it will exalt our wisdom to know that each decent man is probably in most respects like ourselves; and that it is utter vanity in us to consider our case so very peculiar, and that never did man suffer or enjoy as we do. It is well sometimes to go into the crowd for the sake of learning humility; and important as it is for each man to preserve his individuality, he must remember that other people are individuals too, and that thousands and millions of them quite as much as he need the earth's plenty and God's providence.

There is something indeed at first very chilling in this view; and when we really perceive that we are one of the many, that what we are personally going through is but the common lot, that what we are tempted to regard as peculiarly our experience takes place by general laws, and to a degree that may be calculated by general averages, we are somewhat in danger of losing our faith and courage, as if we were crushed under the iron wheels of fatality. It certainly gives a startling shock to our exacting sensibility to be assured that, on the whole, about the same average amount of pain and pleasure, sickness and health, birth and death, virtue and vice, and even crime exists year after year; and that even great crises and revolutions do not essentially break the laws of historical development, nor universally change the human lot. Social statistics do not very widely vary from age to age; and events that mark our lives most deeply with joy or grief have something of the same range and uniformity as the tides and rains, the heat and cold. War and pestilence are not without method when observed in the long-run, and, like fevers, they have their heats and intermissions. There is a kind of order even in disorder; and the tables of insurance, upon which practical men base their calculations and stake millions of money, show an average liability to tempests, fires, diseases, and accidents. History, it is affirmed, is becoming an exact science, and its periods may be defined, like the stages of vegetable or animal life. Certainly the more attentively we study nature, man, and events, the more are we impressed with the idea of universal law; and now, while war has come upon us like a whirlwind, we find ourselves applying general averages to its issues, and counting the probable percentage of death by battle or disease.

When we reflect upon this prevalence of historical law or social average, we are at first liable to be depressed, as if we were under the wheels of an iron necessity without consideration or mercy. But deeper thoughts must relieve this depression, and teaching us to recognize a personal intelligence and will beneath or within the system of universal law, it prepares us to rise above a blind and inexorable fate, and gather together as children under the discipline of the Universal Father. What is universal must surely have a providential purpose; and the generalizing of the facts of human life ought not only to enlarge our surface, but to deepen our mind and exalt our faith, so as to lead us to accept the sufficient universal cause. If all our wishes were gratified at once, and the result answered exactly to our desire, we might be more than we are now in danger of forgetting or denying the overruling spirit; for we might readily regard ourselves as the moving power, and considering effects, however wonderful, as the work of our will, not as the act of God. The universe might seem, as the puppet show does to the spectator — all the movements, however curious, being all ascribed to the human showman, and not to any divine and indwelling mind. There is something, therefore, in the union of benignity and universality in the divine method that saves us from mere humanism, and compels us to own an overruling power which cares for us upon principles that sometimes cross our wishes, that they may in the end secure the utmost good.

We may have a fair illustration of the compatibility of universal law with personal intelligence and overruling power by reverting to our subject. What better expresses the antithesis between private feeling and public law than the flag at the window ? The window opens into the house, where private affections prevail and love appears in its most exclusive form. The mother clasps her son to her arms as hers, and is slow to believe that any power can take him from her side. The flag, on the other hand, symbolizes the power of national law, and in its defence her son enrolls himself in the army and marches away to the war. Look upon him as he marches by the window with his regiment, and is there not something in the rhythm of the step and the recurrent order of the ranks and companies that symbolizes that tremendous law that pervades nature and history, and whose recurrent cycles mark the periods of planets and ages that march ever on at the word of Him whose voice is the harmony of the worlds? How different the movement of the young soldier in the regiment and in the house! In the ranks he has his fixed place, and he moves with the many, and advances or retreats, faces about or wheels, at the general command, without regard to his own wish or will. In the house he is quite at ease, and sits or lolls, dances or promenades, plays or reads, as he pleases. But who shall say that in submitting to military discipline he quits the sphere of free-will and personality, and submits to inexorable necessity? The social will, the national mind, is embodied in that discipline, and he finds that his spirit rises instead of being crushed by the discipline of the camp and field; and even if he is wounded he may know that it is under laws that are essential and benign; and even if he gives his life for his country he can feel that it is better thus to die in a good cause than to breath out an ignoble existence upon a bed of dainty indolence. Whatever may be the philosophy of the fact, the fact itself is sure, that the more thoroughly we enter into the idea of prevailing law, and submit to the rightful discipline, whether human or divine, instead of losing our individuality we exalt it, and our personal life is magnified, not lost, by being united with the social and civil order or the divine kingdom.

It would be indeed most disheartening if the power of law, whether natural, social, or divine, were always, or generally, mortifying or destructive. We know, for example, that all men must die, and this necessity, that is decreed of God, is often, as of late, hastened by national decrees, and thousands fall before their expected time by the fearful chances of war. But in order that men may die, it is necessary first that they should live, and if they live as they ought to do, death itself opens into higher life, and a universal law, written not only in Scripture but upon the human soul, saves us from the dreary sway of materialism and the fearful sting of death. The more we try to perceive and follow this supreme law, and ascend from the order of material nature to the higher plane of the divine thought and the infinite and eternal love, the greater will be our strength and our comfort. In the apparently inexorable march of events we shall hear the music of humanity and of God, that shall stir our hearts with blessed faith, and assure us that without the supreme wisdom and will not even a sparrow falls to the ground.

Our flag ought to teach us, as it waves from our window, that the public necessity that controls private caprice, and sometimes seems to sacrifice private interest, is full of benign influences and lessons. Let those thirty-four stars teach us to discern the higher meaning of our national life, as it has been forming for more than two centuries, and gathering to itself the truths and powers that all ages have been preparing for us as gifts of the Old World to the New. A divine order more and more distinctly enunciates itself as the years roll on, and it is evident that, while we are scheming and toiling, planting and building for ourselves, the Lord of the vineyard and the Master of the house is using us for His own far-seeing and majestic purposes, and uniting our little doings with His own gracious and comprehensive plans for this new continent and its new civilization.

To say no more of purely national law, but considering the bearing of our private life itself, what is more evident than the fact that every true home is under the influence of an enlarging and spiritualizing power, whose source is divine and whose sweep is boundless and unending? Wherever there is a Bible or a hymn-book, a sermon or a prayer, the divine kingdom is acknowledged, and the flag is but the earthly symbol of the spiritual empire that is to be militant until it is triumphant. In this way our private life is enlarged and evangelized, and our private feelings become part of the great and universal Christian conscience. When we read the household life of the nation thus, and see in it the workings of the moral and spiritual laws that are to move God's people for time and eternity, we accept them as we accept the laws of nature, the tides, the air, the light and heat, the changes of the seasons, and we are mightily comforted by the conviction that religion is a great social fact as well as a divine revelation. Our family is seen to belong to the great family of God, and the flag of our civil Union becomes the ready symbol of our higher spiritual fellowship. National law, with its duty and privilege, is seen to be a stepping-stone to the law of the empire of God, with its truth and grace. Protected at home in our national birth-right, we the better understand our Christian birth-right; and the gospel, hymns, prayers, and sacraments of religion, as they come home to each of us, not only express our personal faith, but join us to the great company of brethren and fathers who have gone before us. They speak to us in time of need, but of a divine will instead of a material necessity. Their word is both human and divine, joining man's wants with Heaven's fullness in everlasting union. We still have the flag at the window, and love it all the more because above it we see the snow-white banner that shall win the earth to the sway of the gentle and the sceptre of the peace-making; for in war itself, war is no permanent end. The most ambitious invader professes to make war only to gain thereby a more secure peace; and our war is waged solely to preserve the unity of the nation, without which there can be no permanent peace on this continent.

We have, perhaps, taken pretty wide liberty with our subject, and moralized a little too freely upon a very common thing. There is no danger, however, that the truth that is so called for by the times will be too commonplace — no danger that public life will be taken too near to our homes and hearts, or that our homes and hearts will open too generously into fellowship with the nation and with mankind. Let us each look from our window wisely, with fellow-feeling for every citizen, especially for all who suffer in the common cause, not doubting that in this we do much to educate our own children to be good citizens, and breathe a temper that shall be the strength and the blessing of the land. Let the house be the watch-tower from which we observe all that concerns our country, and interpret every hopeful event and worthy character with humane feeling and personal sympathy.

Nor let our gaze be wholly passive, but let what we see move us to do our part and train our children to do theirs. The *watch-tower* should be also the *fortress*; and wherever our flag waves, it should be over families that mean to live not for self alone but for their neighbor, their country, and their race. For good or ill we must share in the common lot, and whether we live or die we do not belong to ourselves alone. Wave on, then, old banner! Float from every frontier fort and sea-girt citidel, every camp, and every fleet. When war shall cease and the soldier returns to his home, still cheer and stir us in our homes; and whenever the nation keeps her festivals, float in blessing from our windows and our spires, in token of the union between the private affections and public spirit of the people, the patriotism and religion of the nation, to the end of time!

VIII.

Learning Statesmanship.

LEARNING STATESMANSHIP.

I CONFESS to having brought home a new sensation, and perhaps a new idea — or one new to me, at least — from the ballot-box at the late Presidential election. There was something in the look and manner of the crowd there gathered that was peculiar and most impressive. Nothing, or next to nothing, was said, but the great thing was taken for granted. I found that just after sunrise, when I expected to find the coast clear, so that I could drop my votes into the boxes without delay, a long line, not likely to pass away under an hour was in advance. The prospect of waiting so long without breakfast compelled a retreat. Two hours later — when it was said that the crowd would probably be the least — I went again, and joined the end of this *queue* of freemen, and in about an hour and a half I reached the ballot-box, somewhat naughtily taking comfort in seeing the rear-rank as full as when I came, and therefore requiring of the new comers the same delay.

What memorable demeanor in that whole company! Every man seemed at once to affirm his own duty and his neighbor's equal right. There was no crowding, no bad temper, no dispute, no profanity, not even any show of partisanship except in the mottoes quietly presented upon the placards on the two little stands of the rival vote distributors. The person directly in front of me was a handsomely-dressed young man, apparently a merchant, who barely indicated his political preferences by modestly saying what candidate in his opinion would win the day and the White house — a prediction which, as I supposed, proved to be wrong, yet was not in the least offensive. Behind me stood a man in a plain and well-worn dress, with the look of a working-man, quite intelligent and kindly, but with something in his face and bearing that said that life was not wholly sunshine with him. He said nothing as to the candidates yet I felt quite at one with him on the subject, and was quite drawn to him when the rain began to fall and he held over my improvident head the umbrella which he had wisely brought. The only noticeable change in our ranks was made by the approach of an easy, smart-looking gentleman, who stepped up before my front neighbor, and took the place next above, which was vacated for him by the occupant, a plainly dressed-man, who fell back to the extreme rear. Nobody complained of this arrangement, by which a leading German merchant thus secured an early vote by sending his coachman to keep a place for him till he came, for the coachman too was a voter, and could have held the place for himself, and nobody was defrauded. On we passed in tranquil order, and all the proof I had of the presence of the mighty arm of the law was a bland request from one of the policemen near the ballot-box

LEARNING STATESMANSHIP.   169

to tell him how long it took for each person to vote on the average. In reply to my remark that the time varied, according to the voter's quickness and the number of questions put to him, from twenty seconds to about a minute, he said that, according to his calculation, ten men voted on an average in seven minutes, which would amount to about eighty-five an hour — an allowance sufficient to accomodate all the voters in the district between sunrise and sunset.

This simple story of facts is given merely to serve as text for the thoughts that are to be presented. The question comes. What does this mean — what idea, what motive, what destiny are before the thousands and tens of thousands of people who meet thus quietly, in this great and sometimes tumultuous city, in unison with the millions of freemen who at the same time, from the Atlantic to the Pacific shore, are casting their suffrages that are to decide who shall rule the nation with a royal authority, though without a royal name, for four years during this fearful civil war and all its attendant burdens and anxieties? It may be said that the more than Sunday quiet of the city was owing to the military force at hand to quell riot. But not a soldier was to be seen, and no well-informed man can for a moment suppose that the voters at large needed any such restraint, however much it might be called for to keep down a certain ruffian class of inhabitants, or look after rebel intruders. I called at noon on the commander-in-chief of the National troops, and chatted half an hour with him as pleasantly as on any New England Sunday, and was well

H

assured that he had no fears of what was coming, confident as he was that the people at large meant no ill, and that the malcontents and traitors dared do no ill. I confess to being greatly comforted by the visit, quite confirmed in the faith that the nation is sound and strong, and that the sword is in the hands of men, who know and love the law, and will not see it trodden under foot.

The explanation of the marvel of this great election lies in the simple fact that our people as never before, went to the ballot-box as a nation deeply conscious of the solemnity of the issue before them, and transformed from partisans into patriots, and rising above the shifts of politicians into the calm attitude of statesmen. We are impressed as never before with the truth that our people are learning statesmanship, and giving noble fruits of their training. It may be, and doubtless is, true that their conduct was deeper than their theory, and their act was wiser than they knew. This is the case with all earnest action, and there is much in our great impulses that passes our understanding. Yet our people can not be accused of acting blindly, and never has the discussion of great principles entered more largely into public debate than of late. Nor would we exclude either of the great parties from our commendation, for both professed fidelity to the same essential laws, and both held themselves bound by the issue of the ballot. Nothing better expresses our sense of the spirit of the people than an illustration from the great motive powers of nature. The atoms and globes are held and moved by certain elementary forces, and each particle of the crystal, each pebble of the globe, each globe of the system reveals, if we will rightly interpret it, the dominant powers that keep the universe in due rest and motion. Pick up a pebble from the shore, and we can deduce from its history and phenomena all the great laws of the heavens. So take a voter, and analyze the mind that moves him — and the history, idea, and destiny of the nation speak out from him at once. Consider somewhat carefully the National Idea and its practical development in our Manifest destiny, in the light of the late movement of the people.

What do those millions of men all over the country — from New York to San Francisco, from Chicago to New Orleans — take for granted but the characteristic idea of the nation, of the *Many in One, and the One in Many*. Every man feels that he is rightly among the many, under a government that claims the many diversities of places, persons, and parties, under the unity of its jurisdiction? He has been educated to understand very well the organic relation between himself and the nation. In fact, every school-boy knows the simple facts that seem to puzzle most of the political wiseacres of Europe, and can read in every national election the steps of the process by which the individual is related to the town, the town to the country, the country to the State, and the State to the Nation. Our bright boys and girls too are learning that this complex relation has been evolving itself, under God's providence, for more than two centuries, or from the very beginning of the American colonies, instead of being the result of a specific compact. In its present form, indeed, the written

Constitution shaped our National Union, but by no means created it. The Constitution expressed and embodied the previous dispositions and life of the people, whom God has been forming into a nation, and its authority rests more upon the habits and institutions which it completes than upon the specific compact which it enacts. We accept the compact, but not as a mere bargain between the States, that may be set aside at the pleasure of the parties. Our people do not believe that any paper of itself creates obligation, but honor the paper because of the inherent worth of the obligation which it recognizes. They believe that national life *grows;* that it had been growing for centuries, under colonial neighborhood, French and Indian wars, Revolutionary struggles, Confederate articles, Constitutional law; nor did the growth then end, for nothing stops growing until it begins to die. The nation has been growing these seventy-seven years since the Constitution was formed — growing not only in *extent* but in *intent,* or in spirit and idea, and can not deny this fact without abjuring its own life or laying hands upon its own being. Our people are feeling as well as thinking this great truth, and it is idle to try to make them believe that their life as a nation rests upon arbitary compact or optional partnership, not upon a providential evolution and a solemn covenant. They believe that nations, like families, are under Divine rule, and that civil ties have as much sanctity as household ties between those whom God joins and man is not to put asunder. It is evident to us that this faith entered largely into the recent contest, and more and more do our people insist upon the first article of true American statesmanship, that we are a nation, under God —and such, under Him, do we mean to continue.

This conviction expresses itself in the calm assurance with which the millions go to the ballot-box without the least misgiving, as the nation's right and duty to be and to prosper. Distance of place serves but to confirm the conviction; and our hearts beat warmly, but not strangely, as we note how closely the remotest regions answer to our own pulses, and East and West annihilate space and faction at one blow, as loyal word flashes from ocean to ocean that the nation is up and doing, and liberty and law walk hand in hand together. So far as space is concerned, the national domain is practically less in danger of separation than when the Constitution was adopted; and San Francisco is nearer New York in thought, aud will be soon nearer in exchange of goods, than Boston was in 1789. Chicago is nearer New Orleans than the Ohio was to the great Lakes at that date; and the whole country now is one as never before, in the growing sense of the unity of its geographical lines and the true fellowship of its commodities. The people are feeling that in territory we are a nation, and rising above sectional narrowness to statesmanlike enlargement.

The diversity of persons, as decided by locality, education, or race, offers a harder problem to the statesman, and Europe gives us over to destructoin as being bound to go to pieces through so many distracting and heterogeneous elements. Our people do not seem to have any such fear, but have solved practically the problem of national oneness with such personal varieties. We have taken in foreigners enough perhaps to make two nations as large as our whole population at the Declaration of Independence; and while we can not say that the foreign element has been all that could be wished, it surely has not been our foremost danger; and the two leading emigrant races, the Irish and the German, have done much good by their agricultural and mechanical labor, while they have marvelously counterbalanced each other by the reaction of Irish clannishness and ecclesiasticism against individualism and free companionship. A portion of the Irish, indeed, have seemed to have a mortal and dangerous antipathy to the negro; but this trouble has come to a head and has been settled by the riots of 1863 and their summary end. The negro is not to be hunted down and murdered in our streets. Of this our soldiers are quite sure, and we believe that the class that furnished the rioters are also sure. Our people are firm in the faith that mobs are to be put down, and that bayonets and grape-shot are shorter and more merciful medicine than soft speeches or Quaker guns.

The hostility between North and South is the greatest of our dangers of a personal nature, because so many circumstances of climate, trade, and history combine with personal dispositions to set the two at variance. But our people have never believed in any inevitable, irrepressible antagonism between Northerners and Southerners. In old times the two sections mingled freely together, aud the great men of both sections had a peculiar liking for each other, as the nature of things prepares us to believe. Since affinities thrive in the midst of contrasts, the reserved, laborious Northerner took comfort in the genial, indolent Southerner, in the ancient days of national loyalty. The one has always, perhaps, tended more to pride and the love of power, the other more to culture and prosperity; but the two got on very well together so long as their interests led the same way, and the planter's power was helped forward by the manufacturer's enterprise and thrift. The same congeniality will return when the cause of discord is removed. Already one obstacle is out of the way, and that is the mutual contempt that had begun to exist on account of the supposed shiftlessness of the South and the supposed cowardice of the North. The two parties have learned a certain respect for each other in the stern ordeal of war, and both have been too effective and too brave to foster any more contempt upon that score. Our soldiers bring back no fierce hatred for their antagonists, in spite of their too frequent cruelties; and our officers have apparently little fear of the rise of amicable fellowship as soon as the Secession leaders are out of the way, and the people return to their elective affinities.

But the negro — what shall we do with him, and how can the nation be one again, with such a barrier as those millions of blacks between the two sections, with the apparent antagonism of emancipation on one side and perpetual slavery on the other? Precisely what is to be done with the negro we do not profess to say, clear as the principle is that he is a human creature, and ought at once to have the rights of person, property and family that civilzation, even in despotic countries, secures to the humblest peasantry. Emancipation has been the inevitable issue of the causes now at work in both sections. Jefferson Davis himself has affirmed the negro's manhood and his love of freedom; and the rebel President, by his assault on Sumter and by his last proclamation, became practically the prince of abolitionists, and struck a blow at the Southern institution that Abraham Lincoln could never strike. Our people have always believed that emancipation would come at last, but they never looked for it or wished it in this way. The enemy hath done this, and compelled the nation thus to free the negro to save the white man. So let it be, and let slavery fall under the stroke of its own friends. Its fall must bring North and South together by mutual need; for the millions of blacks must be the curse of the whole people unless they are made the blessing of the whole.

Our people have already settled the statesmanship of emancipation, and are in the main as free from negromania as from negrophobia. They are understanding the negro's defects and excellencies very well, and seeing his fitness for the careful training that he needs and accepts. They are seeing that the way to get rid of him is to accustom him to help himself. Our people have never had that disease of *negro on the brain* that has so afflicted the slavery propaganda and their Northern allies, for they have been disposed to let him alone, and have not been eager either to tread him down or to glorify him. The war has given him new consequence, by showing — what our fathers well knew — that he can be a good patriot and a good soldier. Our people are for giving him a fair chance to find his own level. We are in no danger of having him on the brain so long as we give him fair play; and injustice is always sure to haunt its authors with the ghost of its victims. Do a man a wrong, pick his pocket, fire his house, forge his name, or poison his coffee, or even cherish any grudge against him, and we are quite sure to have him on our brain day and night. The only sure way to lay the ghost is to cease the wrong and set it right.

There were undoubtedly immense difficulties in the way of successful emancipation, but they are greatly lessened by recent experiences. It is clear that the negro is more docile than was anticipated, far less fierce and dangerous; and if less proud and intellectual than the average white man, much more mild, amiable, and reverential. It is clear, too, that the Southern horror of destroying the white man's social position by putting the negro on the same level of civil right is wholly idle. Liberty gives every class its proper level; and whatever the negro is or can be, he will be when emancipated. He will be himself, and not the white man. The war did much to set this matter right, and no observing man can suppose for a moment that freedom destroys all elective affinities, and confounds all minds and tastes in one indiscriminate mass. In our army, where all are under the same flag, our men kept their social affinities; and character and culture, whether in officer or private, are sure to tell. Our negro soldiers had a character and worth of their own; but they are themselves, and not white men, and they are content to be themselves, with their own associations and aptitudes. It is so here at home, where labor follows its own law, and party passions are silent. No man thinks his social position injured by the fact that our laws protect our colored people as well as himself. Nor do our colored servants claim undue rank because of their freedom. In the country black and white laborers freely meet together under the proprietor's eye, and no white man thinks himself at all in danger of degradation by the company. A few weeks ago, after finishing a rustic tower upon a high rock, to serve as a kind of Temple of Loyalty, that should lift up the banner and cross aloft in honor, I had need of a team of oxen to drag great stones to complete a rough wall along the base of the structure, and no team could be procured as readily as one belonging to a colored man, a small farmer in the neighborhood. He came with his two oxen, and worked all day with our own excellent man-of-all-work, an excellent specimen of Erin, as trusty as capable. The work was admirably done, and in a way to shame the law that denied him the right of suffrage. The oxen were driven skillfully and gently, the rocks were adroitly handled, the chat between the two men was playful and friendly; and when, at the close of the day, the dark man came cheerfully and resolutely with a huge block of white quartz upon his drag, and deposited it snugly in its place, near the foot of our Union tower, it seemed to me that there might be an omen in the event, and that, under God's providence, it might be the mission of the dark race to finish the temple of our American Liberty and Union by removing the old stigma on our shield, and bringing North and South into new and lasting fellowship. Our people are willing to believe in some such issue, and the robust, healthy instinct of the nation has never been afraid that freedom could destroy any inherent faculty or taste, or set any race above or below its natural and proper level.

The gravest danger to our national life threatens us from the quarter of party-spirit. Parties, more than differences of places or persons, have been and are our sorest evil; yet, in some respects, the evil has been less than was feared. Socialism has not troubled us, as was predicted; and it is marvelous that there is so little antagonism between rich and poor in our current politics; and the inanities of Communism have no hold of our people. The chief cause, probably, of the quiet feeling between the rich and poor is the fact that there are no fixed classes of rich and poor, but there is such free passage from one to the other, that he who makes war on either class may be fighting against his own children, and even against his own future condition. It is a striking fact, moreover, of our social condition, that the very order of persons who have been thought, from their lineage and condition, most dangerous to our civil order, are very fast becoming land-owners, and showing something of the conservatism that goes with property. As far as our observation goes, it appears clear that our laboring class in the country are bent on owning land; and within a few years we have seen many an acre of ground, with cottages, barn, pig, and cow, purchased by men who, in the old country, would never have aspired beyond a piece of hired land and a miserable shanty. No socialistic terrorism threatens us yet, nor has religious rancor risen to such proportions as to endanger our liberties. Our people have an instinctive sense that religious as well as civil liberty is safe, and the moment they see any disposition to interfere with it they will let the intruders know that freedom has weapons of its own, and knows how to strike as well as how to let alone.

Political parties have come near destroying us; and the present rebellion is the work of a political faction that has for thirty years been preparing for its accursed work. Yet no fair-minded, philosophical man will accuse either of the great historical parties of the country of originating secession. Andrew Jackson was as good a Union man as Henry Clay, and General M'Clellan affirmed the nation's right to defend its unity as emphatically as Abraham Lincoln. The two great historical parties have started from different poles of the same nationality — the first affirming the *one* organism, and the second affirming the *many* members in our national being, yet neither of them of necessity bound to deny the other's position; for if we believe that there are many in one, we must believe that there is one in many. Secession sprung indeed from one branch of the party of the many; but it is not a legitimate growth of that party, for it repudiates an essential of the Democratic idea, and insults and degrades the *many* States and people by assailing the unity that gives to the many liberty, dignity, and peace. Our people have seen from the beginning that secession is national suicide, and must be put down. Hence the persistency of the war spirit for four years, and the marvelous indorsement of that spirit at the late election. Neither party at the polls avowed secession, nor intended to favor it; but the political tricksters who drew up one of the platforms basely shrank from declaring openly the power of the nation to defend its life by arms, and foully insulted our slain and wounded heroes by declaring their sacrifice a failure and a folly. Our people would not stand such disloyalty and nonsense. They smelt the rat with their nostrils before they had time to speculate deeply upon the philosophy of the offense, and they would have nothing to do with any candidates who were mixed up with its abettors. Our people re-elected our President for many reasons indeed, but mainly from the best of all reasons, because they believed that he represented the vital, historical, Providential life of the nation; and that, with all his defects, he was a sound, old-fashioned American, and meant to live, and have us all live, under the old flag in spite of all rebeldom, even with England and France as its backers. The people were right, we believe; and it was the best statesmanship to re-elect Abraham Lincoln.

He took his honors modestly enough, and understood his position and what was expected of him. He intended to prove that his Unionism means not the ruin but the salvation of the States, and it will ere long show that in the Union, not out of it, even the now rebel States will find a prosperity, peace, and security that they could never win by being torn away from their historical and normal relation. He proved that the *many* were meant to be *one*, and time will prove that the *one* will protect and encourage the *many*, so as to secure to our great future a variety in unity such as we have never before known in the palmiest days of the republic. Our true policy will bring out all positive elements of local character as well as wealth, and in due time it will appear that the very traits that have done us wrong and moved our indignation can do us good and win our admiration. When Southern valor again becomes loyal we too shall be proud of it, and the Stonewall Jacksons of the future shall rank as do the Andrew Jacksons of the past. Even Southern Rights may cease to be an offensive word, and may enlist our enthusiasm and strength, when sought for and enjoyed in the Union, against all oppression and all misrule.

So we believe that our people hold fast to our great National Idea of the Many in One in face of all the differences of places, persons, and parties that seem to threaten it. Their religious sentiment is evidently accepting and exalting this national principle as never before, and singing and praying and preaching patriotism as of the essence of true faith. Our reading of history, our trust in Providence, our discipline of labor and sorrow, our sense of our mission in God's kingdom — nay, even our study of the variety and unity of nature around us, the law of differentialism and integration, the plainest teachings of God's bounty to us, and through us to the world, all combine to lift loyal conviction into an inspiration, and to make us hear the eternal Word confirming our great habit and popular instinct of nationality, and assuring us that God hath made us, and not we ourselves, and we have no right to abdicate the dignity to which we are called.

Our *manifest destiny* is substantiating our *national idea* by exhibiting its practical development in the great spheres of *industry, government, morality,* and *religion.* We are not speaking now of any ambitious theories or adventurer's visions, but of the obvious drift of affairs, and of the dispositions and work of our people.

We are a working people, and never since time was has there been a nation in which so many persons have taken a direct interest in the welfare of the country, and identified its welfare with their own. We all believe in getting a fair living; and our industry and enterprise have told wonderfully not only upon our national prosperity but our national spirit. An idea is nothing or next to nothing without some corresponding spirit; and what Plato calls spirit, or the irascible quality, is a necessary trait of the rational man if he would be practical or do any thing in the world. Now surely our labor has been a great school of public spirit or of national will; and while we have been severally thinking of getting a living, and opening springs of industry to please ourselves, Providence, by its own prevailing laws, has been connecting these together, as it connects the rills of the mountains with the brooks of the meadow and the waters of the sea, until what seemed dribbling weakness and feeble loneliness swells into combined majesty, and the grandeur of the all flows out from the little offerings of each. How magnificent is the wealth of the country, and what patience and strength and persistency have entered into the spirit of the people under this long discipline of toil! Power, like substance, is not lost, but only transformed; and what a startling manifestation of national power has sprung from the rising of industrial energy into public spirit!

The *wealth* of the country feels the pulsation of its great heart, and a unity of life is seeking to assimilate its commodities together in a true economy and fellowship. What wonders from the mine, as iron, copper, lead, coal, silver and gold, come up from the dark earth; and not demons of darkness, but spirits of light, they join hands in benign activity, and distance the legends of magicians by the miracles of their harmonized utilities. Our fields and orchards join them in their ministry, and enrich and unite the nation with their gifts. Our grain, wheat, corn, rye, are all loyal servitors, and bind us to the sugar and rice and cotton of the South by a thousand affinities. Our products make us one nation as well as our lakes and mountains and rivers and seas, and our political economy is an important part of our manifest destiny. Our people are seeing this; and not only do industrial statistics now enter into common education, but our mechanics' and farmers' fairs and festivals are teaching the magnificence of our resources and the Providential unity of our domain. Even the burden of taxation has pressed upon us the conviction of our national ability as well as need; and the purse is regarded as the loyal defender of the flag. Our laboring class are feeling a new sense of proprietorship in the soil and its products; and the mines of Pennsylvania and of the

Pacific coast not only swell our statistics of revenue but animate the courage and loyalty of the people, as if each man had interest and honor in the affluence of all. So let it be, until we wörk out our destiny to the full, and He to whom the earth with its fullness belongs enables us to see that His will is done in our fullness, and prosperity is the handmaid of humanity and religion.

We take as cheerful a view of the development of our national idea in the sphere of *government*. We have been learning to govern and to be governed for more than two hundred years, and our native American people especially have the hereditary spirit that reconciles liberty with law, and so unites two master forces, obedience and authority, in our loyal temper. The spirit of good government was nurtured in the old colonial townships, and went up through successive steps to the chair of the state and the nation. Never, probably, in history has there been so much schooling in the function of government as here within a century, and a mighty habit of order has been formed that has taken possession even of the rude border regions, and won the wild passions of the rough populace to the restraints of law and the blessings of civilization. California, when cut off from the direct control of the national arm, became a law to herself; and her own people, not a mob but a Vigilance Committee, like Saul of Tarsus, were won by an inward manifestation of the rightful rule to true loyalty and they carried to the sister States, as Paul carried to the Apostles' college, the commission of membership, which came not so much of flesh and blood as from above. Our national order has been a constant schooling of public spirit, and our statesmen have been the generals of our peace, as our generals have been the statesmen of our war.

Undoubtedly the chief source of our satisfaction in our strong men is in their power to bring out the purpose that we all cherish or do what we all wish to do. A great thinker or speaker charms us by bringing out our own latent *thought*, and the word *comes home* to us, we say, because it touches a chord all ready to be touched. So a hero, whether in the Senate or the field, *comes home* to us by bringing out our own latent *will*, and doing for us what we can not do of ourselves. Our leaders in peace and war lead our *spirit* as well as our *idea*, and while we are proud of them, we thank them most for their mastery of heroic force, their power to win us by their very command. So now we delight in our great generals, as they cheer, and strengthen, and integrate our own wavering spirits, and the national pluck is embodied and organized in their will. We are no more afraid of being trodden on by them than we are afraid of being oppressed by a great thinker; for the hero ceases to be himself the moment he ceases to be possessed by the public will, just as the thinker ceases to be himself, and loses his charm the moment he sacrifices truth to passion or policy, and private feeling displaces intellectual loyalty. We rejoice greatly, therefore, in our noble generals and their brave armies. They develop powers that are to live in the life of the nation; and our people feel the truth even better than they know how to express it, and believe that peace will make us braver, as well as more loyal than ever, from the permanence of the spirit of discipline that goes from the camp and field to the household and school and Senate. There are, of course, bad soldiers; and war of itself is a sad evil, yet its temper is not selfish, but social and patriotic; and they who fight bravely under the flag affirm the law of the land in every blow, and declare the first essential of peace by the sword. War is the necessary act of government when assailed, and is as justifiable in certain circumstances as the police of our cities, which defends our persons and property by making constant war upon crime. We accept the military discipline of the last few years as part of the manifest destiny of the Nation, and are convinced by it that we have a heroic will as well as a leading idea. We have been laughed at as a set of braggarts half drunk with reveling in the wealth of a land that came to us by chance. We shall be laughed at no longer after such valor by sea and land. We do not laugh at our antagonists, for they too are brave, and are our own countrymen, and are to be again under our flag. We had rather fight with them than against them, and again, as of old, count their blood as part and parcel of our own.

We have no time to treat of our national destiny in its highest sphere, the region of morals and religion; and we must be content with the merest glance. It is becoming every year more evident, that while with us Church and State have been, are likely to be, distinct in organization and function, they are to have great influence upon each other, and that religion is feeling as well as shaping the character of our people and institutions. Recent struggles have brought out the temper of our great churches, and done much to bring them together in a certain fellowship of thought and feeling, if not of name. Take, for example, the most widely contrasted branches — the branches of extreme centralization and extreme individualism — the Roman Catholic and the Puritan Independent, the former with its historical priesthood and polity, its national council and far-seeing conservatism and its fixed authority; the latter with its popular will, congregational freedom, subjective mind, aud radical temper. How strongly the Puritan Independent has argued and worked and fought for the national life, and given largeness to his method by loyal fidelity. How much he has done to connect the stubborn individualism of which he has been the sturdy champion, with the national fellowship without which individualism runs mad with self-conceit and self-will. The Roman Catholic, with the other prelatical bodies, has helped us perhaps more than he has known by keeping in view the historic unity and progress of true civilization, and never consenting to surrender the integrity of his church organization to party passions or sectional strife. The Roman Catholic Church, as is the case with all prelacy, has been too timid in some respects, and not all of her prelates have, like Purcell and Timon, spoken out fully the word of humanity and patriotism that the nation craves, and Christendom should give now as of old. Yet Catholicism has done us good by keeping open great lines of fellowship between the beligerents as well as presenting us with noble specimens of generalship. She will do us more good when we, as a nation, study better the secret of her organic power, and master the arts of administration which her leaders have so well understood not always in the interests of liberty and progress. Between the two, the Independent and the Catholic, dwell a great company of thoughtful and well-balanced Christians, who can help the nation vastly in the present need by uniting depth of personal conviction with breadth of vision and force of will, in such a way as to bring out the resources of American character and fulfil our destiny in the kingdom of God on earth. Not in form, but in fact, the American Church is uniting the radical idea of the many with the conservative idea of the one.

We are near some crisis that is to call out the higher principles and powers of our people as never before. We have been at war with States who speak our language, profess our religion, and share our history and laws with us. We must not only subdue their rebellion but reclaim them to loyalty. The religion of the country must affirm the sanctity of the national idea, and exalt the public will by homage to the Supreme will, so as make even the enemy respect the motive, and discriminate between brute force or sectional pride, and civic virtue or moral heroism. The religion of the country must help on the coming reconciliation by a spirit as gentle as it is brave, as merciful as it is just and true. A great work is to be done in this way, and it is too much to expect of our rulers to do the whole of it, or look even to Presidential Messages, or Cabinet Reports, to say all that the best heart and culture of the people craves. Precisely what is to be said or done by Christian influence we will not undertake to say; but sure we are that the time is near for a Christian mediation that must leave its mark upon the national life, and show that not only in the age of miracles did living waters flow from the flinty rock.

The American's character itself is to be invigorated, softened, and enlarged, and lifted up, by the discipline of war and pacification. He is to have a certain individualism, but not like the German, who hates organization; he is to hold fast to institutions, but not like the Englishman, who dreads change; he is to love universal ideas, but not like the Frenchman, who makes ambitious abstractions bow the knee to imperial pride. Independent, steadfast, cosmopolitan, the American will keep the post to which Providence has called him, and his manifest destiny shall bring ruin upon no other race or nation, but serve the welfare of mankind and the glory of God.

Thus, near the 4th of March, 1865, we interpreted the cheerful lessons in Statesmanship that were taught us by the 8th of November, 1864.

Merciful Heaven, how overwhelming the events, disasters, successes, fears, hopes, strife of arms and words, peace of treaties and of tempers since that time. Thank the God of our fathers, that Abraham Lincoln's "plain people" still remember his teaching and their Presidential training. They have the country in their hands and mean to keep it for their children in the face of all destroyers, whether dainty gentlemen, raving agitators or dirty ruffians.

A Happy Christmas or New Year to our fellow Statesmen, the people of our America. They are our great success and hope.

IX.

Off-Hand Speaking.

OFF-HAND SPEAKING.

A TALK WITH TWO COLLEGIANS.

YOU are soon, my dear fellows, to leave college, and enter upon a more direct course of training for the work of your life in the great world. You R., are to take after your good father and go into the ministry; and you, are also to follow the family bent, and be a merchant, as is your father, as well as your grandfather, whose well-known name you bear. We are to have a little talk together now, as of old, upon your career, and the proper preparation for it. Some matters might, perhaps, be now profitably discussed that have come up between us before; but it is best at present to take a new subject, and one that is not only interesting and important to you, but to hundreds of our young men of your years and prospects. I mean off-hand speech, or what is usually called extempore speaking.

The fact that you have been through college by no means implies that you have learned this art; for many very good scholars, according to the college scale, are unable to say a word for themselves without the book or manuscript; and I have known admirable linguists, mathematicians, and essayists who blush up to the eyes and stammer and flounder the moment they are asked to speak without written preparation even upon a familiar subject. Perhaps it is generally the case that bookish men are more troubled to find words in time of need than practical men who have been trained in the world to speak as the occasion calls. The cause is obvious, and one that by no means disparages book-learning, but urges constant training in applying book-knowledge to things as they are. The scholar knows more of words than things, and he is in the habit of depending upon the written word to suggest to him the thing, so as to be sometimes sadly puzzled to name or describe the thing in the absence of the written word. His own language is to him very much like a foreign tongue that he has learned to read but not to speak, and in which he can easily read the masters of its literature, without being able to muster words enough to tell his most common wants in conversation. The man of affairs is not troubled in this way; and however deficient he may be in a classic vocabulary, he has at his tongue's end all he knows. and his words rise to his lips the moment he sees the things which they designate. The farmer can talk farm, and the sailor ship, and the merchant shop very glibly, and they are never troubled to find the connecting link between the thing and the name. Sometimes unschooled men have a rich and ready vocabulary by large observation and experience that gives them a unique eloquence; and scholars may almost envy untaught orators and poets the homely, and vigorous, and pictorial speech which comes to them from learning of nature and life at first hand without the mediation of books. There is something in such spirits as Bunyan and Burns that books can not give. That dreamer evidently had studied the Slough of Despond and the Delectable Mountains from sloughs and mountains before his own eyes; and this poet had seen the Daisy and Mouse for himself before he put pen to paper. The same principle holds good of ready and eloquent speech; and the preachers and orators who have learned words from things do better, other matters being equal, than those who learn things from words. We are all coming now to a perception of this truth, and applying it to education from the nursery upward. Say *apple* to a child, and he will say it after you, after a fashion; but show him a ripe, red apple, and let him taste of it, and he will tell its name with gusto, so as to carry the color and the flavor in his tones.

Undoubtedly a great cause of the relative inefficiency of many highly-educated men as popular speakers comes from their dealing with nature and life at second hand, or through words, instead of taking them at first hand from the very things. Of course this is not the necessary result of education, as such, but only of what usually passes for education. A well educated man will not be content with being a mere wood-monger, but he will insist upon having every word answer to a thing; and he, moreover, will not think himself master of the word until he can go to it from the thing, as well as from it to the thing. In order to be rid of the verbiage that is so apt to trouble students they will do well to bear in mind two rules. In the *first place, let them live as far as possible in contact with reality;* see and hear nature and the world with their own eyes and ears, and verify the words in the book by the word that is in human life. Some scholars are so shadowy and ghostly as hardly to verify by their own observation and experience the most commonplace terms — being hardly able to say for themselves what flesh and blood, bone and sinew, horse and boat, woods and river mean. The moment these words are mated with reality they have a wholly new expression, as if the soul had found its body, and sent its life through the whole frame. It is encouraging to note how fondly and readily such words then come to mind, and how well even a child will talk of objects that have come before the senses, or stirred the will and the affections. There is far too large a portion of the vocabulary of students that is without this living commentary, not only from the seclusion that shuts out too much of the material world, but from the indifference that ignores the great principles and duties of society. The words of home, and country, and religion are not alive upon the lips until the things themselves are alive in the soul, and personal loyalty, domestic, national, and spiritual, makes them burn with meaning and love. It is well, therefore, for a young man to shun the perils of the mere book-worm, and to make a genial and worthy life run parallel with his studies, so that he shall not be a stranger to any of the verities and virtues that make up so much of the soul of the great body of literature. Some religious writer has spoken of the importance of the orator having an eloquent experience, meaning, undoubtedly, that he who feels much will speak strongly on spiritual matters — for out of the abundance of the heart the mouth speaketh. But why limit the remark to one class of subjects? Why ought not all experience to be eloquent? Why must not all words shine and burn that speak our living thought or repeat our personal experience? Cicero well and wisely said that the good orator must be a good man. This holds true for many reasons, and, among others, for this reason — because a good man has all human affections within him, and the language of human life is to him a living language, a vernacular tongue, and every noble sentence has an interpreter within his own soul. The diction and the elocution will both profit by a true experience; and the true man's word will not only be the right one, but the strong one.

It is a somewhat curious study to look over the few thousand words that make the staple of human expression, and see how much experience they imply — how much knowledge of truth and falsehood, good and evil. The English language is said to contain about a hundred thousand available words; but, of course, many of these are too technical or strange to be used in common speech, and a well-educated man employs but a few thousand words in writing and speaking upon ordinary subjects. Shakspeare used but fifteen thousand, and Milton has in his poems not more than eight thousand. Estimate our vocabulary modestly, and say that in our speech and conversation we employ or ought to employ some five thousand words, and try as nearly as we can to make out a list of them. How instructive and startling is that simple catalogue! and one might think even the dictionary interesting reading, if we could allow its simplest terms to question us closely, and make us tell how faithfully our own life has been interpreting their meaning by studying whatever is good and true and shunning all that is evil and false. We might find that our vocabulary is in some respects incomplete, because our experience has been so beggarly, and while there are some words to be learned, there are others to be unlearned. Most of us, veterans of the pen and the voice, undoubtedly have great defects in our vocabulary. and some of us use a few pet words everlastingly, while we are strangers to some of the noblest terms in the language. Young men like you have their vocabulary to form, and your present habits will have much to do with the phraseology that you domesticate upon your lips. In your college course, in reading, translating, and writing, you must have employed a pretty large portion of the language; but the words that you have used once or twice are not a part of your vocabulary, and may never recur to you again. That is vocabulary to us which comes home to us, and is familiar and easy; in fact, our mother-tongue. It is important to make this as large and effective as the demands of truth and duty. The present is eminently a formative period with you, and you are to decide what words to drop and what to adopt. Educated, as you have been, under judicious masters, you will not need to have me argue with you upon the importance of preferring the simplest, strongest terms to such as are fanciful and euphuistic, and of wedding to your lips as much as possible of the homely, hearty old Saxon. It has strength and beauty too, like the rock that can be built into solid walls or polished into shining gems. Homeliness you know how to distinguish from vulgarity; and let me urge you to throw out of your common conversation the vulgarisms and whatever passes as slang in college or in the world. These will taint even your public speech, if not by stealing covertly into your sentences, at least by making you constrained, and robbing your delivery of that easy colloquial flow, that is so great a charm in off-hand utterance, and which is easily acquired if you can put yourself upon your habitudes, and let the thought move in its wonted way without fear of its playing off any uncouth antics or mortifying laxities. Let the memory be full of the choicest words from the ample treasures of your study and your observation, and you will find your mouth richer far than you knew, as day by day you bring them into use, or as they start unbidden at the touch of nature or the stir of life.

I spoke of two rules for guarding against the pedantic verbiage that crams the student with mere words; and have illustrated the first of these in what I have said of the importance of making nature and life the interpreter of language, so as to have words stand for things. *The second rule* relates to *such mastery of language as enables us to lay hold of it when we want it most,* or learning to go from the thing to the word, instead of expecting always to have the book before us to lead to the thing. To command language is not merely to have it, but to have it within call, and he surely is not master of this learning who can not use it at will. No kind of property is more deceptive than that which is literary, for there is none that so tempts the owner to call his own what he can do nothing with. Money and lands, if we have not mind or force to use them, can be loaned or given to others; but our literary stock becomes dead rubbish if it is not quick with living thought and an earnest purpose. Our college education is often sadly deficient in the practical training that enables the student to bring his resources to bear upon real life, and the mind as well as the body suffers much from the neglect of the muscular force and suppleness that give calmness and strength to the overwrought nerves, and help them translate their sensations into deeds. The great point, then, is to utilize what we know by a practical spirit and method, or by a thorough discipline. As to the best discipline for the powers of speech there are a great many prescriptions, and we are quite willing to have them all tried, and that especial way preferred which best meets each case. The books on the subject are without end as to number, and the chief of them may be read by you with profit, and read again if you have ever studied them at all. Cicero de Oroatore is a masterly treatise, and Quintilian has admirable thoughts. But the best book on the topic for our day is that of Bautain, a French abbé: this is written mainly for preachers, but does well for all public speakers. Books, however, amount to little unless you practice upon them for yourselves, and this word *practice* is the root of the whole matter. If we would learn to speak, we must begin to speak; and to stop short of this, in order to prepare, is to refuse to go into the water because we have not learned to swim.

I advise you to take every *proper* opportunity to speak for yourselves. It is not well, indeed, to speak for the sake of speaking, but whenever you have any thing to say. It is not proper to mistake gabble for speech, and fall into the monstrous habit of talking against time, without regard to sense or spirit. I think it was Lord Brougham who advised a young aspirant to oratorical fame to begin by acquiring volume or spouting words, at any rate or any how, and afterward minding exactness of thought and expression; just as a miller must have a mill-stream to begin with, and as soon as the water runs freely he can look carefully to the waterwheels, and millstones, and all the apparatus for using the water. It certainly is dangerous, and may be fatal to a man to begin to speak loosely and insincerely merely for the sake of hearing himself talk; and nothing makes a man more sure of being voted an intolerable bore than the name of being such an interminable talker — one of those everlasting prosers who keep running on like a neglected hydrant, simply for want of power to keep the mouth shut. In our day we had one such speaker, who never pretended to believe what he said, or to ask others to believe in him, but made a joke of talking against time. He could discharge an enormous volume of words within a given limit, after the most florid pattern, without ever being conscious of a conviction or an idea, or giving such consciousness to others. He meant to talk and be talked of; and, sure enough, he did spout himself into a conspicuous office somewhere down in Dixie, but he dearly won his honors by sacrifice of much that was noble in his birth-right. When, after years of absence, he returned to the old college halls, he did not even seek out his own class, but sat at another table, and when cordially greeted by his familiar name, he stared at his old cronies and pretended not to know them. He probably at this moment is playing off the same game toward the land of his birth, and joining his rebel boon companions in curses at New England with her schools and churches. His case so well illustrates the consequences, and perhaps also the cause, of heartless speaking, that I can not but allude to it here as a warning. Let him repent and he will be forgiven, and we will remember and encourage his good points; but at present he seems to me to have done the meanest thing that ever was perpetrated by a decent graduate from our college halls.

Do begin with speaking honestly and faithfully your own sincere thoughts in the best possible way, and taking every just occasion to express yourself well. Common conversation is good, alike for the voice and the vocabulary, and nothing is better discipline than the unaffected, sympathetic tone, and the easy colloquial language that good-fellowship gives. I need not warn you of the danger of mistaking discourse for conversation, and haranguing your companions in lengthened words and sonorous periods instead of pleasantly chatting with them. A thing is good when it is good of its kind; and discourse, which pretends to be talk, is not good after its kind, and is in danger of encouraging the very affectation and deceit that we have been condemning. Often, indeed, talk readily and properly rises into discussion, and while you are at table, or in your walks, you find yourself speaking at length before you know it, and some of the best lessons in expression come to you unbidden at such times. Your latest studies and reading come fitly and happily into such discussions; and I remember nothing more fondly in our training for professional life than those free-and-easy chats that expanded so naturally into grave colloquies. Our Commons fare was much sweeter from this seasoning; and who of us would not give a great deal for a full and fair report of those chance talks over our beef and pudding? The fact that we were not wholly as knowing as we now are lent fresh zest to conversation, for nothing so spices expression as the talker's honest faith in what he is saying; and while we were making our first acquaintance with the master poets and thinkers we could venture, with earnest and amiable simplicity, upon a great many loving and believing assertions that would stagger our now harder temper and credence. We have not forgotten, indeed, Plato and Aristotle, Aquinas and Duns Scotus, Descartes and Malebranche; but I am afraid that we who are now near fifty could not discourse so magisterially upon those worthies and their works as when, like you, we were just out of our teens, and proud of the beards that were hoisting the sign of manhood upon our faces, and tempting us to parade it in our thinking.

All young men should be in the habit of speaking deliberately among their associates upon topics of importance, and in our day the college clubs were most important schools of training. I am afraid that they have in some respects degenerated now, and that far more importance is given to the elegance of their equipment and the frequency and costliness of their banquets, than to the good sense and earnestness of their debates, and the finish and nobleness of their essays and orations. The Law and Divinity schools continued these discussions, and our candidates for the bar and pulpit did almost as much for each other in friendly debate as their professors did for them in grave lectures. In such discipline we learned to think and talk upon our legs; and we have been carried through many a hard trial and critical emergency by that pleasant and companionable training. Some of us made a point of speaking somewhere as often as once a week, and we were glad to vary the audience and the theme as much as possible. We began in the Freshman year — so long, long ago — and made our début with a dozen or two of beardless boys like ourselves in the room of one of our class-mates. We took no name, but consented to be called, in fun, the "Literati in Fumo," because our debates generally ended in smoke; and perhaps the fumes of the cigars were a fair symbol of the haziness of our ideas. Year by year the field expanded, until we saw our own pet speakers the favorite orators of the great University Clubs, and not a few of them have won signal honors in the high places of professional life. Sometimes we tried our gift in new and strange quarters; and great was the gusto with which, in our Senior year, we frequented the Lyceum of the village where we kept school. The subjects there were more popular and practical, and the audience was more varied, and in some respects more sympathetic. The mothers and maidens smiled favor upon the new-fledged orators from the college nest; and lest our laurels might be too easily won, some very shrewd and tough reasoners from the bush joined in the debate, and made us do our best to keep from being put down by their strong sense and pithy speech. Afterward we enlarged our sphere still further; and in jails and prisons, as well as in church schools and social conferences, we tried to stir up the gift that was within us. Great was the day when our two schools of Law and Divinity joined together in a Moot Court, under Judge Story's presidency, and one school furnished counsel and the other the jury. One of the most voluble of the orators was a Southern fire-eater in a suit of flame-colored home-spun; and we little thought that the nullification that the costume then symbolized would afterward swell into secession, and that flame would light the fires of this fearful rebellion.

In advising you to use all such occasions for practice in off-hand speaking, I know very well that a more stern and exact culture is required to save you from winning ease and copiousness at the expense of correctness and beauty. It is dangerous to speak much without also writing carefully; for however happy you may be in spontaneous expression, you inevitably tend to looseness and diffuseness, unless you sharpen and rectify your words by your pen and carefully purge and point your style. Close and elegant written composition not only tells upon your manuscript but upon your conversation and speech, and is as vital to oratory as the drill is to war. It will no more rob you of fervor than faithful drilling robs the soldier of his fire, and the sentences that are best knit together transmit the glow of passion as the solid and well-trained phalanx burns with martial fire, and launches itself like a lightning flash upon the enemy. It is well to unite careful writing with free speech, and to go into debate with the mind filled and clarified by the pen and the tongue at the same time, free to move at will. For all important occasions this is the best preparation, and he who is habituated to it will find that his writing gives him breadth and sequence without shutting him up in his manuscript, and giving him the constraint of manner and thought that are so apt to damage mere *memoriter* speaking.

A capital exercise in elegance and exactness of expression is to be found in your classic studies. You probably went through much of your Latin and Greek as mere taskwork, without entering with great zest into the merits of the thought or expression. Recur now to the great masters, and take up your Virgil or Horace, Livy or Tacitus, Homer or Sophocles, and render the choice passages into your best English. Try this plan with a classic friend if it becomes irksome to you by yourself. This exercise does far more for you than merely to give you the sense of the original. It enables you to select and handle the richest words and idioms of your own tongue. It is a lesson in extempore speech by setting you to work to find not only fit terms for given idioms, but suitable graces to answer to the graces of the original. In one sense it is a better exercise than original composition, for it gives you a clue to niceties or elegance of expression that you would not be likely to hit upon of yourself, and at the same time it relieves you of the servility of being a mere copyist. You have a model before you then, and this suggests much that is important; but you are not to copy it exactly, much less mechanically, and you are to retain and portray its very life in a different material or medium. You are not only to use a different canvas for your picture, but different pencils and pigments. So you learn to be an artist yourself in presence of the works of the great masters.

The forms of speech are so many, and language is so far the voice of our almost infinite thought and life, that no school-training can exhaust its various movements or give you its wonderful art. The sword exercise is the combination of a few passes, and dancing is taught in a few steps variously combined; but who shall presume to number the passages of the human voice, or name the steps taken in speech, whether verse or prose? The best models are here the true masters; and no man who is not a thorough student of the great authors who have shaped language can catch the true movement of words, and understand and apply their countless variety. Take for example an oration of Cicero, and what a drill it is in variety of terms and idioms! The page swarms with a mighty host in every process of evolution. You see a battle-field, the words marshalled like troops of every grade and arm, and manœuvring in every phasis of tactics. You must be there yourself if you would know what is going on; and you can not but be there, and under the general's own eye, if you follow his order with your own, and render faithfully his programme into your own living translation. The study of such masters will give us new freedom of movement, and if we are careful to catch their inspiration and guard against imitative mannerism, we learn to break up the plodding monotony of a merely closet style, and infuse the freshness of life into our diction and tones. It is well to try the influence of all classes of writers in this way, and to go from the florid magnificence of Cicero to the sententious point of Tacitus; to hold converse with the dignified and sometimes sombre Virgil after the gay and witty Horace; and to muse on Fate with Aeschylus after singing jolly songs with Anacreon and triumphal odes with old Pindar. We scholastics tend sadly to run into ruts, and the more is the pity, since we have at hand such ready methods of correction; and the whole life of literature, ancient and modern, is asking to take us by the hand and to lead us its own way at the moving of its mighty and various and genial will. How can we mope on so in the dumps with such stirring spirits within call?

It is the peculiar privilege of the scholar not only to know *languages*, but also *language;* or to catch the form and spirit of that great humanity that has been voicing itself in words from the beginning, and which speaks to us now in such fullness in the Historic Word that informs all the master tongues whether living or dead. Philosophically speaking, there is virtually but one language, which is the soul of all dialects; and what we call the dead languages are called so because they are the real roots of speech, and, as such, are under ground that they may the more effectually sustain and quicken the new tongues that have branched from them. A generous classic training enables you to see and feel this continuity of life; and if you not only study well the great models of antiquity, but also keep yourself alive, genial, and active in present affairs and keep your tongue in vital communion with living society, you will find that you are entering into the grand affiliation, and your diction is blooming out and fruiting from the majestic tree of speech planted by the Lord of ages. There will be to you an increasing element of gracious inspiration in speech, and your words will have new and cheering relations with the eternal Word. How language begun we do not know, and the same mystery attaches to this as to all origin, whether in nature or mind. But as we use language freshly and well, and find how full of spirit and life it is, we come to something like a satisfactory idea of its origin, in our experience of the vital powers that preside over speech, and which are as independent of our understanding and will as the air and the lungs, that are so essential to utterance, exist independently of our doing or thinking. Philologians like Muller seem to think that speech came at first by a certain inspiration; and that man, who, of course, was created with organs of speech, found himself uttering words when he first felt the mystery of existence, and the new-found world first touched the springs of life, and the spontaneous forces of his being came into play with a fullness that no artificial schooling can reproduce, How speech was first generated we will not undertake to say. but we are content to illustrate its generation by its regeneration; and surely every man who is true master of language, and who finds his own thoughts and affections in full communion with the historical word of his race, his own mind voicing itself spontaneously in the standard voice of mankind, and the spirit of mankind flowing back into the soul from the spoken and written word — the scholar who has any thing of this experience has a literary regeneration that will help him mightily toward his interpretation of the genesis of speech. You, my dear fellows, will know this experience more and more as you enter earnestly into life, and you will find in that great school a light and a fire that seldom wait on college themes or exhibition platforms.

Perhaps you think me thus far dealing too much in generalities, and you would like to have me come more to the practical point, and tell you what to do when you wish to meet an especial occasion, or when you are cornered unexpectedly and have to stand up and speak for yourself or be ashamed. All that has been said bears upon this point, for whatever makes a man master of language makes him master of the occasion that calls him out. A good speaker, like a good soldier, is always ready — his powers never broken by servile dulness, nor unstrung by indolence; his armor always bright, and his weapons at hand. I allow that some especial training is needed in view of unexpected emergencies, as the good soldier is taught to prepare for surprise, and to be always on his guard. Yet it is utterly idle to hope by any code of rules, much less by any tricks of memory or little arts of speech, to supply the place of that thorough training which is the only guarantee of success and security against surprise. You must seriously study every subject, and observe every object with a practical eye, and merge, or rather complete, the *connoisseur* in the man of affairs. You have already taken one step forward in your method; for while you begun your college course by studying *books* as such, and confining mainly yourselves to your manuals, you have now for some time been busy with subjects, and your most important exercises have compelled you to form and state your views of certain subjects from various references and meditations. You are now to take a second step forward, and study not only *subjects*, but for *objects*. You are not only to write themes and rehearse essays, but to make arguments and plead causes. There is a vast deal of advantage as well as of difficulty in this transition; and your way of meeting it is in great part to decide whether you will plod on in the old school-boy routine, or strike out freshly and manfully in the paths of practical life, with your eye fixed upon the work set before you. A good speaker's eye and tone tell you in the beginning that he knows what he is about, and not only has something to say, but something to say it for; and he is not as one that beateth the air. The habit of studying subjects thus for a practical object will give you a method of arranging, illustrating, and urging your thoughts that will become to you a second nature.

How to divide a subject is a point of much importance, and one that has been much discussed. The masters of rhetoric give us valuable suggestions; but these amount to little unless we illustrate, and correct, and enlarge them by our own experience. It is always well for you while reading or hearing a speech, or oration to analyze it into its constituent parts, and see clearly the members and their bearing on each other and on the main point. You will find that there is a comparative anatomy in the limbs of speeches as in nature, and that a few types constantly repeat themselves with variations. But every wise and earnest speaker will have the principle even if he have not the theory; and books of rhetoric no more originate the idea of the Exordium and the Peroration, etc., than they originated prose itself. The best of these books are good helps, as already hinted, and no young man of your age can do better than to review what the masters of eloquence say of proper preparation. No little work will stir and help you more than the admirable treatise of Theremin upon "Eloquence as a Virtue." It will not only give you excellent ideas of style and arrangement, but quicken your manliness, and do much to shame you out of the shambling slipshod habits and bloodless expression that so often characterize bookish men, and make them compare unfavorably with men of less culture, and with more fire and better aim.

If you find yourself caught before an audience, and have

little or no time to prepare a speech, just put yourself upon your previous training; look at the subject in its main features; see how much, how worthy, how important it is; apply, if you will, the categories of your logic as to quantity, quality, and relation; make the most simple and obvious arrangement of your thoughts, beginning with some statement of principles of truth, following with some leading point of duty, and closing with urging the thoughts home with persuasive sympathy and personal regard. You may be sorely troubled by being taken unawares and not knowing what in the world to say. I believe that it is Quintilian who says that every practiced orator should have a supply of *loci communes*, or commonplaces, which he should fall back upon whenever he is in danger of breaking down from loss of memory or want of preparation. This may do in desperate cases; but a shrewd audience will soon find out the trick, and know when a speaker is drifting on the tide and does not know where he is, and when he is making headway; and it is far better to express the first genuine conviction that really belongs to the subject and the hour than to launch forth into the most ambitious generalities. A vast deal depends upon your beginning, and if you start with a sincere, unaffected tone, and with a genuine conviction, you are almost sure to get through with credit. An earnest man will be pretty sure to have something to say upon any important subject; and even if he is at loss at first what to say, he knows how to confess his inability or ignorance, or to ask help in such a way as to give grace even to his defects, and make them more eloquent than a pedant's learning or a blusterer's declamation. In fact there is nothing better than naturalness; and a man who is accustomed to speaking may be sure to meet every crisis tolerably well, if he will only be content to seem to be what he is, and to make sincerely any remark that really comes to him, and add to his sincerity modesty and good-will. Sometimes truthfulness to his convictions will not allow him to say much, and very little thought rises to his lips. Better far say that little truth than a whole volume of rigmarole forced up for the occasion. Truthfulness is a virtue that wins favor in the end and keeps it when won; and brevity is a failing that men forgive far more readily than prolixity.

To speak well you must be in *rapport* not only with your own mind, but with your subject and your audience. It is really wonderful that this connection is so rarely complete, and that such mishaps come from its absence. Sometimes you are out of joint with yourself, and your mind seems no more to jump with your tongue than the mind of the man in the moon, and you feel that you have no hold of yourself. Again your thought, although quite active in a certain way, does not enter into the subject, and you are very much like an eager horseman who wants to ride, but finds the horse refusing to be mounted, or when mounted, insisting upon standing still or pitching the luckless rider over his head. Sometimes, moreover, when you and your subject get on very well together, you fail to connect with the audience, and without having any positive quarrel with them, you find yourself as far apart as if they were a thousand miles off. You will use every means to establish the true relation, to keep your own mind ready at your call; to make it dwell faithfully upon such leading principles as are fundamental to all important subjects; and to take vital interest in men, not such as belong to your clique only, but in men as men in all the various tempers and conditions of the common lot. He is happy who masters this connection thoroughly, and agrees with his own soul, his subject, and his audience. He is the good rider who is master of himself, his good steed, and the road, and he goes forth conquering and to conquer.

Some very interesting and curious phenomena occur when this *rapport* is complete; and some of the signs that spiritualists ascribe to supernatural agency are constant attendants of good extemporaneous speaking. A strange and cheering and powerful influence rises up within the speaker, and is met and quickened by the subject and the occasion. The calmer he is, and the less elevated and blown about by passion, the more profoundly he is inwardly moved. Thoughts and emotions come to him of themselves without painful seeking, and the subject opens itself to him as if it were a part of his own brain or heart. Words and sentences of unusual fitness and beauty come to him of themselves, and seem to speak of themselves without fatigue of voice or exhaustion of brain or nerve. A remarkable bond grows up between speaker and hearers; the audience light up with a mild glow, and a lambent brightness almost transfigures each head in the speaker's eye, as at the great Pentecost; while the whole assembly seems to be informed with one life, and the thousand souls are drawn together as one spiritual body.

I have talked with a great many distinguished extempore speakers, and while they are almost universally reluctant to trust to any marvelous influences, and disposed to insist upon careful thought and frequent and exact writing to guard against looseness and repetition, they allow that there is something in their best oratorical experiences that passes their understanding. Our friend C——, who is unsurpassed by any living preacher in extempore power, alike of language, thought, and tone, affirms that he sometimes, in his best hours, loses all conscious hold upon his mind and speech, and while perfectly sure that all is going on well in his attic, it seems to him that somebody else is talking up there; and he catches himself wondering who under the sun that fellow is who is driving on at such a rate. Carpenter, the physiologist, speaks of what he calls "unconscious cerebration," or states in which the brain works without any conscious effort to do it, and without any consciousness of what it is doing of itself, as when a man wakes in the morning and finds his thinking much in advance of where he left it when he went to sleep, or even some hard problem solved or knotty questions answered. The cause of these phenomena undoubtedly lies somewhere in those organs that are allied to the heart and stomach and lungs, and are moved by the sympathetic nerves, so as to be more automatic than voluntary, more powers of nature than of volition. How far this involuntary action can be extended, and how far carried up into the higher plane of intelligence and activity, we can not say; but it is evident that whatever partakes of the character of habit partakes of this power, for habit, however painfully formed, becomes a second nature, and is automatic, or goes of itself.

This automatic action rids the extempore speaker of much care, anxiety, and toil, and carries him forward through much of his work without solicitude or conscious effort; but it is full of dangers, and if he trusts wholly to it he loses his higher inspiration and force, and sinks down into an automaton, like a barrel-organ, that, when wound up, can play over all its old tunes. Some speakers and hosts of talkers are spoiled in this way, and they think themselves inspired because by practice they have so much of the "gift of the gab" that they can run on without limit and without fatigue, until all but themselves are tired out. The good speaker may cultivate and use this automatic power; but he must never trust wholly to it, nor even be satisfied unless in every thing he does he is conscious of putting forth some fresh effort and earnest thought, and rising higher than before, instead of drifting away upon the easy level, or floating down the still easier descending current. He may, perhaps, through constant striving and interior faith, make such connections with the Supreme Wisdom and Will as to rise into a higher region of light and peace, and so partake of a motion and a rest that are not of himself or of nature, but of God. Great eloquence has always something of this character, and all great words come from and return to the World Eternal.

Every speaker, however unpretending, needs *faith*—

I do not mean faith in himself alone, but in God and his own vocation — to make him speak well and to carry him through difficulties. It is really wonderful what relief you find by simply renouncing anxiety after you have done what you can, and by putting yourself tranquilly upon your devout trust. This acts like a charm upon the powers of the mind, and rallies them very much as a moment's loss of one's self in sleep sometimes makes a new man of us, and refreshes all the springs of feeling and action. Without going into the theological question of the effect of faith in winning divine grace, it is clear that it marvelously dismisses worry and unrest, and calms and quickens all the faculties, and especially recruits those automatic functions of mind and body that are so vital to all easy and effective action.

There are plenty of anecdotes to illustrate this fact, and every man of experience can add somewhat to the collection. Bautain, whose book is, on the whole, the best on the subject of extempore speaking, as already hinted, gives an interesting account of his escape from a terrible perplexity by a simple act of devotion. He was to preach before the royal family, and made the accustomed careful preparation, thinking out his entire sermon, and drawing up an exact and elaborate plan, but not taking any manuscript with him into the pulpit, for this is forbidden by French usage. On entering the church he chanced to see some unexpected or offensive person, and at once the whole subject and plan of the sermon went out of his head, and he could not get the least clew to it by any process of association. What should he do? To break down was public disgrace before the court and the world, and dishonor to his profession. To go on seemed out of the question. The time came for him to offer the usual prayer before preaching. He calmly knelt down and prayed for grace, either to bear the mortification or to unseal his memory and his lips. In a moment the spell was broken that had bound him, and his subject and plan came fully to mind. He preached effectually, and thanked God for his benignity.

Undoubtedly his calmness did much to rally his powers; and it is an indispensable requisite to all extempore speaking that, however careful your previous meditation, the moment you rise to speak you must dismiss all anxiety, and comply literally with the precept of Christ to his disciples when he sent them forth to preach: "Take no thought what ye shall speak, for in that same hour it shall be given you what ye shall say." True it is whatever may be the cause, that the tongue is more fluent and the mind more collected precisely in proportion as mistrust is put away, and we surrender ourselves in peaceful faith to the subject and the occasion.

God bless you, my young friends, in your opening career. You have cheering prospects before you; and I almost envy you, Tom, your opportunity to carry a scholar's culture and principles into our great mercantile world, and bear your witness, as the years may call, for all the great interests of business, patriotism, humanity, and religion. Very few merchants among us have a thorough education, and are able to speak with force, depth, and elegance upon elevated subjects, although there are many who can give you lessons in practical sagacity, and read character and circumstance as keenly as any of us students can. Do not shrink from your position, but be indeed a high-minded merchant, true to all the loyalties that ennoble character and give dignity to trade.

You, R., begin your profession at a signal period, and you will need all your strength, learning, and enthusiasm to speak to our restless, inquisitive, but not godless age, upon the momentous subjects that are now challenging public attention as never before. Your professional training will be thorough, without doubt, and your learning will be apt and ample; yet you will bring little to pass unless your voice and pen catch the living spirit of mankind, and whatever is truly human kindles your love and enlists your labor. As your tongue burns with the true fire your pen will borrow its glow; you will write more eloquently and easily as you speak more earnestly, and you will speak more exactly and eloquently as you write with greater care; and tongue and pen will educate each other, and carry out the work of these years of scholastic study.

Your father is a practiced and effective extempore speaker, and he will give you the light of his experience. I can only quote my poor doings in this field to encourage you to persevere in training yourself for your work, in firm faith that you can overcome all difficulties and do great good and enjoy great comfort by this accomplishment. I do not see how I could have lived to this day without being freed from the bondage of the pen, and without having learned long ago to speak easily when called on for a word. The relief is incalculable; and while most of the occasions for casual speaking are better met by off-hand address than by elaborate writing, there are numberless occasions when it is impossible to write, and a man must be dumb or speak as he is moved. For over thirty years I have kept up this habit, week by week, sometimes day by day; and sometimes have been carried through odd passages as well as sore perplexities by the practice. A man is sometimes ashamed of the favor he wins by a few chance words fitly and accidentally spoken, and your father will probably tell you instances without number from his own eventful and distinguished career. One or two incidents I will allude to, in order to illustrate the power of off-hand speaking in helping a man without his knowing it.

I remember, many years ago, not long after leaving college, being at a philanthropic meeting in a church of the straitest sect, when a terrible storm broke over the town. The lightning flashed, and the thunder pealed, and the wind blew a gale. Suddenly the whole church seemed in a blaze, a great crash was heard, the glass shivered in some of the windows, and we thought the building struck by lightning and the spire falling into the roof and upon the pews. The audience were in a panic and too much alarmed to move. Youth as I was, I rose to speak without knowing why, but I suppose from the mere habit of saying my word when called upon; and now God himself seemed to be calling. I did not say much, but did little more than ask the people to be calm; tell them that God rode upon the whirlwind and directed the storm; and even now we might see his pillar of fire and hear his trumpet of jubilee as we were discussing the needs of his children and the great exodus of nations. It was a good Providence or a great luck that prompted those unstudied words. The people were both calm and kind, and the church got off with no harm but the smashing of a huge front-window, without loss of limb or life or steeple, while the grave minister did not rebuke the young volunteer.

Later in life, I remember once being present at the memorial tribute to our great novelist, Cooper, and taking my seat on one side the stage, in an old coat and rumpled shirt, without the least expectation of speaking. Why should one so obscure be heard in such an assembly as that now presided over by Webster, and honored by Bryant, Bancroft, Irving, and other lights of letters? But it happened that some of the chief personages who had been relied upon failed to appear, and perhaps it was Ash Wednesday that kept away the clerical dignitaries who were to represent their profession. The Secretary — who was a strange man, and now gone from the earth, where we trust he finds and makes less trouble than here — probably gave my name to the President, and Daniel Webster called your poor friend to the floor, before that blaze of intellect and beauty in old Tripler Hall. That I survived that ordeal, and did not run away, nor sink into the floor, nor make a fool of myself, nor lose all my friends, was owing to the grace of God and the habit of off-hand speaking, that had become so inveterate as to act unconsciously upon me before being called up, and make a little speech probably in the brain as covertly as the heart secrets its blood. I blessed the old days of the "Literati in Fumo;" thanked God, and took courage. Now dear T. and R., I bid you do the same. Faint heart never won fair lady nor made a fair speech.

X.

Art Among the People.

ART AMONG THE PEOPLE.

WE are glad to write this word now in a generous and popular sense, and to speak of "Our Artists" as if our people knew whom we mean, and wished to know more about them. We can remember the time when art had no public position among us, and there was no very sharp line of distinction between a painter of signs or houses and a painter of portraits or landscapes; and very likely if the merits of the two classes had been tested by general vote, the former would be the winning side, because appealing to the more universal want and covering the more surface. The change is now quite decided, although not as emphatic and universal as it ought to be; and there is often an ugly proximity of popular association between art and artifice, or the artist and the mere showman, the close student and faithful workman, who takes the truth of nature for his standard, and the mere trickster whose aim is, by some cunning slight of of hand, to make things appear what they are not, and to leave nature to the dogs. Undoubtedly real artists still suffer keenly from the stings and arrows of the rude and ignorant, and many a gifted and well-trained painter finds his very excellencies set against him by the superficial observer, and hideous patches of green, and yellow, and scarlet preferred to his modest tints, and really brilliant, yet wisely subdued climax of tones. But we must all suffer if we aspire, and artists must not think that they are the only people against whom the world has a spite, and whose toes were born to be trod upon. All men who have fine natures, and who do fine work, are in the same box, and often chide their stars that they were not born on a more celestial planet than this mother earth. So far as sensitiveness is concerned, a large number of us all are of the artistic temperament, and most of us must suffer from the world's coldness without having any original genius to carry its fire into the enemy's country, and to keep our feet warm at their hearth-stones. This experience should give us more of a fellow-feeling for artists, and make us rejoice in their having fair play dealt out to them for our sakes as well as theirs, or in the hope that all sensitive natures may in the end have better appreciation under the wings of art and its genial muses.

Many signs encourage us to believe that the day of Art, as a high intellectual, social and moral interest, has already dawned upon our country. The word itself is its own introduction and proof. The time has been when people started at its three mystical letters, and did not know what under the sun they meant, whether the art of printing, or baking, or cooking, or farming or what not; and even when they learned to recognize the several classes of artists, they were not prepared to accept the truth that embraces them all, and salute *Art* itself as master of all the separate beautiful arts. Even now there is not so full an understanding of its meaning as there should be, and the fact of art is more obvious to most people than its philosophy. They see clearly that a large number of persons of widely various tastes and pursuits associate together congenially in the love of beautiful arts, and that an important body of literature is rising up to illustrate and reward their affinities. Our young children, moreover in their way get some idea of the new and purer tastes that are showing' themselves in their school songs and lessons, and even in their plays; and there are few of our bright girls and boys who do not find out while in their teens, that the Beautiful in the method of God himself has a place between the Good and the True, and that the study of the beautiful, or æsthetics, is a part of all generous education. Kind Heaven itself bountifully helps out the illustration not only by so flooding the earth, and waters, and skies with scenes and elements of loveliness, but by liberally bestowing more interior gifts, and endowing a considerable portion of the young with decided tastes and talents for the beautiful arts. Every year some new spark of genius is flashing out from the spirit of some unobtrusive girl or boy, who hardly dares to believe the truth that great nature whispers into the ear; and there is no more encouraging view of the future of our artists than the prospect of their being constantly the educators of a new and susceptible generation who can generally enjoy, and in time study and rival in part the master-pieces set before them.

We are not indeed satisfied with the present position of Art among our people, but we are sure that it is now put upon the right way. No pursuit amounts to much of any thing until it is made a regular profession, and as such is respected by its own members. Even genius needs its own circle of fellowship for its defence and comfort; and although its great productions may at last challenge the world and fight their way to fame, there are long and weary periods of preparation and experiment, in which friendly and judicious association is invaluable, and genius is consoled and strengthened, while common talent is educated and almost formed under the kindly auspices. We need only ask what the learned professions would be without fellow-feeling and common usages, in order to show how desolate and limited must be the path of our artists without professional association. We rejoice to see so many proofs of their growing respect for their work and for each other. No corner-stone has been laid within our remembrance that has cheered us more than that under the foundation of that noble temple of the beautiful arts, the National Academy of Design, lately erected in this city. The readiness with which the requisite funds have been subscribed is an encouraging sign of the state of social opinion as to the claims of Art, as well as an honorable tribute to the worth of our artists. In one sense, indeed, they are luckier than most other professions, for there is no open split in their conventicle, no schools of practice at swords' points with each other, as among the doctors, nor rival sects as among the clergy. Into this new gate, called Beautiful, the whole tribe will go, and no shibboleth will be spoken to divide the votaries in two. That artists are indeed wholly without envyings and strifes we do not believe; for we have taken it for granted that Paradise was lost a great while ago, and we have known some who could make the old Eden bloom anew beneath their magic pencil, who yet could not exorcise from their own heart and home and social walk the hissing serpent who brought discord into that first garden of celestial innocence and love. It is something, however, that these strifes do not break fellowship, and the guild of Art is one in form and name. We trust that the little feud between the old and the new school of Art in our city will be healed, and the old will be more progressive, and the new more gentle and catholic. The "New Path" ought not to break away from the old, nor the old from the new.

We confess to being very desirous to have our artists recognized by our people at large as an essential profession, and to have Art itself ranked among the substantial interests of life. It is not enough that their best works are to a certain extent appreciated, and do not go begging for purchasers. Their work, or calling, ought to be esteemed like that of the great professions, and generous place should be given to it in society, patriotism, and religion. We are not satisfied to have any true man estimated merely by a fortunate hit or two before the public; and any lawyer, physician, clergyman, or merchant would be aggrieved at having no standing accorded to him except what he wins by striking or exceptional successes, or even by any conspicuous works, without regard to the habits, tastes, and convictions that they imply. We are all of us most happy when we are treated as good for something in ourselves, as belonging of right to worthy society, without being obliged constantly to show our ticket of admission, and to confess thus that we were let in by purchase or favor, and do not of ourselves make one of the circle. Nothing is more mortifying than to find that we are prized merely for some artificial act or casual accomplishment, and not for the culture and experience that have cost us so many years of careful study and thought. What can be more insulting, for example to a cultivated and high-minded clergyman than to be treated as if he were intended merely to say grace at table or help out the stateliness of a funeral or the elegance of a wedding by his pleasing elocution and graceful gesture and attitude. He is not at ease until he is received among gentlemen as one of them, and his place is recognized and honored, whether he happens to have anything official to do or not. Now in precisely this way, or according to this principle, our best artists ought to be recognized; and not merely for their conspicuous works, but for the culture from which they emanate, the tastes and associations which they imply, they are to be sought and respected. As a class, we need them in society, and the ideas and principles of study and practice which they follow ought to be carefully cherished in conversation and instruction.

We are confident that both parties will be gainers by giving to our artists more to do with the education of our children. The rules and laws of æsthetics are as important as any branch of liberal study, and there is no good reason for limiting them merely to the art of rhetoric, when the other beautiful arts are so much more winning to the young eye and ear. Drawing is the true art of seeing, and the hand is as flexible in childhood as the tongue, and may learn to make form as easily as the tongue makes speech. How many of us who are fair linguists and good arithmeticians have cause to lament that our fingers are so ignorant of the pencil; and we are puzzled to give the slightest sketch of a landscape, house, or tree, or even to draw a rock or a gate well enough to give a stranger a tolerable idea of the original. Hardly any accomplishments do we more envy our children than this — the power to take nature upon the wing, and bring home from their rides and rambles little sketches of the pretty things they have seen. If color is added to drawing the greater the charm; and undoubtedly a judicious teacher will find some taste for the beautiful in most of our young people, and can help parents much in deciding the aptitudes of their children for useful and ornamental arts.

In this way the range of employment might be much extended among artists themselves, and a vastly wider scope be secured to school education. There are a great many excellent men, of good literary gifts, who could very profitably vary their labor and enlarge their resources by teaching, without in the least interfering with their professional standing. Nay, why may not the teaching of Art be of itself a vocation; and thus the title Doctor of Arts, as well as of Medicine, Divinity, and Laws, find its way into our Academies ? We are confident that the tone of education and society would be vastly elevated by such influence, and taste would gain delicacy and sentiment upon all matters of life. We are often in a very bad way because we do not know what the beautiful really is; and every little city in the land wastes in a single year in miserable shams, poor artifices of showy dress and unmeaning furniture, wealth enough to build a stately hall of the beautiful arts, and fill it with fitting paintings, if not statuary. Our whole standard needs reforming, and the sooner our children begin to note the difference between art and artificiality, the substance of the beautiful and the mere show, our purses and our principles will be much the better for the change.

True it is that all fine tastes are costly, but not nearly so costly as the mock tastes that are usually called *superfine;* and Miss Flora M'Flimsey is a far more expensive companion for our girls than any of the old Muses or their votaries. If dress is the ruling love, and if the dress must be in the height of the reigning mode, each costume must cost a tolerable picture or marble, and becomes worthless almost as soon as it is worn; while the appetite that it feeds, unlike the taste for beautiful art, becomes more and more impatien of the simplicity of nature, and more and more ravenous for extravagance and ostentation. It would certainly be a great gain every way if we could apply the true æsthetics to our houses, dress, tables, and way of living in general. We could then seek the things that are best, and often prefer what is very cheap and simple as being most beautiful, while the vulgar rich rush after folly and ugliness, thinking it must be charming because it is so very dear. In fact, the really beautiful is cheap in comparison with the merely showy; and a truly artistic eye will find untold riches in every landscape, water, and wood, and may teach the skilful hand to cull or to copy rare charms of color or proportion on every side, and adorn the home with a *naive* simplicity that wealth itself might covet. No homes are more winning to us than those pretty little nests that are so bird-like, with all their rustic adornings of colored leaves, and airy grasses, and trailing vines, and the like natural gems of art. When the pencil adds its skill, and a gifted son or daughter enriches the walls with a few spirited drawings or paintings the charm is complete, and Art and Nature help each other out delightfully. The culture implied in such tastes is a valuable part of education, and the homes where our best artists are intimate win from them a kind of atmosphere of refinement that favors all beautiful growths and sentiment. What better can we do for a bright girl, next to forming her religious principles, than to open her vision to the loveliness with which God has been pleased to fill creation, and make fact of what the poet says:

> "To her there's a story in every breeze,
> And a picture in every wave!"

When ample means allow, the home may welcome the artist in more substantial shape, and set up his choicest works among the household treasures. It is not as expensive a luxury, relatively, as it is often thought to be, to indulge in this taste; for a picture of high merit can be had for a less sum than is often given for a mirror or a set of curtains, and the picture is for all time, while the furniture may be worth little or nothing when the mode changes. Good pictures are a legacy from father to son — or, to use a more financial figure, they are a good investment; and a really first rate collection of paintings is as good as silver and gold for time of need, and less liable to the thieves that break through and steal. We have friends who have tried this experiment to the astonishment of their acquaintance, and found that, after being laughed at for extravagance in spending fifteen or twenty thousand dollars upon choice pictures, they could get their money back, and even more, after the dark day had come upon them; while the mere modists, who had spent all they could spare in dress, furniture, and feasting, found that little was left, and they could not have their cake and eat it too.

We often wonder that our men of wealth do not give more subjects of native interest to our artists, and try to fill their walls with more of the riches of our own rivers, lakes, vales, and mountains. Every man who has lived in the country and made his fortune in the city must be haunted by charming scenes about the old homestead that he would gladly keep before him in his more artificial life. What would you or I give, dear reader, to get hold of Kensett, Hart, Colman, Whitredge, Inness, Haseltine, Cropsey, Casilear, Gignoux, Bierstadt, or Church for a month or two, so as to have them take suitable sketches of the charmed spots about the old country home, and in due season enshrine them in gems of choice art that would make great Nature our household friend, and carry into the shady side of life all the sunshine and witchery of our early days. Human life, too, how rich it is in subjects, exacting though they be; and too few of our artists may be able to put a merry girl or boy, or a lovely wife or daughter, upon canvas and make them altogether at home there, in speaking form and attitude. Yet some can do it, and those homes are happy who can have the work of their hands and embalm the dying years in unfading beauty — nay, rather keep the passing years alive, so that no hue nor trait nor smell of death shall be upon them. We know that all this care and cost will be called needless by some, and the photographer will be raised to the place before held by the painter. All honor to the photograph; but it is no substitute for high art; and saying nothing of the fact that it takes an artist to make a good photographer, we must have an artist to complete the work, and virtually take the portrait over again, since the camera is bound by its own nature to distort and falsify in respect to proportion and foreshortening. Art only, original art, can hold the mirror up to nature, and bring into play not only the form but the life of beings and things. The fact is certainly so, whatever may be its philosophy; and the photograph of any living thing, whether flower or face, is tame and dead compared with the sketch of a true artist. Upon stone-walls the camera is mighty as it is minute, but upon living things it insists upon putting something of that same look of stone.

No photographer can give the real man, as our best portrait painters and designers can do. Elliott, and William Hunt, are truer to the face of human nature than the sun, and Eastman Johnson, and Leutze, Church and Bierstadt put more truth into the canvas than the camera does.

We are for opening to our artists a wider range in our households, alike as teachers and workers, and what we say especially of painters we would say of the whole craft. We would be as hospitable to them in our national and public edifices; and we are by no means so straitlaced as to look upon religion as wholly outside of their province. The wonder often is that we have not more of true national art, and we allow that there is some room for the wonder, respectable as are our galleries at Washington, Philadelphia, New York, and Boston. The answer probably is that we have had no great national enthusiasm since the recent great progress of art-culture among us; and that now we have resolved to be a nation we may look for something of the patriotic fire in the pencil and the chisel. Great things must be done before they can be carved and painted; and the sculptor and painter are now called for to immortalize valor and public spirit on hundreds of battle-fields and in thousands of villages and towns. There will be no dearth of material now, and the artist and photographer have sketched our heroes and their deeds at first sight, so as to put all the needed materials before the eye of the genius that is to come or has come. There is nothing in our native sculpture, in a modest way, finer than the groups of statuettes by our gifted young friend Rogers, and his "Union

Refugees," his "Scouts," "Recruits," and others, are a cheering promise of what his chisel, with others, will do for us when the new generation catches the rising inspiration, and marble as well as canvas plays the historian and poet to ages yet to be. Some of our artists, such as Gifford, Colyer, and the like, have themselves mingled in the strife, and not only their hand but their spirit will do much to animate the whole craft. As a craft they are evidently very patriotic, and some of the best things that they have lately done have been done in honor of the country and the flag.

Religion in America is no stranger to art, yet ecclesiastically speaking, there has not been much relation between the two except in architecture. A very few churches, indeed have some fine statuary, but these, for the most part, are almost apologized for by being made to serve a sepulchral use. We think highly of memorial art, whether in the chapel or the cemetery; and since our gifted young friend Gambrill designed for us a memorial of a dear sister that enshrined her saintly life in stone we have loved the whole craft of architects and sculptors, and prayed for the time when they may show their taste and genius in monumental marble. A mural tablet or a modest tombstone may be a speaking biography, a sculptured poem, and may be worth more to the heart than a costly pile of soulless stone-cutting. It would be well if, even in this way, the sculptor, and with him the architect, could find entrance and larger liberty in our churches, as the emancipation from the old thralldom, once begun, would not end there, and it would soon be thought as proper to put a historic or ideal head on the porch or by the side of the altar as upon a tomb. Pictures are very rarely introduced into our sanctuaries, except in stained glass, which are, after all, more glaring and ostentatious than any of the masterpieces of the pencil, either ancient or modern. Yet we have never seen any offence taken at a modest altar-piece over a Protestant chancel, and have no doubt that a church that would fitly present a few choice Scripture paintings upon its walls, in the vein of our best Christian art, would meet a positive want in any of our great cities. We should hope to be saved the infliction of worshiping in constant presence of many of the customary ecclesiastical monstrosities that cover cathedral walls. Tortured saints, pinched and starved hermits, grim inquisitors, ghostly monks and nuns, are not to us the best impersonations of the Christian religion; and we like much better the humanity which God made and His grace has redeemed and consecrated all around us. If our best Christian faith and life could be fitly translated into art our churches would need no better adorning. Childhood and womanhood and manhood could be presented in an ideal truth as well as beauty that would edify the affections as well as educate the taste; and the good old Scriptures, both the Old Testament and the New, could come out of the ancient parchment and look us in the face, and talk to us again in very spirit and life. The better study of the Bible has made it virtually a new book, restored its freshness without impairing its essential sanctity; and when Art will do for the church walls what criticism and travel and thought have done for the minister's homily, it will be a new day for lovers of the beautiful in our hallowed shrines.

Probably most thoughtful people are ready to allow sacred art a place in the education of their children; and Bible pictures and statuettes are marked and abounding features of our time. It is surely no great stretch of liberality to assign a suitable place for the collection, and already the Sunday school-room is in many cases becoming a rich repository of art. Some of our toughest old Puritans have made up their minds to this innovation; and, while they would perhaps be horrified at the sight of a picture or statue in church, they take positive delight in worshiping with their girls and boys in a pretty chapel, where the fountain plays, and the roses bloom, and fair scenes and faces look out from the canvas on every side of the walls, as if to ask why should any thing that God has cleansed be called common or unclean? We believe in a new day of Christian Art, and are quite sure that it will come as soon as the ban is taken off from its works that has already been lifted from the head of Nature, and the soul is as free to enjoy the worthy works of men's hands as it is now free to enjoy the handiwork of God.

It might be well for both parties if Art and Religion could be brought into closer personal relations, and our artists and clergy could see and know more of each other. Some wit, in one of our late morning papers, makes fun of the odd juxtaposition of the two at some of the late art réunions, and seems to think it the absurdest thing imaginable. We are not of this mind, and we presume that the painters would not ask the parsons to chat and make speeches if the company was not to their liking. In two respects the professions are somewhat alike. They are neither of them in danger of accumulating surplus wealth or given to the world's sharp ways. The greater part of both professions seem to us to be what are called capital fellows, and able to enjoy genial and instructive conversation together. Each can help out the other's culture vastly. Every fair-minded preacher would at once allow that many of his figures of speech would be greatly tested and corrected by having them tried by the painter's pencil to show whether they were made of wood, stone, fish, or flesh, or all together, and every writer may get grand hints from the thoroughness of a painter's study and the freedom and breadth of his handling. The artist may, perhaps, learn to think more deeply from the theologian, and win a seriousness and earnestness that the profession much needs. We are not about to mount the pulpit and call Art into the conventicle, much less decree that every day shall be Sunday; but we are sure it would not hurt the whole tribe of the easel to hear a good sermon at least once a week, and stay out of their studio one day in seven, and give its hours to the better affections of the family and the altar. Such fine spirits as abound among us would be sure to come under a higher motive, to take hold of a better class of subjects, and draw far nearer the home life and devout sentiment of the people. The free and easy method may be carried too far; and true geniality would gain instead of losing, if our artists generally were in the way of more thoughtful and devout associations, and in harmony with their own best exemplars. All the inspirations are surely akin to each other, and he who seeks the spirit of beauty in nature and society does well to seek it at the fountain-head of Him whose being is the perfect loveliness, and whose work is the perfect art. In fact we have of late inclined, in our way of philosophizing, to number all the arts among the virtues, and rank them as skilled powers of the will in their several degrees and kinds. According to this view a noble manhood, gentle, wise, and loyal, is the highest of arts, and shapes all that it touches according to its own divine ideal. Each of the beautiful arts is a form of the educated will, a power of well-doing after its own kind. To paint a good picture is to do a good thing, and not merely to dream of doing it; and the mere sense of beauty, without the power of producing it, is no more true art than the sentiment of right is acttve virtue, or than that he is a charitable man who says, be warm and clothed and lifts no finger to help the poor.

We do not say that fine art is of itself complete morality, or perfect virtue; but it is virtue as far as it goes, or virtue in the æsthetic order, and having the same relation of active service to good taste that moral rectitude has to good feeling. Great gain will come from a better study of all the virtue which flows from the supreme good through the human will, and we shall thus correct the error of denying a moral quality to artistic excellence. Why had not Fra Angelico's pictures as much sanctity as the prayers with which he ever initiated the work of his pencil? And if the painter's sancitity exalts his art into virtue, why should not his truthfulness and fidelity, his courage, humanity, friendship, patriotism, or whatever worthy trait puts power into his pictures, have place among the virtues? For ourselves, we believe that the true artist, like the orator, must be the good man, and his work it is to present things good and true in the forms that are beautiful and sublime. His art is the virtue of true taste in its active energy, the excellence of the æsthetic faculty in its force as well as its sensibility. He surely is a favored man in this, for he works in God's school and is one of his favored children. He makes his wares after the divine pattern; and if he makes them well, each little flower, or rock, or tree, or face from beneath his pencil is worthy of a place in that creation upon which the Maker looked with favor and saw that it was good. We do not deny moral excellence indeed to the useful arts, and have respect for every rake and spade, every chair and table, that honest industry turns out. But obviously every work rises in the spiritual scale as it implies a higher range of the intellect, will, and affections, and the art that moves in the light of universal ideas, inspirations, and fellowship, ranks above the mechanism that looks only to special ends and rests in individual instincts and appetites.

One great glory of Art is the universality of its power as a principle of association or assimilation. When men come together they must have something to keep them together, and the first thing always is to occupy their minds. In barbarous times this is done by games, often of cruel spirit; and not only savages, but people nominally civilized, like the Romans, liked nothing better than to see a wrestling-match or a sword-fight, *secundem artem ;* and fair women were in glee when an adroit fling was made or a scientific thrust was given, no matter how limb or life suffered. The Spanish bull-fight is a specimen of the same monstrous art of amusing; and our own fairs and elections are apt to turn up something of the same temper, in a milder or coarser sort of fracas. We have learned, however, generally to keep our hold on the animal man without sacrifice of his intellect and heart, by setting the grinders to work; and the probable cause of the almost universal custom of social eating and drinking is not for the sake of the things themselves, but for the sake of enjoying them together. We are made one in sympathy by any sort of social activity, and the ice is broken as soon as all mouths are opened, if only by a bit of cake and a cup of tea or glass of wine. We will not quarrel with these creature comforts, but we may well rejoice that we are finding and using a higher order of assimilatives, and making our artists provide them for us. The beautiful is the fairy-land of good-fellowship, and where Art opens her lists and lifts her pennon, all the Graces are ready at once to dance and sing and make merry. The beautiful is the play-ground of the fancy and affections, and all gentle hearts are opened, and quickened by the arts of beauty, whether architecture, sculpture, painting, the drama, music, poetry, or, what is perhaps master of them all, and fit companion of them all — eloquence. How powerful as an assimulant or socializer is our noble Central Park! Fifty thousand people there are met as quiet as a family under the charm of the landscape and the spell of the music. How cheap and lasting is that banquet of the beautiful! The band may cease to play when night comes on, but the melodies still haunt the ear, and return in dreams by day and night. Darkness comes down upon grove and water and meadow and hill, but the landscape is there still, and will reappear with the dawn, a perpetual feast of inexhaustible loveliness to the end of all time! Change the entertainment into coarser materials, and try to feast that multitude with food and drink, and how much lower the plane of fellowship, and more frequent the outbreak of rudeness, to say nothing of the vast cost of loading the tables with good cheer, and repeating it with every reunion. But where beautiful Art holds her feasts her guests are humanized while they are pleased and assimilated; and however many come, the marvel always holds, and the table is always brimming with plenty, as if none had seen or tasted those sweets.

How rare is that privilege of high art — the privilege of always being enjoyed and never lost by fruition. The old monks in the refrectory that rejoiced in Leonardo da Vinci's picture of the Last Supper might well say, " We are the shadow, and they — those figures on the wall — are the substance." Much more might they have said that the painted table was the most abounding one, for it was spread with unfailing stores, and surrounded with undying life, while the convent board had to be supplied anew after every meal. Every picture surely is a lordly dish that thousands taste without exhausting, and every fine sculpture is a rich goblet whose juices ages do not drain nor dry.

We like to meet once in a while with our artist friends, and chat with them over the social table about the pictures that line the walls; and as we last had this pleasure, at the Artist Fund Exhibition, an occasion of unusual enjoyment and encouragement, we could not but compare the evanescence of the good cheer on the table with that which glowed on the canvas. The sparkling glass was soon empty in the hand, but when shall that brimming cup of beauty be exhausted in the grasp of high art? How many have drunk inspiration from that prophet soul of Allston's creating, and how many shall drink it still! Yet the glow of that eye is not dimmed, nor is that force abated. And look at that other and still more marvelous canvas, in which Rosa Bonheur's touch has put all the dash and fun and fire of the whole horse tribe; who shall exhaust that world of overflowing animal life, or what death shall strike down those prancing steeds and frolicsome ponies? Rosa herself in art is unfading, whatever time may do with her striking face and fingers. Her muse always grasps that same pencil, and looks out from that eye, and speaks from that lip. Muse and Madonna are to the devotee in this respect alike — always fresh and pure. *Ars semper virgo*, the old poets ought to have said, whether they did or not.

We must all be gainers by giving our artists more to do with our social and public festivities, and enabling them to bring their tastes and talents to bear more effectually upon the popular heart and mind. We spend enough surely in trying to give beauty to our private and public amusements, but the confectioner, the wine merchant, the dress-maker, the upholsterer, and the pyrotechnist get far more than their share. We rejoice in all those social occasions with which the hand of art has a leading part, even if it be merely in the grouping and the color and light of shade of *tableaux vivans*, as we sometimes see them. We delight still more in those charming réunions, which are increasing in our great cities, especially in New York, in which artists gather at once their friends and their works, and open studios, and fair women and accomplished men throw around the passing hours the magic spell of art. Would that there were far more of such things, and that our people of culture, position, and wealth would take counsel of the artist as much as they now do of the florist and confectioner.

We know no sociality more charming than that which is largely leavened by art, and our authors and artists and best specimens of the merchant mingle freely and enjoy each other's gifts and graces. The Century Club has much of this merit, and not only in number but in visible works the artists seem to bear the palm; and while the other members are allowed to range over the whole building at will, with no especial abiding place, art has its own favored hall of exhibition for its sons, where its freshest fruits may be seen, without losing its liberty to put its canvas and marble and crayon in any vacant spot throughout the edifice. Some of the festivals held there in past years give valuable hints of what good society might every where be by a little infusion of taste and genius. A Twelfth Night Ball or a Shakspeare's Birth-night Banquet was poetry and romance as well as festivity; and if the times had not been too dark very likely the third centennial of Shakspeare's birth and the sixth centennial of Dante's that were near at hand, would have evoked something of the same good fellowship and genial intellect. The more of such things the better, and they can often be done on a modest scale of expense in a way to charm and instruct greatly. Any bevy of bright girls have grace and talent enough to follow a good artist's lead, and to impress their more awkward brothers and beaux into the work of improvising romance or reviving history or the drama. In fact, if the priest has his breviary, in which he notes the scenes, events, and characters of the year according to his church rites, the artist, whether poet or painter or sculptor, may have his breviary too, in which he notes those aspects of nature, those facts of history characters of art and letters, that make out the ritual of the temple whose gate is called Beautiful. We shall be glad to see some attempt in this direction; and as we are quite ready to allow to the artist his right to a priesthood of his own and a shrine of his own, with a goodly following of devotees, we are also for extending his social sphere, and allowing him a large pastoral walk through fields green and fresh and varied, with plenty of lambs about him. We like to go and see him, and are glad that he is not unwilling to come and see us. We have been pretty free with him in this off-hand chat, but it has been the freedom of a grateful and loving friend, who is willing to be done by as he has done.

XI.

American Nerves.

AMERICAN NERVES.

THE starry heaven gains in interest and power over us with time, and the more we gaze and meditate upon that majestic and well-ordered empire of globes, without haste, without rest, without a single laggard or a single runaway, we can not but be more and more impressed by the contrast between the sublime method of the Creator and the derangement that enters into almost every work of man's hands, and sometimes invades the very citadel of his mind. It is good for us to be star-gazers more constantly and earnestly than ever, and try if we can not read there on high something better even than the astronomer's science, and ascend to that idea of divine order, which was written upon the heavens that it might be copied in the thoughts and purposes and methods of the earth. During these late magnificent nights we have been on better terms with the heavens than usual, and have, perhaps too fondly, thought that Ursa Major and the Pleiades, Venus and Jupiter said something even to our dull ears that our readers would be willing to listen to without impatience.

Walk through the wards of an insane asylum, and talk here and there with a patient; mark them in all their varities from abject melancholy to raging madness, or read some good book on mental disease, like Dr. Ray's recent admirable hints to our people, with the addition of some philosophical thoughts from the great German masters of the subject; then ask the stars to help you toward some simple and comprehensive view of mental health and ailment. You will not be long without the needed light. Evidently the mind, like the universe, has its pervading law, and the soul, like the solar system, gravitates according to the play of balancing forces and recurring cycles. Our earth in her cosmic relations illustrates the affinities, the attractions, repulsions, and periodicities of the life of her children; and the true kingdom of God over men must copy the polity of the Cosmes, which is its ground-work. We do not mean to deal now in dry, far-fetched, or mystical correspondence between mind and matter, the soul of man and the universe of God, but simply to illustrate the laws of mental health by two or three hints from the shining heavens.

It is obvious that the order of the globes is kept by the play of two forces in regular cycles. Thus our good mother earth, towards whom we confess to a growing attachment in spite of her manifesting some of the infirmities common to us her children, keeps her orbit by being attracted toward the sun, and at the same time being driven off by her own centrifugal force and by the concurrence of these two forces in a certain periodicity. Is it not precisely the same with the mind in its own relation to its dominant interests? We surely are subject to a constant attraction toward the world of nature and society in which we live, and a large part of our existence is as much in the passive voice as is the relation of the earth to the imperial sun. So, too, like the earth, we have a certain force of our own, and much of our life is in the active voice, whether for good or for ill. Like the earth too, we have our periods, and our existence is well ordered as it moves in judicious round in habits that repeat the harmony of the spheres. Let us throw out some practical thoughts upon each of these aspects of the subject, and speak of the healthy condition of the *sensitive capacities*, the *active powers*, and the *periodical habits* of the mind with an especial eye to our nerves.

I. In the largest acceptation of the term the sensitive capacities comprise the intellectual tastes as well as the physical and moral susceptibilities, for these tastes come into consciousness by being acted upon, as when the eye perceives beauty and the ear music by the touch of lovely sights and sounds upon the senses. A large part of the perceptive power is sensitive; and not only in the sensation which tells us whether an object is agreeable or disagreeable, but in the perception that records its qualities, the mind is acted upon at least quite as much as it acts; and even in the highest form of thinking there is some reality, visible or invisible, that is impressing itself upon the perceptive faculties. Yet without dwelling longer upon definitions, but taking the facts of our sensitive capacities as they are, it is evident that we do not enjoy mental health until our sensibilities are brought under the influence of their appropriate objects.

The eye must feel the light or it is very unhappy, and pines and worries almost to distraction when long bereft of the element in which it lives. So, too, the ear must hear sound or it virtually starves, and a familiar voice to one who has long been immured in solitude and silence is as welcome as bread and water to the thirsty and famishing. Even the sense of touch must have its object, and after long cessation from action, the fingers clutch the pen or staff or hammer or sword with absolute delight, and rejoice even in the pressure of any weight upon the muscles that bears witness of the mighty power of gravitation to this perhaps lowliest of the senses. Terrible disorders evidently ensue when the senses are robbed of their due objects, and the diseases that abound among people living in seclusion and darkness are owing undoubtedly quite as much to want of healthy impressions upon the senses as to noxious influence upon the body. Pre-eminently are we dependent upon the master senses, the eye and ear, for healthy sensibilities, and the Creator is our benign physician in the wonderful care which he has bestowed upon His provision for refreshing and healing sights and sounds. There is medicine in the brown earth, the green grass, the silver waters, the blue heavens, the golden day and sable night. There is healing not only in the hues of nature, but also in the distances; and after returning from the open country to our city streets and walks, we have a sense of imprisonment within these inexorable barriers, and the eye for a while, like a caged bird, seems to beat against those ruthless bars, and to sigh for the long vistas of meadow and valley and mountain and lake and river. The sounds of nature, too, are healing — the bleating sheep, the lowing cattle, the chirping crickets, the humming bees, the singing birds, and, above all, the human voice, whether in playful children or thoughtful and kindly men and women. Sometimes a single word heals us of a bitter wound, and the despondency that was settling down upon us like a dark cloud vanishes at once, and morning breaks upon the benighted spirit as at the voice of the lark that the poet hears singing at heaven's gate to call up the tardy day. Undoubtedly the world was constructed by the Creator upon hygienic principles, and we make sad mistakes in so often turning away from His benign school for the dementing artifices and deceptive nostrums of man's device.

We sin against God's method of treating our senses alike by apathy and intensity. If we fail to accept all this wonderful provision for our intelligence and comfort, and close our eyes and ears to what he sets before us, sad derangement at once follows, in the form of apathy, whose sullen and stagnant waters close in not around death alone — the death of the higher sensibilities and affections — but around the life, the monstrous and abounding life of the sensual appetites. Idiotic apathy may coexist with the most appaling sensualism, and the bestial instincts of gluttony and lust may run riot in their dark caves, while the lordly towers above are wrecked or scaled, and the daughters of music and vision are shut out or driven away. We see cases of such stolidity and sensualism wherever the higher sensibilities are neglected, and the vital point settles down into besotted earthiness. Our own danger, however, probably lies in the opposite direction, and our senses suffer from being drawn away from their natural and healthful objects, and being exposed to all kinds of morbid stimulus. After we have been a month in the country, it is a trial of our nerves to pass a day in the city. The tumult and hurry and noise of Broadway almost distract us; the very air surges like an angry sea on which proud ships ride forth to conquest, and wrecked crews are always hoisting the flag of distress or firing their minute guns. We feel an electric thrill in the very presence of the great multitude by day and even by night, and we almost sleep upon our arms, half conscious that life is a constant campaign, and every hour an alarm-bell may ring. True, indeed, we become in time used to all this excitement, and like it, and even add to it; but this fact is no proof that it is good for us. The drunkard loves his cup, and we love ours — our habitual excitement — too, the most fondly the very moment that we are nearest ruin.

This fast life surely is not good for us. It may be, and undoubtedly is, better than swinish apathy, but it is not healthy. Our men do not live long in cities, and threescore and ten years is becoming a very exceptional age among our elderly people. Many who hold on to life pretty stoutly are yet very shaky, and seem to keep alive like patients whose soul and body are held together by spirits and anodynes. Many an elderly man, who aught to be in the full exercise of his judgment and the calm enjoyment of his affections, is slowly wasting in a fever that is fed in the morning by greedy money-getting, and in the evening by free potations. Between the counter and the decanter a great multitude are digging unconsciously their graves, and from time to time they fall into the open pit without giving or taking a word or sign of warning. The physician may note their symptoms, and read in the trembling hand or tongue the disorder of the nervous system and the perils to life or sanity, but even if he ventures upon timely hints, they may lead to some slight precautions — a little riding, a few weeks' diet, a journey to the Springs, a voyage to Europe — but seldom to any radical change in the whole method of living.

It is not merely the physical senses, of course, but the whole range of sensibilities, social, and religious, that need the attraction of their appropriate objects, and are deranged by the lack or the abuse of them. Our whole social nature is now eminently sensitive, and besides those several instincts that determine specific social relations, as in the family, there is a great social sensibility, a dominant sympathy of race, that craves human fellowship, and can not live alone. This exists wherever man is found, but is peculiarly intensified by our modern civilization. The ancients felt deeply the great loyalties and affinities of family, country, and, in a measure, of religion; but they knew no such power of public opinion as now sways the world, and decrees the cut of a coat, the trimming of a bonnet, the turn of a treaty, the fame of an author or the fashion of a religion. We live not only upon the air of heaven, but upon the breath of opinion; and in our cities, life, in a great measure, follows this mysterious and almost inexorable social law. Country people seem to be more independent, and almost indifferent; but they too are often given to the reigning idols, and in the farm-house city ways and thinking win great attention and force the moment the sons and daughters are in question, and the future of the family is to be decided.

We do not say that moderate sensitiveness to social opinion is in itself an evil but quite the contrary, for utter indifference is far more likley to lead to apathy or eccentricity than to manly independence; and we hardly know of a recluse or an odditiy who would not be vastly humanized by a tolerable leaven of sympathy and companionableness. Yet it is clear that immense danger wait upon this instinct, and far more of our people languish and die of mortification and fancied neglect than of starvation or want. We are well aware, indeed, that a certain amount of difference and competition is necessary to give a healthful stir and pleasant zest to society; and that where all the elements are wholly monotonous, stagnation and disease inevitably ensue. In the general relations of society, as well as in marriage, a certain diversity of blood and experience is necessary to health and sanity; and as those families and districts that constantly intermarry with each other tend to degenerate, so it is, in a great measure, with the households and cliques that associate only with each other until they are so assimilated that wholesome variety can not exist, and they settle down into a dull routine that is more like dead mechanism than living harmony. We believe that serious mental diseases sometimes result from this monotony of households and neighborhoods, and many a moping woman or hypochondriac man would be made a new creature, not by a brief change of air and locality, but by a permanent change of the whole plan of living, through more genial associations and varied pursuits and recreation. In all monotonous homes and haunts, as in all stagnant waters and marshes, deadly miasmata lurk; and nothing is more frequent, among persons who are compelled to be constantly together without due change, than the alternation of gloom and irritability — fits of sullen silence broken by flashes of petulant temper, like forked lightning from the dark and heavy cloud. Such association, or rather conglomeration, is like the earth without the sun to cheer, and vary and transform its elements and existences by solar gravity, light, heat and electricity. The soul, quite as much as the soil, needs the solar influence, and a wise economy of life will copy the arts of good husbandry in its use of the blessed sunshine. We must remember, however, that there is moderation in all things, and even the sunshine may scorch our gardens, and blind our eyes, and dry our springs. Happy is he who can feel the wholesome attraction of all social forces, and yet keep his mind lightly poised upon its own centre, and true to its own orbit.

Terrible evils come from giving solar centrality and attraction to some equivocal if not evil power, such as often goes by the name of fashion or the world. In one way or another we are all more or less subject to this sway, and our spirits rise or fall, are gloomy or giddy as our great arbiter smiles or frowns upon us. Much even of our hard work and anxious scheming looks for its reward to this pitiful demi-god; and success in business or a profession has its choicest reward in the eyes of wordlings from the breath of social opinion, and but for the spur of emulation, the sting of rivalry, many an eager competitor would rest upon his laurels or his gains, and save something of himself both body and soul, from the wasting fever that is burning him up. To all of us there is some social power that tends to be our central sun, and be the solar arbiter of our destiny; and evidently our modern manners that so discourage the old-fashioned rural independence and muscular hardihood, and herd such multitudes together in cities with so many and so incessant excitements from financial and social competition, heating atmospheres, enervating amusements, enfeebling and inebriating habits at table, stimulating books and arts. tend very much to intensify our social sensibilities and throw us into the arms of the world in which we move. That world, indeed, may take many shapes, whether of business, politics, pleasure, vice, literature, or religion, and we must allow that a great city presents some forms of social attraction that are solar in intrinsic worth as in actual importance. Probably the best society in the city if well understood would help its clients forward in true life, and the thorough gentleman or lady has not only the charm of refined manners, but the grace of gentle breeding and high principle. Yet every where a yielding, dependent nature is in danger of some malign fascination, and we all need to say our prayers whether strong men or sensitive women, that alike in body and soul, in nerve and spirit, we may be saved from this tyrant world that insists on being our idol, the central sun of our worship and our life.

Our sons and our daughters feel the attraction, and before we can say definitely what the matter is with them, we know that something is the matter, and a power is at work upon them, and not mainly for good, not mainly according to the lessons of the home, the school, and the church. Our daughters, as being the most sensitive, may sooner indicate the tendency of their dispositions, and interpret to us the code of the social arbiter that claims homage. We see something of the world within the world, that so mightily presses its decrees and plies the overtasked nerves and spirit with its incessant appeals and stimulants, that ransack all nature and art for materials and methods, and touch every sensibility of our being, from the senses and passions to the taste and imagination, and make it the part of prudence to play upon every responsive string of this magnificent but not over-strong organism with which the Creator has endowed us. This new sun worship, this new honor of Baal and Astarte, has its retinue of priests, its splendid ritual, and its orders of teachers and artists. Wonderful is the paraphernalia of pomp and luxury that waits upon its will, and perhaps the most voluminous portion of modern literature, the novels and romances of society, is devoted to its service, and does its best to turn the heads of our young people with morbid

L

love dreams and fortune hunting. Apparently a large part of the place that was once filled by books of devotion is now held by romances and stories of the world and the heart, or what goes by that name. The old confessional is not so much abandoned as transformed, and the circulating library puts questions and hears secrets such as were seldom on the lips or in the ears of ghostly priests.

What is coming of all this new ministry to the sensibilities which now begins with little readers in bibs and tuckers, and is continued sometimes by mothers and grandmothers in caps and spectacles, we can not say, for we have not seen the end of it, and it takes at least a full human lifetime, threescore and ten years, perhaps more, to show the entire run of a social usage, especially of a mental epidemic. It is very certain, however, that there is a great deal of morbid sensibility both of body and mind that comes of this excess of sentimental and passional stimulus with the attendant diminution of the old-fashioned outdoor exercise, household thrift, and muscular activity. Whatever be our solar attraction, whether the world of romance or the world of current society, it is a very fickle and shaky luminary, and sad are they who make it their light and guide. In some respects the old *regime* of the Court and the Church were better, for they were more steadfast, and the solar quality of stability is an offset to many of the limitations and rudenesses of the ancient times.

Even our religious world has not the solar stability that should belong to it, and we believe that a considerable share of the mental unsoundness of our time comes from want of a fixed foundation of faith, and regular nurture of the higher affections. Not many people run mad from fanaticism now, and the authentic reports are ample proof that a very small percentage of the insane become such from fear of having committed the unpardonable sin, and lost the hope of salvation. But we look for the fruits of religious unsoundness to the too general fever and instability of the people, and regard all ill-temper, gloom, and discontent, all apathy and excess, as more or less connected with a fundamental defect in religious training. Almost all the mischiefs of an ill-built house may rise foom a bad foundation, and they who build on the sand must expect all discomforts and perils in the superstructure, no matter how fine the material and careful the work. Now we certainly fail of the true stability in religion in these days of universal questioning and agitation. Even good religious people carry their religion too much in the upper story, and too little in the affections and habits that are the basis of life. They are reasoning, talking, bookish believers, and they are satisfied with a fine theory of light and warmth divine, instead of going directly to the fountain-head in an affectionate, genial, practical, orderly church and home life. We are not pleading for the restoration of the old fixtures, and for anathematizing modern thought, or calling all doubt the child of the devil. But sure we are that if our reasonable scruples could be more satisfactorily met, and our tastes and dispositions could be duly considered, and the ministry of religion could be brought to bear upon us with something of the ancient stability, order, solemnity, and variety, our age would be greatly a gainer, and health and spirits would be vastly nearer the true mark. As things are, religion too often frets and fevers us. It is too critical and subjective, calling us to spin faith out of our brains, and grow grace from our own emotions, instead of finding all that we want in Him who asks to be the all in all to us, and in whom we are to live, and move, and have our being, as does our old mother earth in the sunshine. Every age has its form of morbid religious sensibility; and we suffer in our way, not so much, we think, from any prevailing fanaticism or superstition as from a general mobility, a critical unrest, and an introversial uneasiness. All self-consciousness is more or less morbid; and whether we fix attention on our stomach or our conscience, our heart or our affections, an unhealthy current sets toward that quarter, and we are not well until we forget ourselves and our organs and frailties in the service of God and his people.

II. Thus we come to the active part of our nature — to the will, the centrifugal force that checks and counteracts the excessive and morbid play of the sensibilities. Here we are still subject to danger; and the active impulses, as well as the more passive senses and affections, are liable to great derangement. Very likely the barbarous races, that seem to have been so free from our ailments, had peculiar infirmities; and those savage warriors, instead of sighing like our sentimental swains over imaginary troubles, and pining for coy beauties until they lose their wits, if they ever had any to lose, lived a life of continual madness, and their war fever was a bloody mania that haunted them like a remorseless fiend. Barbaric times are full of the traces of fearful cruelties and demoniacal possessions, which perpetuate themselves even in the temples and rites of religion. The martial spirit itself mated with two evil spirits, widely contrasted, and found distraction now in monstrous fanaticism, and now in the grossest sensual indulgence. If we suffer most from unstrung nerves and sensibilities, they suffered most from unsubdued impulses; and if folly is our besetting ailment, madness was theirs. In fact every active power may be beside itself by overexcitement, and even the simple instinct of muscular motion may be crazed either by long suppressed exercise or overexcitement and the arms, legs, and features may make chaos come again by their wild and discordant play.

All the social impulses are exposed to similar disorder, and what are called irritable tempers are such often from the suppression of healthy social impulses. Let any of us keep in the house a day or two without active exercise, and how our muscles rebel against the prison walls, and are craving to upset every thing in their way, and to seize hold of every stick or toy that can be made to call into play the suppressed energies. On the same principle, let the active spirits be kept down, and what mischief comes! How cross is the child that is not allowed to play, and how madly the little creature rushes at the first opportunity, and seizes hold of the first available playmate as an oasis in a desert, or a loaf of bread in a famine! We grown children are quite as impatient of restraint, and we fret and fume like madmen if we are cut short of our accustomed activity. What a wild beast an active man generally is when kept away from his usual pursuits, and in the fullness of health! He can not keep still, and his muscles and impulses are as ravenous for exercise as the stomach after fasting is ravenous for food. In fact the human will has its own appetite as much as the senses, and hungers and thirsts after its appropriate objects; nay, it pines and starves without its proper aliment, and starvation of the will is one of the frequent forms of mental disease. This truth is very obvious whenever men suddenly renounce their active pursuits, and lead a life of comparative seclusion, as in case of the sailor who goes to live upon a farm, or the merchant who gives up business for unbroken leisure. Immediate discomforts, and generally in the end alarming maladies, follow. The impulses and the will, bereft of their accustomed play and nurture, clamor for their objects; and when disappointed turn upon their masters, and tear them, as the old demoniacs of Gadara were torn by the fiends that possessed them. Something like *delirium tremens* ensues, and all the active powers, like the fearful appetite for stimulants, have their form of delirium when their indulgences are cut off; and even common business becomes as necessary to its votary as liquor is necessary to its victim; and the hypochondria of the retired merchant is very much, in nature, though not in degree, like the madness of the restrained inebriate.

The inference from this principle of our constitution evidently is, that every active power or impulse should move in its proper orbit, alike for the sake of its own healthy development and as a check upon the excessive sensibility to which it is so nearly allied. Instead of quarreling with the more tremulous and morbid forms of sensitiveness, we are to study them carefully and tenderly, and consider what capacities they denote and what activities they demand. It is the part of wisdom not only to satisfy and soothe them with their appropriate objects, as by bestowing kindness upon the gentle, comfort to the lowly, encouragement to the desponding; but also to set them to work in such way as to stir nervous delicacy to healthy effort, and remove nervous tremor by muscular training. It is a new study to some of us — this study of morbid sensibilities with an eye to corresponding healthy activity. Yet how rich in lessons in this science is our common life and how vast the field is for the application of the true science or art of checks and balances! Take, for example, the nervous delicacy and morbid sentimentalism so common among girls of a certain age. We do not make light of it, nor slight the gentle manners and methods of soothing a sensitive temperament, nor the bracing discipline that brings muscular hardihood to the relief of overwrought nerves. Yet God's method surpasses ours by calling all those trembling sensibilities, both of mind and body, into the active voice, and woman is a new creature when her affections go forth on their providential mission, and as wife and mother her love is unwearied labor, and her labor is unwearied love. In constitution, temper, mind, and spirit, she puts forth new power, and she does not surrender, but transposes, the delicacy of her nature in this benign school of her Creator, as the magnet does not lose but quickens and steadies its trembling life by pointing strongly and loyally to its polar star.

It is well to question every sensitive capacity in the light of this same large philosophy, to discover its wholesome, active sphere. We are not for making fun even of the vanities that are so tremulously alive to social favor; and we have long been convinced that many of the most gentle and valuable characters that are capable of feeling the best moral and intellectual influences and following the noblest leaders, are those that are in danger of being laughed out of countenance, if not trodden under foot. The vines are as important as the oaks, and bear richer juices and have more flexible and perhaps as strong fibres. Let the vines be taken care of, and beautify the oaks by their clusters and their climbing. All this excessive susceptibility in modern society, in many men and in most women, should lead us to look for some appropriate career, such as shall not shock delicate tastes, and shall carry out fine dispositions to fitting objects. The heart must have its own mission to fulfill, and the arts of charity as well as beauty must open paths for its activity, give music to its marches, and lend glow to its pulses. A beginning has been already made, and whatever is best in our modern humanity and culture proves that mercy is twice blessed, and they who heal others are themselves healed, as the spring that healed the sick was itself healed by the visits of the troubling angel.

All true art we regard as eminently sanative, because it calls out the active powers in fellowship with beautiful tastes and delicate affections. Even rude manual labor has a share in this healing ministry, for it braces the nerves, and strengthens the limbs, and gives point to the hours, and works off the moody humors that else might be morbid and dangerous. We tremble to think of what the gathering animal spirits of fifty thousand workmen in a great city might do, if this enormous electric battery were not every day and every hour discharging itself upon some stubborn and insensible material of wood, stone, leather, cloth, iron, or the solid earth. The daintier classes have the same needs to meet in their way, and all the arts of business, culture, accomplishment, humanity, and religion, are needed to keep them with sound mind in sound body. We believe that the progress of the beautiful arts in the higher classes has been very conducive to their health; and even music, which is usually ranked among the soft and enfeebling arts, has done much to train the will as well as to quicken the senses; and an expert pianist or vocalist must take a vast amount of physical and mental exercise to keep in tolerable practice. Is there not a compensation in this for the perils of our new social refinement, and are not the daughters, and in a measure the sons, of the affluent to open new paths of culture and distinction, that shall feed the sensibilities, and train the powers, and elevate the position, without interfering with the usual market of labor, or robbing the poor of their bread? Let all the beautiful arts then live; and it is no small comfort to know that the benign muses that solace weary hours and give zest to lives not subject to the spur of want or the strain of oppression, may be a precious stay in times of trial or adversity, like the bright blooms of summer gardens that may be the sweet and healing balms of the dark and cold winter days.

The highest and fairest of all arts is that which devotes the life to God, and trains the will to its highest office of love and duty to that Supreme Will which is the end of our being, the infinite object and blessedness. We will not presume to limit the forms or varieties of this art. We are willing, nay, glad to have all earnest people follow it in their own way, and we confess that we are ourselves trying to take lessons in it every day of our lives from some of the many proficients in this benign art, and our list of adepts and exemplars follows no party lines, but rejoices in a wide fellowship of loyal sons and daughters of God; comprising, in friendly closeness, names most diverse, from the obedient Catholic to the independent Quaker, and running through the whole intermediate scale. To us he is master of the art of arts and of the noblest of sanative schools who can so lift his own will to God in piety and charity as to bring other souls within the saving attraction, and join them thus vitally to the only true church, the blessed company of the children of God. This art is not yet exhausted, and it has finer issues and deeper treasures to open than any that physical science can open; anodynes beyond the power of narcotics or anæsthetics, tonics beyond the range of drugs and electricity. He alone is by eminence the Good Physician who came to heal souls by teaching and moving them to love and do the will of our Father in heaven, in sympathy with his children.

III. We have given these hints upon the discipline of the two spheres of human life, the more passive sensibilities and the more active energies, and shown in passing how the two counterbalance and check each other in a wholesome method like the forces that draw the planets to the sun, and send them off also by centrifugal weight, and so keep the harmony of the spheres. It is obvious that a judicious method will accept this principle, and so rule life as to give each side of our being its rights, and combine the passive and the active elements in due association and succession. Here the Creator is our teacher, and we are wise as we copy the order of nature in the method of life. Thus consider the interchange of day and night — the one for action, the other for rest; the one more in the tone of striving will, the other more in the tone of the genial affections, tranquil meditation, as well as of physical repose. What a disaster it would be were either day or night to be perpetual, and we were compelled to lose the benign alternation or to imitate it by our poor arts; to illuminate night into the look of day, or to darken the glaring and perpetual day into the semblance of night! The result would be not only inconvenience and discomfort, but disease both of mind and body. Let us read then, the majestic lesson, and allow our life to have its day side and its night side, as also its intermediate twilight, by wisely uniting active labor with tranquil rest, and interposing the twilight of genial recreation and soothing conversation between the two.

The Creator is teaching us the art of mental health, too, in the round of the seasons. The year, like the day, needs its variety, and suffering and disorder ensue whenever we do not yield to the influence, or we allow care or pleasure to set aside the benign ministry of the changing months, which are as essential to our human life as to the uses of the soil and the trees. Health and spirits alike feel the variation in this grand ritual of creation; and the old church did but copy the work of God in the varied order of its year, and base the priest's breviary upon the pages of the almanac of nature. In the ancient times great good was done to the people undoubtedly by the rich variety and benign alternations of the church year which copied inversely the order of the seasons, and made the long and dreary winter of nature the blooming and varied summer of the Church, in a round of feasts and fasts without ceasing from Advent to Pentecost. There is still much power in this ancient method, although it is too pedantic and antiquated, too much bound down by obsolete ideas and usages, and too little adapted to the thinking and action of our age. Without picking a quarrel with any of our neighbors of the old régime, we do not hesitate to say that we believe in a more reasonable and generous order of the year than has hitherto prevailed in the old church Catholic or the new church Protestant — a method that shall develop our present convictions into practice as the ancient church developed the convictions of its own leaders from the fourth century to the fourteenth. We do not believe indeed in forcing the matter, and we know very well that the best things grow, and are not manufactured ; that life is born, not made.

We should like, however, to have our wisest heads try their hand at planning or maturing the true order of the year for humanity and religion. As matters now are, money is the ruling power, and capital, taking advantage of the indifference of the masses to the old religion, is gradually and perhaps unconsciously shaping society to its own policy, and dividing the year, month, and day so as to make the most profit out of the method. We do not denounce capital or capitalists, yet we believe this age of gold lacks some elements that redeemed the old ages of faith ; and we are not altogether pleased at seeing banks, work-shops, stores, and factories lord it over life in place of the old priories, colleges, and churches, and at having the year of merchandise and manufacture supplant the year of religion. We are not, however, for going back but forward. Suppose then, dear reader, we startle you with a closing hint, and suggest calling a grand council of health to tell us how to use better the time that life is made of, and divide the months and days so as best to copy Heaven's merciful law. We are willing to be very liberal, and let every true thought and generous interest be represented.

We will give the body a fair voice in the council, and not only shall the doctors of medicine send their best men but the *roughs* shall not be crowded out; and the German Turners and the English Cricketers shall have their say for the arts that are manly, and the sports that are genial and strengthening. All trades and professions shall state their grievances and wants, and suggest their remedy for monotony or overwork. Woman shall be justly and generously heard, especially her plea for more joy and nobleness in her social life, and such order of church and home as to bring higher motives and associations to bear upon her daily lot. Children shall not be shut out, and bright girls and boys from our schools and play-grounds shall be heard, especially in their protest against the utilitarianism that makes religion of politics and trade, and installs dogmatics and metaphysics at the altar in place of the living God and the loving humanity. The artists should have their place, and plead at will for the worth of their vocations, and the importance of bringing music, poetry, the drama, architecture, sculpture, painting, eloquence, to bear habitually upon the common life, and enlist and convert the old muses to the new catholicity of the children of God. The clergy we would deal with most liberally, and seek the most earnest and judicious of them all from mitred Archbishops to radical Puritans, from Cardinal Wiseman to Henry Ward Beecher, bidding them, in the name of religion, devise some method by which worship may resume its place in the affections of mankind, and the year as it rolls may bear all its interests and blessing to the mercy-seat, and call all men to find in God the all in all. As things now tend religion is making more and more of its old heritage over to the world, and losing its hold over the masses that were once its strength without succeeding in gaining any proportionate power over the wealth and culture which are its pride and ornament. The general health both in body and mind suffers from the want of some dominant wisdom that ascends to universal principles, and rules life under its solar influences, in the sensibility and intelligence, the earnestness and strength that are Heaven's own law, and can alone bring Heaven's kingdom to our earth.

The great consummation, however, is coming, and in various quarters the thinkers and actors are moving to their aim. We believe all the more in their success, because we believe that they have a leader not of their own appointing, even Him who made the world and marshaled the hosts of heaven. Every hour of idle star-gazing is a comfort to us, therefore, trying as this last hour of star-gazing may have been to the patience of our readers in suggesting this humble essay.

XII.

The Ethics of Love.

THE ETHICS OF LOVE.

EVERY BODY will allow that it is well to talk of the Romance of Love, the Sentiment, the Poetry, the Enthusiasm, or even of the Tragedy of Love; but who ever heard of such a matter as is implied in the words, "The Ethics of Love?" Yet there they stand, good reader, and there they will stand until you see and like their meaning. No thought is more vital to our own well-being and to the very salvation of society than that which they indicate. The world will continue to be a sink of iniquity until wisdom and virtue rule the springs of feeling and action, and the relation which is first of all others as cause and consequence is regarded in its just dignity, and comes within the jurisdiction of morals and religion.

I know very well what the whole host of Sentimentalists will say, whatever may be their differences of temperament or character, whether moonlight dreamers or wide-awake enthusiasts. "What would you make of this life of ours, thus to rob it of its enchantment, and put prudence in the place of passion, enslave emotion to duty, and insist on boring us to death with your moral lectures, instead of leaving the heart to the freedom and sacredness of its own inspirations? We believe in being good and doing good as much as you do, but there is a time for all things; and we insist that the affections are their own highest law, and you take the very life out of them the moment you begin to prate of authority above them. Let us alone, and you will find that all will come out right at last, and Nature takes good care of her own children who follow her imperious law." We have heard a good deal of such stuff as this, and have lived long enough to see its utter folly and its wretched fruits.

I confess, indeed, to having attained somewhat grave years and long since to have passed the heyday of young romance. Yet I would not write to disparage youthful enthusiasm, but rather to honor and pepetuate it. Those of us who have passed the meridian, and kept constant company with our own children and their young friends, think as much of the heart as we ever did, and probably more. In the best sense of the word we are willing to be thought younger than ever — as ready surely as ever to enter into the glee of childhood, to play and prattle with merry girls and boys, to go among the wedding guests without carrying a funeral visage thither, and to take our share of the wedding cup and the bridal kiss. It is precisely because we believe in the heart that we are to see and vindicate its sacred law, and show forth the solemn fact that it denies itself, and strikes at the seat of its own best life, the very moment it rejects authority, and sets up its own sentiments and impulses as the supreme standard.

The best natures apparently feel this truth before they have philosophized upon its principles and sources; and whenever they are moved by an engrossing affection, they almost instinctively seek the protection and sanction of the highest law, the Supreme truth and love. It would be a paradox were it not sober reality, that the deepest of passions rises gladly into the highest of loyalties; and not prudential foresight only, but devoted love, asks that solemn vows may be spoken that invoke the majestic rule of God over the uncertain sway of human feelings.

A great deal of mischief is done, and in high life as well as low life, by ignoring this fact, and taking it for granted that love is to be regarded wholly as a private experience, and that the world and the church, and perhaps even parents and friends, have nothing to do with it, or at least have no right to interfere with it. We are not speaking now of persons so utterly unprincipled as to set human laws at defiance and offend the first principles of social decency. Yet of those who conform to public opinion — at least to its external laws — not a few hold very false views upon the subject, and miserably mistake the essential truths of social and religious order. Misery beyond account comes from making a god of a very equivocal impulse, and holding every relation and duty second to its movings. Thus a girl of fair character and education sometimes imbibes from trashy novels, or as trashy associates, the preposterous notion that the first man who wins her fancy and haunts her dreams is her predestined husband; and that if thoughtful parents, who have watched over her for years, present objections or ask any hard questions, it is perfectly justifiable for her to turn her back upon them and the old homestead, and run away with her lover, who may be a knave or a fool, or may possibly settle down into a decent and commonplace man, with nothing of the hero except what he had in the imagination of his silly bride. Sometimes worse results follow, and the deification of passion brings forth its bitter fruits of shame.

Allow that love is an emotion, and one quite private and personal, and in itself alone concerned only with two parties, the lover and the loved. Are not all the feelings in themselves private and individual, and do we not cease to be rational and moral beings the moment we rest in mere emotions, and fail to rise into the region of thought, where universal ideas dwell and universal ties are recognized? What would be the consequence of treating other impulses as romancers and sentimentalists treat love? Suppose that our sons and daughters should swear eternal *friendship* to every acquaintance who happened to take their fancy, and form fixed associations with them, instead of waiting for time and reflection to pass judgment upon the fitness of such an intimacy? Certain mischief, and often utter ruin would follow; and our sons surely are likely to find in some of the school and college friends who most fascinate them at first the most dangerous temptations and vices. If it will not do to base relations of friendship upon impulse or passion, why rest the relations of love upon such a sandy foundation? These relations, from their very nature, need more caution, as the consequences of error are more enduring and fatal, and lovers, husbands, or wives can not be thrown off or set aside like false friends.

Instead of according to the impulsive or passional school of love the supreme honor, on account of its fervor and its unselfish devotion, we rate it very low, and deny to it the true human worth. Impulse, mere passion, is in a low plane, the plane of mere nature, and allies us with the animals, and with the *idiots or naturals* to whom irrational desire is the imperative law. Animal impulse runs its own course without being troubled by any thought of what reason and conscience dictate, or social and religious order demand. The *idiot*, as the word denotes, follows merely his private or individual desire, as if he were his own man, instead of belonging to duty, society, and to God. He eats, drinks, sleeps, vegetates, and animalizes himself as the mood takes him. He becomes truly human only when he rises from impulse to reason, and learns to connect his individual feelings and desires with the laws of society and religion, so that he becomes a social being, integrated or made whole by living in the family the nation and the church. He does not escape his *idiotic* condition by carrying his impulses merely into a higher plane, and exchanging animal passion for impulsive sentiment, however refined or mystical. He is not a rational and moral creature, a true man, until he completes himself by ruling his impulses and passions in reason and conscience, and living not for himself alone, but for his neighbor, humanity, and God. He is essentially idiotic so long as he cuts himself off from the higher fellowship of his race, whether he grovels like a brute in the sty, or dreams himself into a phantom in the cloister, or heats himself into a furnace in his chamber. No matter what the impulse may be, whether it is horror of water, or longing to jump into the river, to eat dirt, or to drink poison, or to run crazy with love, so long as the impulse of itself rules him, he is not a whole man, not truly human.

We do not quarrel with impulse as such, but we deny it the supreme honor, and allow it no worth apart from the rule of reason and conscience. These benign and majestic guides do not crush the impulses, but accept, purify, and guide them; so that a rational and just man, instead of being a calculating machine, is the most affectionate, genial, and earnest of beings, holding all his senses and susceptibilities open to the best influences and under the best control. He does not deny the emotional or mystical element, either in love or religion, any more than he denies that element in the charm of eloquence or music. He does not shut out the mystery of art or nature, or of social fascination, but accepts it in a more open eye or ear and well-trained mind and temper. He does not pretend to explain the mysterious power of a landscape, or symphony, or beautiful face and form, but is able and willing to appreciate it truly without mistake or hallucination. In fact reason and conscience are the conditions of the purest and highest mysticism, for they make a man alive to what is loveliest and best in nature, art, and religion, and enable him to hear the blessed word and see the blessed vision that are hidden from the vulgar sense. We will not say that a man must be a poet,

THE ETHICS OF LOVE. 289

saint, or philosopher to be in love; but sure it is that the highest qualities, instead of preventing, deepen the experience; and he who is the most of a man can most appreciate the best gifts of God, human and divine, and of course therefore can best appreciate that good gift of God, that gift both human and divine, true womanhood. A great deal of nonsense has been said and sung and written upon this subject; but the nonsense does not lie in the mere fact of mystical emotion; and all thoughtful people are ready to own that in love and religion true experience passes understanding, and does not come of calculation, but of the spirit that moves as it lists. The spirit, however, moves each soul accoding to its affinities and aptitudes, and a man of sense and principle, whether before bright eyes in social fellowship or under ghostlier influence in the sanctuary, discriminates between truth and falsehood, and is not likely to be bewitched by a fool or harlot, or converted by a knave or an ass. True susceptibility is not insanity; and while it is open to whatever is true and lovely, it opens the gates of reason, conscience, and affection, not the doors of Bedlam, with its madness and folly. "Why is it," said a fine young man, who had wooed and won a noble girl not long ago — "why is it that love is so much like religion, and that it comes upon a man very much like the new birth that the Gospel speaks of, and does not seem to be our own work?" The reply of a Broad Church minister was somewhat thus: "For the best of all reasons my dear fellow: it is because they are very much the same thing in different planes; it is love in the divine sphere that makes religion, and love in the human sphere that makes what is truly worthy the name and calls for marriage as its just and sacred consummation."

Dismissing, therefore, the preposterous notion that impulse or passion of itself is love, and maintaining that this experience, instead of being shut out of the higher relations of reason, conscience, and religion, comes within them all, and needs their guidance and comfort in full communion, we are ready to take more positive ground, and perhaps astonish the most romantic as well as the most utilitarian of our readers with our extravagance. Do not be alarmed as to our sanity when we deliberately affirm that true love is a virtue, and high among the list of virtues when true to its highest standard. How can we stop short of this position without throwing the most vital of earthly relations wholly out of the court of conscience and the shrine of religion? If we merely say that true love is innocent, or does no wrong, we still deny its moral character; for so are the mountains and trees, the doves and the lambs innocent, yet they have no soul, and aspire to no virtue. We are not, indeed, turning ascetic, and bent on carrying the monkish spirit into the marriage market, or affirming that a man loves worthily only when he sacrifices his tastes and feelings to the stern law of duty. We are not in favor of his marrying his grandmother, or any woman of her venerable years and mien, under the stolen name of duty; nor do we think that loveliness, either of person or disposition, is to be put under the ban of church or conscience. But leave the heart free to its own sacred affinities and its true choice, and persistent fidelity can not stop short of virtue.

All virtue, according to our thinking and the best masters of ethics and the Word Divine, comes from the Supreme Good, and partakes something of its mind and purpose. Whatever blessing we have, we have virtuously only when we take it from the Supreme Goodness, the All-perfect Giver, and make use of it under His providence and grace. Love is virtue when it is from God as its source and to Him as its object; and all our affections are virtues as they partake of this affection, and proceed from the Eternal Source toward the Eternal End, or blessedness. Now what decent man, who that is fit to ask any woman to be his wife, can deny that he lives under a moral and spiritual kingdom, and that the marriage bond has the sanction of God in its beginning, and should lead the family nearer to him as its aim? Every true woman understands our position at once, and can not put on the wedding-ring without a profound sense of the sacredness of the tie as a religious obligation, as well as a social compact. The sweetest home virtues nestle within that bridal blossom, although often as unconscious of their worth and power as the apple-blossoms in spring are unconscious of the precious hopes they bear to cheer and enrich the harvest.

Love surely should be a virtue by partaking of the supreme good, the infinite wisdom and goodness; and it should partake of this both passively and actively, or as a motive as well as an affection, and be earnest and strong as well as susceptible and judicious. It becomes all the more genial as well as devoted by taking this stand; and they who believe that the Supreme calls them to each other will be more open to the highest satisfactions, because they mean to be true to the highest duties. They will take more and more of what is best, because they are to make the best of all things to each other, giving as they receive, and receiving that they may give. We do not promise them unbroken happiness; and a marriage that ignores the necessity of sacrifice belongs to the Paradise of Fools, and treasures up ashes in its mirth. We are told that there are seven lamps of architecture that should shine upon every master builder's work. He who builds a house or founds a home needs them all — the whole seven — the lamps of Sacrifice, Truth, Power, Beauty, Life, Memory, Obedience. The lamp of Sacrifice heads the list; and what is the love good for that is not lighted by its ray? Certainly they can not love each other who are not willing to make sacrifices for each other, and to make them cheerfully, both by suffering pain and privation and doing hard service together. The good old Prayer-Book makes this idea plain enough, it would seem, yet it is too often forgotten in the sweetness of the orange-blossoms, the charm of the music, and the revelry of the marriage-feast. Why forget it, or think it a ghost or skeleton that belongs to the grave and not to the bridal? There would be more joy, not less, if the solemn lesson were made more of, and our young people were trained to regard love as having the majesty of sacrifice to grace its consecration, and the "promise for richer, for poorer, in sickness and in health," were made the measure of the affection, and not merely the warning of prudence or the caution of fear. More marriages would take place if this truth were recognized, and the world would not as now keep asunder those whom God would unite, by interposing its pride and vanity and forbidding the bans until it is quite sure that the two will not be obliged to make sacrifices for each other, but will be easier and perhaps richer by marrying.

We all know that there are young people enough who make fools of themselves by rash marriages; but their folly comes not from expecting sacrifice, but the reverse. They marry selfishly, and are disappointed, and often quarrel and part, or else live out a miserable existence of repining and reproach. If they started with a deep-seated and reasonable attachment, taking it for granted that they are to make sacrifices for each other, they would be content to begin life together in a modest and frugal way, without waiting for luxury and without ending in petulance and despair. They would marry for love reasonably and conscientiously, as they enter into other social, civil, and religious relations — not for the sake of amusing themselves, but because it is right, and virtue takes precedence of pleasure, and in fact commands the only enjoyment that is worthy the name. I know well what a revolution this principal would make in society; how many false and ungodly connections it would stop, by putting a test that mere wealth and fashion of themselves can not abide, and giving a warning that indolence, thriftlessness, and sentimentalism miserably neglect. But there would be more marriages on the whole by far, and all of the right-minded sort of young people would be ready to marry as soon as they can be congenially mated, and begin to live in a comfort that answers the claims of reason and the heart, without waiting for luxuries that come only with affluence, and depend upon its uncertain stay. We should soon see a new style of house-building and furnishing, of living, dressing, and entertaining, such as moderate earnings can provide and modest tastes can enjoy. Thousands of young women who now " waste their sweetness on the desert air," or find gay ball-rooms a desert place to them, would find good husbands, and be what God meant them to be, sensible and healthy mothers; and the legion of young men who haunt our hotels, clubs, and theatres, or worse places, would begin to live the life that is truly human.

The mischief now is that self-indulgence is too much the arbiter of marriage, instead of virtue; and in the scale of self-indulgence celibacy seems to win the preference with vast numbers, especially of men. No deep vision is needed to see what is going on in our towns and cities; to show how temptations and vices abound; and how little it seems to cost to open every pleasure to the reckless and impassioned. The mischief may begin with one sex, but is not confined to one; and there is nothing in American life so alarming as the precocity of those vices among us that prevent or destroy the home virtues, and ruin soul and body by their abominations. Paris is perhaps bad as it can be, so far as the vices of its adult population are concerned; but neither in Paris nor elsewhere in Christendom, have we reason to believe, do the precocious vices of youth, and even childhood, so abound as in this empire city of America and its great rivals East and West. Here, as nowhere else, are the young left to their own wills and ways. Nor does the mischief of measuring the work of love in the scale of low gratification bear its fruits only in the nominally degraded walks of life. Men of culture and position abound who are by no means models of rectitude, and who make their plans and habits of living according to principles very different from those that are sanctioned by true morality and the higher laws of the affections. They shrink from the yoke of a loyal union to enter into unhallowed intrigues — blind, apparently, to the fact that a certain sacrifice of selfishness to the welfare of others is the essential mark of nobleness and the condition of the most enduring peace and prosperity. The certainty that loyal love demands sacrifice, and calls not only for the frequent surrender of time and luxury, but of personal ease and self-will to another's good, gives the loyalty its dignity, and in the end secures its happiness. Nothing is worth having that is not worth sacrificing for; and nothing is held worthily that is not held at some cost of means, or time, or thought, or labor.

Virtue in love is a topic that may make prosy preachers draw down the corners of their mouths in sanctimonious severity, and may set wide awake, hearty young people into a titter, as if an intolerable bore were at hand. The mistake lies in regarding such virtue as a poor negation of vice instead of a generous affirmation of the true goodness. Very little is proved toward a man's virtue when he tells us, and tells us truly, what he does not do. Goodness is in being and doing something, not in being and doing nothing. He is a shabby sort of a temperance man who measures his quality by mere abstinence from this or that, and he may pinch or dry himself into a mummy or skeleton yet never come near that just self-control, or right tempering of himself against all excess, which constitutes that cardinal virtue temperance. So in the relations of love, abstinence from vice is not virtue, and may be the easier to some people because they fall below the true manhood, instead of rising above it or even coming up to it. Virtuous love is not a pitiful asceticism, but it is human excellence in the relations which love originates — in short, it is the pure and rational and earnest humanity that should prevail between man and woman. It is no beggarly speciality that prescribes a single duty or condemns a single vice, but it is the whole life of true souls in their relation to each other, under God.

Like all virtues it has two sides according as it is more receptive or communicative, passive or active. On the one side it is susceptible, or open to affection; judicious, or mindful of the guiding principle; comprehensive, or careful of the whole range of fellowship. On the other, or more active side, it is earnest, enterprising, faithful, determined to carry out its loyalty heartily, effectively, and thoroughly. The first part may present more of the feminine side, and the second part more of the masculine side of the virtue, as the Psyche of the old myth represents the sensible, tender, discreet woman, and Eros represents the more determined and daring man. The two traits tend, however, more and more to blend with each other; and man becomes somewhat womanly, and woman somewhat manly when true love unites them, and Eros and Psyche mingle their blood and their life together.

With all good or philosophical moralists we distinguish between virtues and duties, and regard virtue as the force that gives duty its motive, while duty is the path in which virtue is to move. It would be a fine thing for our literature if we had a really good book on the whole subject — a wise and edifying treatise, that should handle broadly, deeply, and generously the relations of the sexes, setting forth the true laws of their life, with due notice of their perils and derangements. The materials abound in various quarters, but they have not yet been brought together. The old books of fatherly and motherly epistles to sons and daughters are obsolete, and are written as if young people did not know much of any thing about themselves or the world, and they have probably less wisdom in matters of the heart than a considerable portion of what is generally stigmatized as light reading. A few pages on the subject may be found in our current manuals of ethics, but we believe that the German moralists are the only ones who have treated it with any thing like its proper fulness and earnestness. The French have handled it well in their way, and their gifted women of the best character have given us excellent hints and helps toward a better understanding of the human heart and its home relations. The majority of Frenchmen, however, whose works on the topic suggest themselves to us, are any thing but edifying or comforting. What can be more corrupting than Balzac on Marriage? and what more frightful than Debreyne, for twenty-five years both priest and physician, in his revelations of the abuses of the love passion? Perhaps the best thoughts may be found scattered through the poetry, essays, and fictions of our time; for literature now has become the great school of the heart, and the novel often takes the place of the confessional, asking questions and telling secrets that of old were not spoken to the general air, but whispered in ghostly presence. Women themselves, to whom love is no small part of religion as well as of life, are now writing some of the best poems and stories, and are giving us, thank God! their side of the truth and often their side of the tragedy. Better days are coming, we believe; and never since time was has so high an ideal of the true relation between man and woman been set forth as by our best authors. Both parties are understanding each other, and being just and generous to each other; and we are no longer in danger of looking upon woman as wishing to be the weak toy of man's pleasure or the strapping rival of his hardihood. They are confessing their need of each other in every plane of life, from the natural to the spiritual; and the chart and compass are before us for a safe and pleasant voyage over the great sea together, if we will use them wisely.

Nothing is clearer than the fact that woman invariably gains whenever love is placed upon its true ground, and her relation to man is regarded in its highest plane. Upon the level of mere material existence or animal life she loses in comparison with man. He is generally stronger, and he can command her, enslave and beat her if he will, and his mere instinct is an insufficient protection for her when sick or infirm from the cares of maternity and other causes. When his interest in her depends upon his passions, his interest tends to cease precisely when her need of his interest deepens; and not only savage life, but what we call our civilized society abounds in atrocities on the part of man toward his victim. Most of the saddest misery that we see comes from the wrongs of women; and while busy with this essay I have had cases come before me professionally that are enough to make a man ask whether we are living in a Christian land or under the grossest paganism. A nice elderly woman, whose widow's weeds have for years won respect, did not appear, as usual, for her share of relief. I found her daughter, a simple, honest girl, with a baby in her arms. "Are you married?" I asked. "Yes," was the reply, and the husband was supposed to be a competent accountant. "How long did he stay with you?" "He staid three months, and I have not seen him since." That tells the story of the tragedy that is going on in our cities and large towns from day to day. The decent American woman in humble life is more strict than her English compeer, and we do not seem to have many of the miserable class that Joseph Kay describes so graphically in his book on the social condition of England. But marriage in form is no security for its proper duties; and in ranks where public opinion is feeble or hardly exists, and religious obligation is not cherished, marriage is the frequent pretext to cover the vilest treachery, and the wife is deserted, burdened and desolate as the harlot can not be. The law promises redress, but what does the redress amount to when obtained at such trouble and cost, and when it may only bring about a second act of the same tragedy whose first act almost took the sufferer's life away? Why women allow themselves to be so entangled is the constant wonder, and the solution probably is, that they see out of their own eyes, and judge men by themselves, and think a man's promises answer to a woman's heart as truly as to her ear.

This very week I have been led to hear the story of three who declared themselves victims of such falsity, and who bore the look of respectability and had its surroundings. The most estimable and cheering of them all, an exemplary and apparently religious woman, with an excellent reputation in high quarters, ascribed no small share of her present cheerfulness to being rid of a miserable man who had married her while two other wives of his were alive. This may have been a dark week as to matrimonial matters, but even this dark week has had other aspects of the subject quite sufficient to keep one from desponding.

As to the question of the equality of man and woman in their relation to each other and before the court of public opinion, we need not say how much we abominate the old heathen notion that woman is born to be man's slave or toy. It is not so easy to meet another wrong done to her on the ground of her alleged purity, and the consequent enormity of her offense when she falls from that purity. Whatever may be the justice of the verdict, it is

THE ETHICS OF LOVE. 301

almost universal and inexorable; and an erring woman when detected is ruined and an utter outcast from society, while her betrayer may keep a certain position of nominal respectability. Strange to say, many women of society called respectable will notice him, while almost all women turn their backs upon their erring sister. There is undoubtedly some cause for this distinction in mere taste and prudence, since a fallen woman falls more deeply than a man is likely to fall, and more of her nature is polluted than his by the sin. More of her constitution, her sensibilities, her affections, is acted upon and degraded. Her loveliness in the highest sense is gone, and the temple of her purity is foully desecrated, whereas the world readily regards laxity of like kind as but an incident in the life of a man, and one that may be atoned for by a life of sobriety after his wild oats are sown.

The higher ethics, however, puts a stop to this partiality, and holds man and woman accountable to the same exalted law. The great principle is the same for both — a life for a life, a heart for a heart. The true love is as exclusive as it is strong, and demands that each shall keep solely to the other till death do them part. Man's nature may make this exclusiveness more a sacrifice from the heat and endurance of his passions; but he is bound by the same principle as woman, and he gains by it in his way as she gains in her way. His fidelity gives him a sincerity, gentleness, chivalry, and spirituality that loose habits are sure to destroy, while her fidelity rewards him with a magnificence of conjugal and maternal affection and devotion that give home its sacredness and bring both nearer heaven. We know something of the world and its ways, but the more we see of its sins the more we love the good old loyalties of the hearth-stone and the altar.

If more humane and effective laws are needed, in combination with more effective Christian influence, to protect the poorer and less educated classes, a purer and higher social code ought to prevail among the cultivated and refined. There is certainly an approach to such a code in the best society, and conduct which might pass with impunity elsewhere is there visited with the general ban. High society may neglect sadly its inferiors, and leave them to the mercy or the arts of its sons; but it guards its own daughters somewhat sternly from insult and wrong. Excommunication is the penalty to be paid by the offender who assails their honor, and even in our peaceful and anti-duelling community death is thought to be the seducer's just doom; and public opinion may blame, but does not denounce, the father or brother who takes the law into his own hands. Yet there are many wrongs that are not guarded against, and many sources of suffering that are left open. We can not say that man is always the aggressor, for we are sure that he is sometimes the aggrieved party; but it is clear that the social code is in many respects wrong or deficient, and it fails to adjust rightly affairs and relations that are vital to social welfare. We have been tempted to laugh at the Courts of Love which were held in the age of Chivalry to settle delicate questions of gallantry, and have been amused to note that the last of them was convened at the call of the great Richelieu, who found some matters too subtle even for his diplomacy, and who called in gentler fingers and brighter eyes than his to see into and unravel the web. Such a court would not be amiss now, and it is certain that the old code of thirty-one articles would be wholly inadequate to the present demands of society. But we need not fear that we shall long be without such jurisdiction, for woman rules society as man rules politics, and sessions formal and informal are constantly held, that tend to adjudicate the rights and duties of love, and to define the just relations between man and woman, whether married or single. It is to be hoped that some day the social law may be digested and the common law of the heart be so codified that he who runs may read. It is to be hoped, too, that, while strictness prevails in duties essential, liberty will be allowed in things indifferent, and the result will be a more free aud varied, genial and intellectual fellowship between men and women, that shall give the charm of the higher and universal love to general society, and help all worthy seekers to find their predestined mates in that form of the affection which is more private and exclusive.

Of all striplings who have been called scapegraces, Cupid is the most hopeful, and he has the whole future to mend his manners and his morals. It is not impossible that he may grow up into a first-class angel, and his wings may be the means of his aspiration instead of the signs of his fickleness, while his bow and arrows may be turned to good account as part of the armament of the embattled cheruhim that contends for God and humanity against the world, the flesh, and the devil.

So ends our essay on the Ethics of Love. Call it too gay or too grave, as you choose, but do not let the poor handling harm the good text.

XIII.

Garden Philosophy.

GARDEN PHILOSOPHY.

I CONFESS to having been moved to throw out these stray thoughts on the wisdom of the garden not in the usual way of the poets and essayists who have made the subject so charming. Not in blooming June nor ripe September, but in dull November, after quitting the country for the city, and in the midst of the bustle and passion of the great electioneering campaign, the fit came upon me while looking at the luscious apples and brilliant flowers upon the tables of our Horticultural Society; and had it not been for this lovely spring day, this essay might have been a kind of digest of the remarks upon the Garden as an Educator that were then thrown out *impromptu* at request of friends, while the Democracy were listening to their pet orators in the great hall below, and thundering out at times applause so deafening that the prize Nonesuches on the table seemed to deepen their blushes, and the radiant cactus to tremble in its sensitive petals at the din, as if spirits of Paradise were appalled by an outbreak from the pit below. But that bluebird's song and these bursting buds have given my pen a fresh start, and I quit the old notes and write from a more vernal inspiration.

It is very pleasant to go among the farmers, florists, and fruitmen — and I will not forget that November reunion now — they are so full of love for their soothing, delightful pursuit, and so ready to give the help of their experience to every kindly seeker as to be quite winning to us men of books. I confess, however, to some little misgiving when asked to enlighten them, in view of my small doings as an amateur cultivator. I am afraid that our few acres have been more a sink of money than a mine, and that our crop of health and pleasure, when compared with our account of outlay and income, would bring more than a smile to the faces of the thrifty husbandmen who are willing to hear a scholar talk of flowers, fruits, and trees with great respect, and take it for granted that his practice is as good as his theory, and his thrift keeps pace with his taste. I am afraid to say how much our potatoes and eggs cost us as compared with the market price; yet sure I am that we got our money's worth, for health and enjoyment that are priceless come into the estimate, and no meney could tempt us to part with the harvest of delights that every year yields from our garden. The most thrifty farmer or nursery-man is always ready to forgive an amateur a considerable share of improvidence if he has only the true love of nature; and on that ground I am able to hold up my head among these good people, and talk and write as one of their gentle craft. What is said will have more point if we consider the philosophy of the garden as a school of science, a workshop of art, and a gallery of beauty and sociality.

Consider first, the school that is opened to us among the plants. The place itself is a marvelous lesson, for it sets before us the first form of organic life, and teaches us how nature rises in vegetation from the earths of the mineral kingdom through the world of plants up to meet the realm of animal organization with man at its head. The garden is thus mediate between the mineral and the animal world and has a wonderful chemistry of its own that transforms soils of sand, loam, gravel, and clay into the juices and fibre of flowers, shrubs, and trees. The last great discovery of chemistry brings out this power in clearer light by teaching us to see that all atoms of organic existence consist of but two general classes, the crystalloid and the colloid; and it is with vegetation that nature passes from the crystalloid to the colloid, and begins to build up her wondrous architecture of living things. How this is done we do not know. We see that the crystals of sand and limestone are dissolved and transformed into the starch and gluten of wheat and corn; but our chemical laboratories vainly try to make the change with all their science and art; and all their retorts, and acids, and blow-pipes have never been able to make bread or bread-stuff — not even an atom of starch or gluten — out of earth. Plants are ordained of God to work this transformation from crystal to colloid, from mineral to vegetable, and each plant has its own line of succession from the beginning, and does its wonderful work in its own way, and with the same costume and implements as at the beginning.

The study of the various soils themselves becomes most interesting in itself and its correspondences. A man of observation may learn wisdom for himself and his children by considering the qualities of his land and what they stand for. The mind is sometimes thick and clayey, or light and loamy, or drifting and sandy, or hard and gravelly — and in each case needs as specific treatment as the soil. Sometimes too, the good yield of most forbidding soil gives us most encouraging hopes for unpromising children and youth. I once had five hundred loads, chiefly of clay, carted from a dirty swamp-hole to fill up a bog, and was frightened to see such an unsightly vacancy in the first locality and such a cold, barren surface in the second. But the empty hole soon became a pretty pond, and the dismal clay smiled and laughed itself into a green and luxuriant meadow. Who will despair either of soils or souls after such an experience.

Then what a lesson a man may learn from the marvelous variety of growths in his garden. Saintine, the author of that charming story of a flower in a prison-yard, has lately died, and the grateful earth might fitly bloom out violets, lillies and roses upon the grave of so loyal a lover of nature and man. If his prison-hero found a world in that one plant that pushed its way up between the stones, and became the subject of that lovely prose-poem, we surely are more favored, aud we all have field enough for our survey and our pleasure. The little plots of a few square feet with vine and roses behind our city houses, or the broad acres of our great park, give us all our botanic garden, where we may be wiser with Ray, and Goethe, Linnæus, and Jussieu, if we will. If the naked eye soon exhausts its range in our little field of vision, try the microscope, and what wonders disclose themselves beneath our feet and give enchantment to the very dust we tread! I once passed the rambling hours of a week in the country in this way, peeping into the grounds at the risk of being thought crazy, and was ashamed of my old ignorance and astounded by the new found-wisdom. Even in the hard paths under our feet there is a world of hidden beauty — flowers of most exquisite tint and form; and never more reverently did I quote Wordsworth's lines that tell us, "Wisdom is ofttimes nearer when we stoop than when we soar."

When we walk through a garden of any magnitude we are surrounded with such a multitude and variety of growths as to be almost oppressed with those riches, and we find it hard to classify them under one dominant law. The lichens and mosses, the ferns and funguses, the trailing and climbing vines; the flowers of all hues and forms, the esculent plants so various, some ripening their fruit under ground and others lifting it into the air and light; the clover and the grasses, the trees deciduous and evergreen of all sizes and shapes, from the low juniper to the soaring elm — what a world is thus set before us! and how shall we bring all this motley crowd of growths to any sort of order, and arrange them under any satisfactory system? This question has not only perplexed simple observers of nature like ourselves, but even the shrewd masters of botanic gardens; and it is still not wholly clear by what marks plants are to be classified. It is still the ruling habit of popular speech to classify plants under the heads of trees, shrubs, and herbs according to their mere size. But careful observation shows the folly of this arrangement, by showing that plants of the most various dimensions belong to the same organic family; the bamboo, thirty feet high, being a kind of grass, and the lowly harts-tongue being of the same general division as the great tree-ferns that rival the palm. But when the error of this superficial system was seen, it took years for naturalists to hit upon the true criterion. The system of Rivinus, in 1690, was based upon the formation of the corolla or circlet of flower-leaves. The system of Kamel, in 1693, depended upon the characteristics of the fruit alone, while Magnol, in 1720, looked to the calyx or outer envelope as well as to the corolla; and at last Linnæus, in 1731, drew his system from the variations in the stamens and pistils or the reproductive organs of the flower. We were brought up to believe in this last system, and some of us remember well how we used to plod over its pedantic terms, and write them again and again from set copy into our writing-books at school. Before Linnæus, however, a sagacious Englishman, Ray, had a glimpse of the better science of vegetation, and in 1703 had grouped plants either as flowerless or flowering, and had subdivided the flowering into dicotyledons and monocotyledons, according as the germ is nourished by two or one seed-lobe. The idea of Ray waited for its complete development till the time of Jussieu, who presented the first principles of his Natural System to the French Academy of Sciences in 1773, and finished his great Exposition of this system in 1789, eleven years after its commencement. His system with some modifications now prevails, and plants are divided into the *asexual* or flowerless and the *sexual* or flowering. Without puzzling our readers with learned terms, it is better to take them out into the garden and teach them how to see for themselves the leading characteristics of plants. Consider, first, such as are asexual or flowerless. These are of two kinds: first, those that have stems and leaves undistinguishable, such as the sea-weed, the fungus, the lichen; secondly, those that have leaves and stems distinguishable, such as ferns and mosses. There can be no difficulty in understanding at once these two classes of the first order of plants; for any toad-stool or mushroom shows us a plant both flowerless and without distinguishable leaves and stem. Pluck, moreover, a leaf of fern of any kind, and instead of flowers or seeds, you will note on the back of the leaf little elevations that look like barnacles, and from these come the spores that propagate the plant. Thus you have the two classes of flowerless plants.

I am willing to be laughed at for quaintly simplifying the second and principle order of plants, the sexual or flowering; and once amused an intelligent and good-natured audience by producing a cornstalk and a stick of sassafras as specimens of the two orders of the second of the two great divisions. All the plants that are most important to us are either of the cornstalk or the sassafras family. Perhaps it is best, however, to take a more familiar specimen than the sassafras, and we will hold up the cornstalk and the maple branch before our readers as specimens. The cornstalk is a somewhat homely creature, but has the most distinguished relatives, and is of the family of the grasses, lilies, and palms. All our cereals are of this family, and without its help man and beast must come near starving. The characteristic marks are obvious. The cornstalk grows from within and is *endogenous*, and, moreover, the germ is fed from only a single cotyledon or seed-lobe. In this as in the other plants of its class, there is no clear distinction between the wood and the bark.

Pass to the other or *exogenous* class of the same grand divison of flowering plants, and we have, as in the maple and all our forest trees, and most of our fruits and flowers the constant mark of the formation of the wood from without inward, so as to record each successive season of growth in the rings of the trunk or branch beneath the bark which is distinct from the wood. The germ, moreover, in growing is nourished by two seed-lobes instead of one. It is interesting and instructive to carry these simple principles in our mind as we ramble through our groves, and orchards, and garden with pruning-knife and microscope in hand. We soon find ourselves becoming tolerable botanists without crazing our heads with a catalogue of outlandish names. We can train even our little children to read this grand yet obvious alphabet of nature, and tell whether a plant belongs to the flowering or flowerless division; whether to the family of toad-stools, mosses, and ferns, or to the family of grasses and trees; and to decide to which branch of this last great family it belongs — whether to the grass and cornstalk tribe, or to the tribe of maples and roses. When we have found the place of a plant in the grand division, and its general class, it is interesting to hunt up its especial order and tribe, and say exactly what it is in common phrase. Here, for example, we have a clump of oaks of various kinds, big and little, that have colonized that corner of our ground. Cut off a branch or twig from each. Ascertain by the wood that it belongs to the grand division of flowering plants, and to the first class exogenous and dicotyledonous, and then trace it out to the second subdivision of plants without corolla, and to its order, according to Loudon, among the *urticea* with rough points or stinging hairs, and see its odd affinity with the nettle that gives the order the name; or, as other botanists have it, we may rank it with the *cupuliferæ* or cup-bearing trees among the chestnuts, and beeches, and hazels. Thus we have fixed the place of the oak according to the natural system. Then we can compare the leaf and wood with those of other oaks described in the catalogues or plates, and tell just what kind of oak it is. Every such search will teach us a great deal, and if we have a good botanist at hand great is the gain. A plain farmer who has learned the trees and shrubs by heart is an admirable colleague to the botanist, and may tell us at once what a plant is before the scholar can study it out, and may rid us of a vast deal of trouble by teaching us by its common name where to look for our full scientific description. I am half ashamed to say that in our own little domain there are still many wild plants that I can not call by name, nor identify with any of the descriptions and plates in my books. Very likely that solid farmer or his buxom wife or pretty daughter, whom we sometimes pass on their way to the village, might wholly dispel our darkness by a word as familiar as any in the kitchen and herb garden to the rural population.

We know very well that the knowledge which is generally sought from the garden is not of the scientific kind, and gardening is a very different thing from botanizing. It is not safe, of course, to base our cultivation upon learned classifications; and he would be a funny horticulturist who should portion off his grounds after the system either of Linnæus or Jussieu, and insist on keeping by themselves all plants not found in the same botanic classes. This rule would compel us to keep the cucumber and pumpkin away from the corn, and forbid the rose to show its lovely head near the green turf which best sets off its beauty, or to mate with the lily that so completes its charm. We must bring economy and taste as well as science to bear upon our garden before we combine all desirable variety with unity, and integrate the differences of our vegetation by a judicious singleness of aim. In this way we reach the practical economy of gardening, and are able to bring our science into the service of our art. The true economy must, of course, have in view both utility and beauty, for there can be no good garden without both elements; since the potato-patch and currant and raspberry bushes are none the less profitable by being neatly and even prettily arranged, and the winding paths through fresh lawns or under shady trees are full of healthful influence, strengthening the limbs by inviting exercise, and cheering the spirits by various aspects of loveliness.

As to the complete idea of the garden, the estimate must differ as our point of view or aim differs. If we were writing for a prince with ready millions at command, we might perhaps take Lord Bacon's estimate, and say that thirty acres are not too much for a prince-like garden, without including the forest park or farm. It is easy to see how his plan might be adapted to modern taste, and made quite charming, by doing away his absurd Dutch squares, and set circles, and cumbrous carpentry. If laid out literally by his plan, his thirty acres would become a magnificent baby-house, and confirm his own remark, "that when ages grow to civility and elegancy, men come to build stately rather than to garden finely, as if gardening were, the greater perfection." His four acres of green in the entrance, with two long walks in covered alleys on either side, would be a dismal affair without trees or shrubs to cheer the eye and relieve the loiterer from the necessity of hiding under the covering of carpenter's-work, twelve feet high, to escape the glare and heat of the summer sun. Nor do we see much charm in his artificial mound (in the middle of the twelve-acre garden proper), thirty feet high, for " some fine banqueting-house, with some chimneys neatly cast, and without too much glass." His heath of six acres in the rear, which he would have "formed as much as may be to a natural wildness," is more to our modern taste; and the only trouble with this portion is that, instead of our having all the wild beauty by itself, and all the regular beauty by itself, the two should be intermingled, and the broad lawn should border on charming flower-beds, of various growths, and romantic shrubbery in studied freedom; and art and nature should do their best to help each other.

The case with us, however, is that we are not to devise princely methods of magnificence, but republican plans of economy; and the garden that we have in mind must needs be one that comes within the average means of lovers of nature in America. Any man of moderate means may own a few acres, and treat it according to the most approved principles of economy and taste. We who are not farmers wish, of course, to do as much as we can with our little domain, and expect, if possible, to unite the advantages of park and orchard — flowers for the eye and vegetables for the table. We wish to have the largest crop of market value and landscape beauty. Our rule of utility may be summed up in a single sentence, and be said to be that method of gardening which secures the most products of the best quality suited to our needs through the year, and so produced as to draw out, without exhausting, the various and alternate powers of the soil. To carry out this rule, even in a kitchen-garden of half an acre, will be no small study and discipline to the shrewdest calculator

GARDEN PHILOSOPHY.

and economist. Books have been written on "Our Farm of Two Acres," "Four Acres," and "Ten Acres." I shall be glad to see as good a book as these on "Our Garden of One Acre," or "Half," or "Quarter of an Acre." I have so humble a sense of my own attainments in these economics of gardening that I will not pretend to be overwise, but be more ready to remember the constant comfort and health of our unfailing supply of fresh vegetables through the season, than to school our readers in the art of money-making out of carrots and potatoes, strawberries and grapes.

The economics of the beautiful I am more free to speak of, and am quite sure that beauty is far nearer to us, if we will seek it, than is commonly supposed. The great secret is to follow the lead of nature, and try not to overlay nature by ambition, and not to fall into poor artifice in our search for art. The idea of God in nature is obvious. He unites ever difference with unity, and always brings together a large array of various elements around some central purpose. The great universe, our solar system, our earth, or any large prospect on its surface, or, if we specify particular objects, we may say that a tree, a bird, an animal, or, above them all, a human body, these manifest wonderful diversity of parts in unity of aim — and the study of creation opens an inexhaustible school of beauty. The nearer the garden comes to the variety and unity of nature so much the better for its completeness. There, as in nature, the lines of beauty and utility should be mingled; and while we should not be ashamed to plant our esculents and even our fruit trees in rows, we should study to secure the curve of grace wherever we can consult taste, and allow the generous eye and the easy foot to move in the line of beauty. He is happy who can have enough of flowing or living water in his grounds to help him to dream of the lake, the river, and the ocean; enough of rise and fall on the surface to relieve the scene from monotony, if not to suggest the images of the hills and cliffs of his romantic rambles and reveries; enough of lawn and grove to unite the charms of the open meadow with the forest shrubs; flowers, shrubbery, and orchard enough to present the useful and the beautiful in judicious harmony, and to help the master and his friends to discern distinctly the hand of God — the All-wise and the All-lovely — in the domain. I believe most sincerely in making the garden thus a microcosm, an epitome of nature, a chapter out of the great Cosmos. We read that Father Adam heard the voice of God in the midst of the garden, and our faith is that the same God is with us; and with all our illumination we are wretched scholars if we have not learned to hear His word as it speaks to us amidst the flowers and trees. Lord Bacon well says, " God Almighty planted a garden, and indeed it is the purest of human pleasures." Base surely is the mind that forgets Him in this purest of pleasures, or fails to see His wisdom and goodness in its riches.

One glance at the *science* of horticulture prepares the way for looking at the *art*, and so we pass from the garden as a *school* to regard it as a *work-shop*. It is certainly the oldest of work-shops — older by far than the carpenter's or smith's — and the place where man learned to earn his bread by the sweat of the brow. Strength surely is born of this labor, and the working power of the race comes mainly from the tillers of the ground. Without undertaking to call farm labor wholly blessed, or to think it altogether a luxury to work ten hours a day in the broiling sun, we may surely say that no form of muscular activity is more beneficial than that which belongs to a judicious round of gardening. It compels us to take every attitude, and call every muscle into use. We read of, and sometimes see, ingenious calisthenic exercises that are so contrived as to bring the whole body into healthy motion, but no artificial ingenuity can compare with gardening as a gymnastic exercise. What variety of implement, posture, and movement there may be in a single morning's work! We may sit, or stoop, or walk, or stand, with rake, hoe, trowel, spade, or plow. I certainly never knew what muscles I had till bringing them out in this various work. There is a great deal that a gentle hand may do, and grace as well as health attends the fair woman who plays the Flora or Pomona of the domain, and tends her flowers, vines, and trees, as a good housewife only can do. Beauty is lovelier at this task than at any play; and a rational man on the way to matrimony might be more readily won by the charming contrast between the delicate hand and foot of the fair amateur gardener, and the brown earth and usefel trowel or pruning-knife, than by the brilliant belle of the ball-room with its surfeit of splendors and its monotony of unbroken display. There is nothing, moreover, better for a sedentary man, or student of delicate habit, than moderate practice in the garden. There is variety enough to keep his attention, and effort enough to stir his blood, quicken his senses, and point his purpose. He may profitably try once in a while the harder forms of labor, and learn from experience what hard work is. Let him go at the stones of the little or large quarry with sledge-hammer and crow-bar, or try his hand with the axe at felling some dead or doomed cedar or sycamore, and his aching flesh and bones, and panting breath, and swelling veins will soon teach him his limitations, give him new respect for his rough comrades at the business, and read him a new version of the old Latin saw, "Non omnes omnia possumus," or, "We can not all do all things."

Skill as well as strength is found in tilling the ground, and the horticulturist who is master of his art need not hang his head before any adept in accomplishment. To be able to adapt each plant to its soil and conditions, to train and prune, to bud and graft, and perform all the nice offices of gardening, with the attendant supervision of fowls, cattle, and horses, and the due prevention of blights from the elements and ravages from noxious insects, requires a rare union of aptitudes and crafts, and seems almost to call for all handiworks and vocations in one. Some persons have a charmed touch for trees and flowers. A good nursery-man has his own gift of nature as well as training, and there is something more than superstition in the legend of St. Rosa of Lima, one of our few American saints of the canon, who is said to have had such witchery over the vegetation that the roses and lilies bloomed out at her approach. Some temperaments are certainly in peculiar harmony with plants, and seemed to be loved by them as well as to love them. Perhaps there may be something in the influence of animal electricity over the growth of vegetation that may explain the apparent marvel, though I am not one of those who insist upon explaining all faith away by the materialist's creed or no creed.

If we add the skill of horticulture to the rugged health that belongs to outdoor labor in the wholesome air of the country, we certainly have a work-shop worthy of the school which should prepare us for it. Little as the rural population come up to the proper standard of their privileges, we may be quite sure that we need them to recruit our exhausted city vitality, and that our great towns would miserably degenerate without constant reinforcement from the bone and sinew, the fresh blood and brain of the green fields. So far, indeed, as the science of health and the art of living are concerned the city has the advantage; and were it not for our better knowledge of medicine, ventilation, bathing, cooking, etc., we might all languish and die, until a fresh migration came in from the bush. Undoubtedly the best science as well as art is to be found in the great centres of life, and if we therefore receive much from the country we are bound to give much in return, and carry our culture and knowledge into the villages and fields.

There is probably no piece of ground in the whole land better worth seeing than our Central Park, that work-shop of so much labor and studio of so much art. We ought to rejoice in it not only for its direct pleasures, but for its influence as a model garden upon the whole nation. Every man's acres ought to be lovelier for that careful and magnificent enterprise and achievement. There is something there for every man to learn, whether for the millionaire bent on laying out his princely acres wisely, or the thrifty workman who would know what is the best vine to trail over his cottage or the best shade trees to set before his door. The element of beauty is evidently becoming more and more a popular study with us, and the taste for landscape-gardening is making more general advances in America than any other art except music, which goes so well along with it and seems to call for it as the song of the bird calls for the grove and the flowers, " whose breath," says Lord Bacon, "is far sweeter in the air (where it comes and goes, like the warbling of music) than in the hand."

The beautiful arts are brought before us by this illustration in their two classes — the arts of the hand, that appeal to the eye, and the arts of the voice that appeal to the ear. Now surely the garden is the *atelier* for both classes of arts, and on the one hand invites architecture, sculpture, and painting, and on the other hand rewards music, poetry, the drama, and eloquence. We must have some kind of building there, and any man of the least taste can play the architect upon some rustic bower, even if he has too much good sense or modesty to venture upon planning his own house or stable or conservatory. One may be well amused at the effect that may be produced by a little money, where there is plenty of rustic timber. I built of our own cedar wood two rough arbors several years ago, which cost but twenty and thirty dollars, and now that the vines have covered them they have risen into romantic beauty, and no costly summer-house of the old, artificial pattern can compare with them for a moment. My favorite retreat in the heat of the summer days is in the least costly of the two, and the pomp of millionaires seems ridiculous when I sit with some noble book in hand under the shelter of my twenty-dollar study, with stately oaks and walnuts around, with chirping birds and chattering squirrels, keeping company with the ceaseless murmur and rustle of their leaves. Two years ago I tried my hand at a statelier structure, under the spur of a generous gift, and with the help of a young student of architecture, who is now winning honors in the great school of architects in Paris. His drawing was charming, but the thing itself is more so; and the rustic tower with five pointed arches on its stately rock foundation, is a picturesque feature of the whole neighborhood, and is intended to bear aloft our sacred flag with the holy symbol of our faith. It stands upon a cliff whose face bears the inscription, "God and Country," which was cut by a soldier on his way to the war in 1862, and who brought back his shoulder straps to the stone work-shop in peace. The cost was only about two hundred dollars at the worst of all seasons for building, and in common times it might have been built for little more than half that sum. Who will laugh at me for erecting three handsome buildings for two hundred and fifty dollars? Let him laugh who wins. I am willing to be laughed at by any body who will get more beauty and enjoyment for less money. Our acres are enriched for our lifetime, and our summers are idealized for a sum of money which might be easily spent upon a ball-dress or a dinner.

Sculpture as well as architecture belongs to the garden. It is well to have means to set up fountains, vases, and statutes, for these do much to fill out and integrate the landscape. But little wealth is needed to bring the sculptor's eye for mass and form and light and shade to bear upon the prospect. Every grove and clump of trees or shrubs is a study in form and grouping. Swedenborg says that trees represent men; and whether he is right or not, we know that the finest statuesque effects may be produced by due selection and massing of trees and shrubs, so as fitly to combine and contrast the drooping willow or elm with the spire-like fir or hemlock, or the rounding maple or oak. At night the eye, in some respects, enjoys still more the sculptor's art of giving beauty and grandeur to mass and form. In our little domain it was a new revelation to me years ago, when I began to walk at evening in our groves of cedars and maples, and oaks, and to note the sky-line of shadow and light which so brought out their expression. The place had a solemn, grand, cathedral look; and two or three cedars that had no particular charm in the daytime rose up into romantic beauty then, and their tips seemed to be ready to volunteer to be built into the walls of some old minster, in order to complete or repair the work of the glorious dreamer among the builders of the ancient times. The landscape-gardener must needs be a sculptor in taste if not in talent, and so arrange buildings, walks, lawns, trees, water, shrubbery, and all things in the view as to give all the true measure and proportion, and bring out new power and charm, under all the changing lights and shades of nature. Every man of common sense practices the same art, however, when little conscious of it; and he who trains a woodbine upon a stately tree, or an ivy upon a solid wall, belongs to the illustrious craft that ranks Phidias and Michael Angelo among its princes. He is a sculptor not in dead wood or brass or stone, but in materials quite as ready to obey the call of taste and imagination, and give those effects of form and light and shade that lend the handiwork of the chisel its power and charm.

And who shall tell the capacities of the garden for the painter's art, with its display of figure, color, and perspective. Landscape gardening is landscape painting, with a stouter instrument than the pencil, indeed, and with richer and more living colors than any on the pallet. It may be that the material is so near at hand, and often so ample as to leave little to the invention of art; and he sometimes treats nature most generously who most scrupulously lets her alone in beauty unadorned, and thus adorned the most. But generally the loveliest ground needs clearing and arranging. In fact, rural art is never so perfect as when it brings out nature; and culture of the soil, as of the soul reveals the fairest of its capacities, and lights up the face with its best expression. You must first be able to see your ground properly, and so also to see from it into the distance. If your garden is a wilderness of nature, where you can hardly see a rod before your face, you are not master of your domain, for you can not, either by sight or by imagination, take in its extent or richness, nor own it with your eye, the most imperial of the senses. True art will not show the whole at once, but what it does show will imply the rest, as the hand or foot implies the whole body. The thicket that you let remain will combine with that which you cut away to give the due proportion of seclusion and openness, and your pruning-knife or bush-nook well plied will sometimes do wonders in bringing your tangled wilderness into the proportions of a picture. One of our great painters showed me a few years ago a picture on canvas twelve feet by seven, which embodied only a week's work, and was a noble sketch of a storm in the Rocky Mountains, with all the features of snow-capped peaks, majestic cliffs, highland lakes, browsing deer, running brooks, stately trees, and gentle flowers. If he had been two months at work upon the piece the result before the eyes would be enough to show for the labor and time. Yet I have seen more marvelous transformations than that wrought by the knife and axe. Cut away a few bushes and branches within that grove on the hill, and there is a full view, a grand picture, of the sea, with its changing waters, and its rich effects of storm and calm, moonlight and sunlight, now with broad and unbroken surface, and now all alive with vessels under steam or sail. I have seen an arbor that Eve might not scorn made in a couple of hours by clearing out the interior of a thicket of alders and young cedars, opening a lovely carpet of ground pine under foot and preparing the way for the woodbine, the clematis, and the honey-suckle to run up the bushes of the encircling walls, and to cover them with their rich and ever-varying festoons and arabesques.

The proper application of the principles of perspective to any little domain as simple as ours may not shame any painter's art, and what has already been done there is enough to show that the pruning-knife is ally to the pencil and both may minister to the spirit of beauty. The element of color, too, needs careful treatment, and is much under command of taste and imagination. The hues of nature, indeed, we do not create; but we find them, and, not as the painter finds them, in parcels assorted and labeled at his order, but in natural combination. The rose is not of a single red, nor the pink or the violet of a single pink or violet shade. But there is great choice in the selection and grouping of flowers, shrubs, and trees, so as to bring out the true melody and harmony of color. We may call the color the music of the light, and, as in music, we may find in color melody and harmony. That rose, with drooping head and blushing cheek, has its own native air or melody, like the song of the robin or bluebird; and that fuschia, with pendant and jeweled drops, seems to answer the rose's queenly air with her own gentler tones. But group the whole array of plants of color duly, and what harmony is the result! Sometimes different clusters or beds of well-chosen flowers seem to answer each other like the responsive choirs of the cathedral; and it may not be altogether conceit to say that in a well-concerted garden you may have all voices of color music, from the deep base of the ruddy rose to the thrilling soprano of the violet.

We need to take account of all the changes of season and periods of vegetation to bring out the proper effects of color, and the good gardener will sow his seed and arrange his flowers so as to leave no month uncheered from the time when the bluebird pipes on the advance-guard of spring, and pecks at the swelling buds of the maple, to the time when the sere and yellow leaf gives such glory to autumn, and, the snow-bird is seen on his way to summer skies. All the hues of nature, of course, should be made to contribute their part to the pictured series of months, and great account should be made of the constant features of the landscape, such as the evergreens and the mosses and the rocks that give such charm to winter when summer life is no more.

The vocal arts can not fail to feel the power of the haunt thus prepared for them in the landscape; and music, poetry, the drama, and even eloquence, are ready to catch inspiration from the arts of rural architecture, sculpture, and painting. Nature surely gives us music enough to call out our voices; and it is no slight to the birds to practice their art on true principles, and make their wild melodies the prelude to the finer melodies and harmonies of the voice, the flute, the harp, or piano. We hear of chamber concerts and academy concerts. Why not have garden concerts more frequently? I have certainly sometimes thought even the organ-grinder a godsend in the country, and have there listened with delight to the old strains that I would have closed my ears against in the city, so much does nature set off art, and the trees and flowers ask to be interpreted into music. And as to poetry, we are all ready to be poets in the country; and if our fancy is dull of itself, and has no Pegasus of its own to ride, it is quite ready to mount upon the pillion of some favored son of the Muses, and ride with him into the heaven of ideals. How much poetry has been written in or about the garden, every library is proof, and Parnassus can never be a paved city. Even the policies and passions, the lights and shades, and follies and aspirations of city life come most to mind in the country, as they see the battle best who look upon it from some tranquil hill away from the din and smoke. The drama, too, belongs to the garden; and he who has the true eye may see tragedy and comedy all about him in the airs and attitudes, the loves and the quarrels of insects, reptiles, birds, and beasts, and the various play and mien of the more rational tenants and ramblers of the domain, with their walks and talks, their work and play. It is a good place, too, for actual dramatic scenes, especially for pastoral life, and there are many parts of our great dramatists that can be charmingly enacted in groves or dells, or among flower-beds and grassy lawns. Last year a little association of amateurs of letters spent a day with us in the country, and amused themselves and us with recitations. Among other selections they gave us the melancholy Jaques with his companions in the great scene in the Forest of Arden. The famous words "All the world's a stage" gave our little dell, with its canopy of oaks, elms, and walnuts, quite a Shakspearian dignity, and we were not at all ashamed to have such a scene brought to such a theatre. Nor would glorious Will himself have thought the performance altogether poor.

As to eloquence, the garden speaks for itself, and is sure to make its true friends and lovers speak; and the finest of all speech — that which calls for two parties only, and is very likely to fix the destiny of both — flows more freely and willingly there in some charming arbor or shady walk than in the city drawing-room or promenade. What sacred eloquence the garden may inspire none will deny who revere Him who bade us consider the lilies how they grow, and taught the hidden wisdom of the seed and the soil.

I have been anticipating the last branch of our subject, and have implied that the garden may be a gallery of elegant resort, a saloon of society and conversation. Why should not more stress be laid on this idea?

There is something in the place itself that favors companionship; and when left to ourselves, away from the distractions of the world, we make friends of books or find them in our neighbors. We feel our social nature more when less surfeited with society, and made to hunger and thirst for its nurture and refreshing. There is something, too, in the ready walks and various paths and scenes that invites conversation. The tongue insists on alternating with or relieving the active foot, and the eye, in time satiated with seeing, asks for the voice to give the listening ear its turn. The garden makes Peripatetics of us all, and after we have walked half an hour we are impatient to read or talk the next half hour, and keep up the balance between body and soul.

Then what socializers are fruits and flowers by their taste and beauty! The pear, peach, apple, cherry, and all the smaller fruits of flavor, seem to be half soul and half body, and to mediate between the spirit and the flesh. Who cares to eat fine peaches or strawberries by himself? We must share the treasure, like a choice poem or sparkling paragraph. All persons of gentle culture have this feeling, and every good-hearted man, however rough his hand, is no stranger to it. How obvious it is in all fruit-growers at their gatherings! and although the quantity of the choice fruit under view may be small, they insist upon sharing it in good fellowship. It may be a single choice apple or pear for the whole dozen of amateurs; but out comes the pocket-knife, and all have a fair portion. I believe that the growing of fine fruits has introduced a new element into society, and has made the taste of good things to educate the higher taste that feeds on the beautiful, and brings men together in the fellowship of refinement and intelligence. The strawberry, the raspberry, the peach, and the pear have been great civilizers in America, and yet their work is not done as yet.

The more express beauties of the garden carry out this work, and there is something wonderfully assimilating in all scenes and objects of pure taste. Flowers are wine to the eye, and they who enjoy them find themselves won to genial companionship, that softens and exalts and does not inebriate. When combined with the various charms of the landscape they have a certain enchantment, and the rose or the honeysuckle is a precious poem when it interprets our old homestead or our pet haunt. Then how comparatively small the cost of much of this rare beauty. Buy a dozen or two of roses or phloxes of choice kinds, as you can for some two or three dollars a dozen, and see what will come of them. What exquisite bloom in those bush-roses, in that splendid *Chateaubriand*, that luxuriant *Mrs. Elliott*, that stately *Pius IX.!* and what witchery in those climbers that run like roguish imps upon every thing that will hold them, and are Puck in frolic and Ariel in aspiration! Those phloxes, I confess, amaze me by the perfection of their color and the continuance of their bloom. For two months that *Valery* has charmed us with its rich Magenta clusters, and that *Alba perfecta* has soothed and even evangelized us by those petals of exquisite white, with its interior of pink, as if love and purity were blending together, and the pure in heart were flaming into rapture as they begin to see God. Yet the twelve phloxes cost less than a good bottle of wine, and for two months their cups have been full of nectar, and now are filling again.

Dear reader, I must break off before I have wholly done; and should I say all that comes of itself to the pen on this theme, you might tire of my prattle if you were not moved to take up the word for yourself, and in your own garden at this charming season ramble and dream, and speak out what you and fair nature so well understand together without need of any go-between.

XIV.

Easter Flowers.

EASTER FLOWERS.

IT is one of the obvious marks of our American religion, that we are noticing more habitually and affectionately the ancient days and seasons of the Christian Church. This tendency does not seem to us to come so much from any change of doctrine or discipline as from domestic and friendly and devout dispositions, and often shows itself unequivocally in quarters where the most independent thinking prevails, and even where the straitest Puritan theology is professed. That Christmas should be every where gaining ground, and that Saint Nicholas should be held in honor where all other saints are discarded, is not to be wondered at, so far us the attraction of Christmas festivities is concerned; for children will be children, and parents will be parents, and whatever brings the two parties lovingly together is in the line of Nature, and is sure to prosper. Yet we believe that with the natural glee of that great holiday a great deal of devout faith and affection mingles and the gayest carols and the wildest sports have something about them that does not end with flesh and blood, but which partakes more or less of the higher spirit. Humanity, too, mingles with every true Christmas feast, and the poor are every where remembered, not only for their own sake, but for the Holy Child who became poor that we might become rich. For our own part, we confess to having a great liking to a religion that is not afraid of a little laugh and fun — not fearful that the church windows will break, or its walls shake at the explosion of any amount of innocent natural spirits. We believe that young and old are never in so good a way for enjoying themselves as when they are upon solid ground, and can sing and dance a little without fearing that the earth will cave in under their feet. On this account we can commend a good sound platform of faith and fellowship as giving a safe footing for mirth as well as worship, and are quite sure that we can move more merrily as well as more effectively there than when on doubtful ground; as skaters glide on more boldly and play off their most antic evolutions when perfectly sure that the ice will not give way beneath them.

Whatever may be the cause or the effect we are quite sure that Saint Nicholas is making his way into universal regard, and is likely to stand as high upon the Puritan as the Catholic Calendar, at least so far as home observances are concerned. Less attention has been called to the second great festival of the ancient Church, Easter; yet there are unmistakable signs that it is fast gaining upon the religious affection and public regard of our people. Like Christmas, it is winning our household feeling as well as our religious respect, and is sacred to the memory of departed kindred and friends as well as to the rising of our

Lord from the grave. We have carefully noted the gradual increase of observance of the day, and can remember when it was a somewhat memorable thing for a minister, not Catholic or Episcopal, to preach an Easter sermon. Now Easter sermons are very general in all pulpits, and Easter flowers are making their way into churches of all persuasions. One of our chief Presbyterian Churches near by decked its communion-table and pulpit with flowers as for some years, this Easter season; and we, who have some ways of thinking and acting quite our own, made our church beautiful with lilies, roses, geraniums, camelias, etc., according to fixed usage. We were considerably among the florists at this time, and they uniformly reported that such a demand had never before been known for the products of their conservatories. The resources of the city and neighborhood were exhausted, and appeals were made to Philadelphia and Boston to supply the deficiency, and in some cases great prices were offered in vain, a dollar being the price for single lilies.

The cause for this new love for Easter is to be found partly in the unquestionable growth of church feeling in our people; but this feeling is greatly enhanced, and, in some cases, almost wholly created by family affections. Easter is becoming rapidly the festival of sacred remembrance of departed friends, and the remembrance is all the more sacred by remembering them in God and the Beloved Son. It is interesting and impressive to observe how powerfully our congregations are affected, when this use is made of the day, and the great sentiment of home love is brought into keeping with devout faith. It is quite a revelation to note the response that is made by the people when asked to bring to the altar some memorial of departed kindred and friends. At first we asked for flowers to make the church bright and beautiful for the afternoon festival of the Sunday-school children. The gifts came in great abundance, but even then the flowers often had a memorial character; and no parents who had lost a dear child could fail to think of him or her more tenderly in the midst of that cheerful flock, and the flowers themselves, as they sent up their incense to the mercy-seat, seemed a message to the lost ones as well as our offering to heaven.

The good effect is not lost but rather helped by making part of the service decidedly genial and festive, and quite in keeping with the cheerful temper of children. An Easter carol or two, a distribution of little gifts, with pleasant remarks from the pastor, and other like features, may give the day greater compass and attractiveness, and do much to enlarge the often too sombre and restricted character of our ministrations. It is well to take a hint from good Mother Nature as she speaks to us in these charming pets of her bosom, the blossoms of spring. The blossoms are the pictured cradle of the fruit; and if we would have the fruit we must first have the blossoms. We have too often forgotten this stubborn fact, and expected a harvest of substantial fruit without a childhood of blossoms. We do not believe that the Creator has put forth so much of his wisdom and power to make the earth beautiful with fragrant blooms, merely to amuse our idle hours; and we regard the beautiful in nature, as in art, as the ally and handmaid of all that is good and true. In the economy of creation it is evident that the exquisite tints and odors that attend all vegetation in its fecundating and fructifying seasons are intimately connected with the welfare of the future fruit and seed. It is true, also, that in the germinating seasons of human thought and feeling and purpose, the element of beauty is very powerful, and society and religion are stronger as well as purer by the graces of art and beauties of nature that are enlisted in their behalf.

Children very readily fall in with all usuages that combine cheerfulness with reverence, and do it all the better if treated as if they were expected to acquiesce in church ways as a matter of course and affectionately, instead of being everlastingly argued with or scolded into obedience. It is really touching as well as amusing to see how earnestly very little ones will do whatever is required of them when asked to help out a sacred festival. Three little girls distributed our baskets of nosegays to the scholars with charming grace, and the smallest of them — a four-yearling, who can usually hardly keep still for a moment — did her part famously, and dealt out the bunches of flowers with an odd sobriety, as if she were one of the pillars of the church or shepherds of the fold.

The art that is most characteristic of our modern ages is undoubtedly music, and antiquity is searched in vain for any instrument that can be compared with the organ or piano, or any compositions that can be named in the same breath with our great oratorios, symphonies, and operas.

Vast sums of money are every year spent upon music, and time, far more valuable than the money, is given without stint to musical education. More is to come from this art probably than we are now aware of; and we are not only to be entertained but refined, moulded, assimilated, and uplifted by its influence as never before. The Creator is not chary of the gift, and not only the taste but the talent is bestowed with a bountiful hand among our people; and sometimes the backwoods give us specimens of song from native human genius that are as refreshing to our city connoisseurs as the gushing melody of the wild mocking-bird is welcome to ears sated with the trained notes of our canaries. We were at a little amateur concert a few weeks since, where an untutored girl from the country rivaled the pupils of our first masters in her singing, and after once hearing the opera of the *Trovatore* she gave the famous *Miserere* with a pathos and vitality that would have done honor to a practical *prima donna*.

God has been even more bountiful surely in those elements of beauty that minister to the eye; and flowers, that are scattered beneath our feet almost as freely as the grass, are the music of vision, and their notes can be read by every body at sight without any study of the gamut or counterpoint. Yet within the reach of almost all of us as they are, where land is so abundant and the country so accessible, they not only admit of the most careful and skillful culture, but they may be arranged and employed with the highest art. We need not undertake to show that gardening may be raised to a place among the fine arts, but we will affirm, what is far less frequently acknowledged, that the effective disposition of flowers requires a taste decidedly artistic, and even a good bouquet may claim the dignity of being an original composition. There is all the difference between a well and ill arranged nosegay that there is between a piece of manufacture and a work of art; and the eye and hand of art will make every flower and leaf speak its own word and tell upon the general effect, and so secure to the whole arrangement the essential of all beauty, diversity in unity, instead of the set patchwork of the common bouquets of the shops, which look as if they were made by machinery or colored by blocks, like calicoes or floor-cloths.

In one respect flowers are like music: they both speak a language of the heart that is at once personal and universal, or capable of conveying an individual sentiment, and at the same time appealing to a common taste and imagination. A lover can sing a serenade under his lady's window that shall tell her virtually of his love, and at the same time charm every chance listener, and no more obtrude his own personality on the ear than does the light of the moon, which shines on the swain and the passer-by with the same impartial splendor. Quite otherwise would it be if the swain undertook to tell his emotions in prose speech, which, if heard by a stranger, could not but be ridiculous or impertinent. Equally expressive is the language of flowers; and the bouquet that a beauty carries in her hand or wears in her bosom may speak to her of the love or friendship of the giver, and at the same time delight every beholder with its own intrinsic loveliness. This characteristic of flowers fits them especially for the use of religion, as they at once express the private affections of the givers, and enrich the symbolism of the altar. Nothing would be more offensive to a delicate sensibility, for instance, than an inscription of personal feelings or attachments upon the church walls upon festive or solemn occasions, and the common devout conscience would protest against such an obtrusion of private life upon hours of public worship. But the basket or cross of flowers can say all that the heart wishes to say, and say it without any obtrusion or personal feeling. The beauty that speaks for one worshiper speaks also for all, and each rose or lily is like one of those old litanies that come down to us from time immemorial, and are so inimitable alike by being free from all egotism and full of wholesome piety and charity: thus being common prayer to all devout souls. The flowers are of older birth even than those ancient prayers, and are primeval litanies from the creative breath of the Eternal Word.

We find their eloquence growing upon us from year to year, as our charming Easter festival comes round, and enriches our church with gathering remembrances and associations that enlist our household loves and griefs, in the offerings that are brought to us with unstinted hand. Some of the gifts that were lovely of themselves were most impressive in what they suggested. That beautiful cross of lilies upon a shield of green, and surmounted with a crown of camelias, is a fit memorial of Helen who went from us some six years ago, and who has ever since been similarly remembered in our Easter festival. She was a rare woman, with a mingled delicacy and dignity in her face and bearing that made you doubt whether she was born to be a nun or a queen. God took her to himself soon after her marriage. Her family rightly commemorate her thus in the church by whose minister she was baptized and married and buried. The font too, in its wonderful beauty, with profusion of white flowers of rarest kind in its basin, the ivy and roses and carnations that twine the shaft, and the cross of lilies and violets that hangs in front, is a brother's memorial of his sister, and its Easter adorning is in memory of one of Helen's neighbors and friends, a young wife lately called away from the earth. In those compositions on evergreen shields on each side of the pulpit, the designer veiled a personal affection under the garb of a sacred symbol. The anchor of white camelias, with its top in the form of the cross represents *faith* with *hope;* and the heart of red bavardias and carnations that rests upon the centre of the cross symbolizes *charity*, while it also stands for *Cordelia* — a good old name for a daughter, and derived from the Latin for heart, and in this sense undoubtedly it is used by Spenser and Shakspeare, to mark the loving daughter of Lear from her hard-hearted sisters Goneril and Regan. Over the whole parterre that cheered and scented the entire church, personal affections thus mingled with religious sentiment, and a family that had been for years most generous contributors found their gifts this year ministering to their grief, as before to their joy; and the beautiful offerings that so often had come from the cherished wife and daughter's conservatory, threw the fragrance of the garden over the place where the burial service had been said over her remains.

We are well aware that in all matters of sentiment like that which we are treating, there is great danger of falling into sentimentalism, and pampering a morbid and egotistic sensibility that tempts people to dwell upon their own emotions in a kind of self-pity or self-admiration, very much like that of one looking into a glass and enjoying the reflection of a gala dress or a morning costume. We are not fond of sentimentalism, and we believe that one means of curing it is to be found in giving fitting and healthy expression to every genuine feeling. Every form of true affection should have liberty to manifest itself; and sentimentalism ceases the moment the heart, instead of turning in upon itself in morbid introversion, goes forth to its rightful object in the rightful way. Thus marriage is the honest and healthful utterance of love; and the simple, solemn words of the marriage-service adjusts fitly the relation of two beings who else might have gone mad with passion or silly with sentimentalism. Every great affection should also have its wholesome utterance; and undoubtedly a great deal of discomfort and suffering always exist, in a community where material interests are so supreme, or religion is so harsh and dogmatic, as to shut the spiritual world and its people out of our thoughts, or at least out of the commemoration of the church. We do not profess to have sounded the alleged marvels of "Spiritualism," as it is called, to the depths; but we are convinced that most of its power over our people comes from its recognition of the reality of the unseen world and its inhabitants, and of their relation to us. The adherents of this new faith are said to be numbered by thousands, and even millions, and their existence should, if nothing else, teach us that, in this age of natural science and material enterprise, there is a yearning after things unseen — a craving for some comforting fellowship with souls departed this life. We note signs of this disposition in the palaces as well as the common homes of Christendom; and the beautiful volume of Meditations on the Future State, published under the auspices of Queen Victoria, from the German of the genial and devout Henri Zchokke, is one among the many proofs of the tendencies of home affections and griefs to rise above their seclusion into the fellowship of universal truth and devotion. The church is wise that gives voice and nutriment to all the great human experiences and emotions, and has by no means exhausted her arts of giving comfort to the bereaved.

Every great sentiment tends toward some organic method; and thus it is clear that love, patriotism, and devotion all have their characteristic manifestations in the family, the nation and the church. How we are to treat the dead is a question that every year is doing something to settle for us, not only by establishing and adorning cemetries, but creating new forms of memorial art. Tennyson's "In Memoriam" is thus not only a monument of literature, but a sign of the times, and marks a new era in the consecration of memory. The poet finds that the thousands of readers who can not rival his invention can enter into his feeling; and what he writes of Arthur Hallam is read to mean thousands of cherished sons and daughters and friends, whose graves are found in every land the sun shines upon. It is certainly much to be desired that a taste as pure as this poet's should be carried into all forms of memorial art, for there is nothing for which many are so ready to spend time and money, and nothing in which so much time and money are often thrown away. In this country our monumental art has made great advances; yet a man of taste is often tempted to wish, as he walks or rides through our cemeteries, and looks upon the most costly structures, that the sculptor had stayed his chisel, and the bountiful and graceful hand of Nature had been left to make her simple and beautiful memorials in trees and grass and flowers.

We make a great mistake in limiting the bearing of memorial tributes to persons of public service and name; for even these, although they are known widely, are not as deeply loved by the community as by their own kindred, and the affections never ask Fame to tell them whom most to lament. Often the very qualities that most shrink from publicity most win love; and the eulogies paid to our heroes and statesmen and authors are a feeble expression of the debt of the living which is constantly paid to the dead. Probably most men and most families, if called to name the dearest of all names of those no longer seen on earth, would speak some word that has little meaning out of their own home circle; for love, unlike admiration, lives by nearness, not by distance, and asks to tend a flower rather than to adore a star. We confess to sharing the common lot in this respect; and the flowers that we place in the church at Easter tell us more of dear and lowly names in our own home than of the great characters of history. We may be permitted to speak here a word of personal experience, and our humble "In Memoriam" of a gentle, loving, and devoted sister can not but have heart and scope enough to rise above all personality and come home to the household affections of readers.

Why should we middle-aged, hard-working, practical, and sometimes care-worn people be ashamed to confess that we do retain some relics of what usually goes by the name of the heart, and are very often tempted to believe, in spite of all the world's teaching to the contrary, that this organ gains instead of losing vitality, with time, so as to compel us to love and to crave to be loved more instead of less as the shady hours come on, and the evening of life, like the closing day, calls us home and opens to us anew the thoughts, affections, and sociality of the morning? I have ventured to put this question to many shrewd, well-balanced persons, and have generally found the answers all on one side, and that the affirmative side. I once asked a very pleasant little circle of married friends whether they thought they had more or less heart as the years rolled on, and they all said that they lived more and more in the affections; and I am quite sure that the grayheads in the company, both men and women, said so with the most emphasis. It certainly ought to be so;

and as our nature ripens, and our life enriches its experience, and the living and the dead claim a stronger hold upon us, we ought to love more, and of course desire to be more loved. The old home of our childhood comes nearer to us as we climb the hill from which we can see our whole journey hither at a glance; and all new affections touch the old chords afresh, and waken the music of the old voices and the old familiar faces.

These Easter flowers are a kind of color and odor music that revive my play-days, more than twoscore years ago, in that little garden that was the whole world to me then, and the little playmate who was my constant companion. We were left fatherless in early childhood, she being under four years of age, and I but two years older. With our father's death our means were stinted, and we left the more costly central home for the humbler of our two houses in a retired part of the town. Here, however, we had a garden for our play-ground, and a river-side for our rambles, and with these, children can not be wholly unhappy, and can not, though fatherless, be always under a cloud. I remember very well that little garden — its few grape-vines and fruit trees and vegetables, and above all its flowers. They were not the rich blooms of our recent horticulture, and we could not boast of any conservatory for pet plants in winter. The old-fashioned inhabitants of those beds and walks were of a very hardy, democratic race, and the roses and pinks did not scorn to associate with their plainer neighbors, and the sweet herbs, the balm, the sage, and marjoram were the connecting middle class between the flowers and the turnips, and onions and potatoes. The peony was a great favorite because it was so large and so bright to our childish eyes, and because, moreover, it was the first to peep out of the ground and let us know that spring was coming. The lilac, too, was a dear old plant, and its smell now always brings back those days, and the flower itself has more poetry for me than the rarest and costliest of our new exotics. Then, too, that pale yellow flower, that opened at evening before your eyes, sometimes as suddenly as the wings of a butterfly, and exhaled a sweet and powerful fragrance that filled the whole garden, we called it the evening primrose, was much prized, and although not of any great beauty, it was very suggestive, soothing, and dreamy; quite in the tone of the calm, and pensive, and sometimes melancholy hour, when it unfolded its leaves and sent out its odor, as if to serenade us in its own humble little way. All these old favorites the Easter flowers bring to mind, yet only two or three of them keep their place in our day in favor; and the roses, carnations, and geraniums on our altar, were the only flowers that could claim direct kindred with the growths of that old garden in that long since deserted home.

It is well for our children to know how simple were our pleasures in those days, and how little it took to set young hearts beating with glee. Pennies then went as far as dollars do now, and at any time two pennies would bring from the old dame's candy and fruit shop near by enough of her sweet confection, that went by the name of Gibraltar, to make an Eden in that garden, whose two little children had thus early learned that sorrow and death are in the world, and all is not always paradise here now. Then what a different value was once set upon books from what is now set upon them? A shilling would buy a story with a picture or two that was enough to charm the whole year with its pages read time without end. And a two or three shilling book, merciful Heavens, what a godsend! When could we exhaust its riches, or be sufficiently grateful for the treasure? Museum, circus, theatre, and the like were unheard of for years to us; and when, in time, we ventured upon a visit to the neighboring city and saw the snakes, and birds, and beasts, and wax-figures of the museum, and, most marvelous of all, went for the first time to the theatre, and beheld the melodramatic splendors of Timour the Tartar, we had as never since the idea that we had found the world, and our wisdom-teeth were cut. I have never yet got over that play, and am still of the opinion that it is the gteatest of dramas, and am afraid to test my impression by sight.

We grew up, my little sister and I, and had a good education from elder brothers and sisters, who were in the place of parents, and whose care deepened after our mother's death. My little playmate always kept the humility of her character, and sometimes her humility bordered on timidity. Yet, in all matters of positive duty, she was plucky enough; and no storm nor heat, no pleasures nor dangers, could keep her from her post. The lowliest of us all, she rose above us all in the scale of worldly privilege; and the shrinking little girl learned to rule her hundreds of loving pupils by her persistent, judicious kindness, and in time passed from the school-room to a goodly mansion of her own, with all the comforts and kindness that heart should desire. Her garden always smiled under her touch, and she was one of those, like St. Rosa of Lima, who have a charmed hand and eye for flowers. She loved our Easter festival, and when with us on visits she contributed generously to its beauty. To me its coming always brings her near, and these sweet blooms and odors are full of her words and smiles. Since she died, her favorite flowers in her garden and conservatory seem to have something of her life, and to speak of the loving hand that so carefully and wisely tended them. When I look at her pet plants — such as her fine collection of fuschias, which were in bloom when I saw them last — I can almost believe what some theologians teach, that all creation is waiting the hour of deliverance, and plants and animals have a dormant soul, that one day shall show itself and rise into the life of our humanity. It would have been no absurd transition, had those fuschias, with their drooping, pensive heads, passed first into song-birds, then into fawns or antelopes, and then into playful children.

Her death was sudden, but not surprising; and in this, as in all her trials, her gentle spirit proved its strength. On the night before she passed away, when her watchers thought her asleep, she started them by repeating, in a sweet, and clear, and penetrating voice, some exquisite lines that a friend had lately brought from England, and which deserve a place amŏng the permanent treasures of our language:

> "Oh! for the peace that floweth as a river,
>   Making life's desert places bloom and smile;
> Oh! for that faith to grasp the glad Forever,
>   Amid the shadows of earth's Little While!
>
> "A little while to wear the veil of sadness:
>   To toil with weary steps through miry ways;
> Then to pour forth the fragrant oil of gladness,
>   And clasp the girdle round the robe of Praise.
>
> "And He who is Himself the Gift and Giver,
>   The future glory and the present smile,
> With the bright promise of the glad Forever
>   Will light the shadows of earth's Little While."

I arrived in time to see my sister before she died. We spoke cheerfully as well as devoutly together, and remembered the old times, and plays, and talks in the intervals of our Scriptures and prayer. She was the same gentle, lowly, faithful, devoted, loving creature when she was dying as during her whole life, and even the approach of death could not put away from her look and lips the pleasantry that always mingled with her comforting. Her brother repeated to her as she died the ancient communion hymn, "Therefore with angels and archangels, and with all the company in heaven," etc.; and the blessed comforter of so many years, the most angelic spirit that I have ever known on earth, went to fulfil her ministry in brighter worlds. Very sober and prudential people say that her monument tells only the simple truth when it says of her,

> "She kept God's Commandments
> And lived Christ's Beatitudes."

At our Easter festival we usually send to bereaved families some little memorial of those who have gone. Besides the tokens sent to her husband on the Easter after her death, we sent to the Orphan's Home, of which she was the presiding Manager, an illuminated tablet with words of Scripture and a cross of unfading flowers. I saw it there in the parlor last summer, while the orphans were heard singing in their school-room beyond.

Her eldest brother who looked upon her death-bed bore ever after in his look and life the power of the scene. He never afterward spoke with indifference of divine things, and seemed to look to a good angel who called him to her with a sister's deathless love. He was a peculiar man and of talents far greater than were called out in his business life. He united with Franklin's studious thrift the love of nature that he delighted to trace in St. Pierre, and the pleasure in studying animals that he so appreciated in La Fontaine. He was quite a master of French Literature, and in his last days he amused himself, as for years, with his favorite authors. I parted from him a few hours before his death, and our last day together we rode through his favorite old haunts, and saw the fields, hills and waters that he loved; and called at the country home of friends, who gave us flowers that meant for him more than was intended, and bore a presentiment of the last Easter when flowers were placed upon the altar as memorials of his passing away. The eldest and the youngest of our family are now remembered together, the first and the thirteenth children of parents whose twelfth child now pens these words.

I know very well that it is very perilous to indulge in personal griefs and remembrances apart from great principles and associations; and this very peril we would shun by making our home and church life such allies that all our private affections may be consecrated instead of being crushed at the altar. We need a religion as large at least as the human heart; and we protest against that prosy, dry, technical theology that is forever making the sanctuary a battle-ground or a logic-mill, and shutting out the facts and affections of life, the living realities of man and God and heaven. We do not ask for sentimentalism, sensationalism, scenes, or pageants in the sanctuary; and we believe that whatever is against good sense can not help religion. But we do claim that whatever is beautiful, as well as whatever is good and true, belongs to God, and is of the essence of the Christian religion. We are confident that the new age is in some way to restore to the ministry of the beautiful its rightful alliance with goodness and truth, and that we can make no greater mistake than to take it for granted that religion must be of necessity rude and ugly, and leave to superstition and priestcraft the work of illustrating that there is such a thing as the beauty of holiness.

As a nation we are learning to express our public spirit

in beautiful symbols, and our war and our peace have been rich in æsthetic lessons. How much of practical as well as moral beauty was associated with the event that so separated, yet united our war and our peace, the death of Abraham Lincoln. The Nation laid their Easter Flowers on his tomb, and the civil life strangely repeated the lesson of the Church life. I found our good women gathered in tears on that terrible Saturday for the usual task of adorning the sanctuary and doubting, whether to wreathe the roses and lilies, the pinks and geraniums, or to drape the church in mourning. The pastor advised them to follow the wisdom of the gospel and church, and connect their sorrow and their comfort with their Lord's death and rising, and enter more deeply than ever into the true Easter joy, reserving mourning for the coming funeral season. The usual service went on in all its sacred beauty, and central within the chancel under the great cross of white lilies stood a stand of rustic work, twined with rich wreaths and drooping with pendant vines, and bearing a pyramid of white flowers, inlaid with Abraham Lincoln's initials in violets and tipped with the Cape Jasmine, whose rare fragrance was thought to be a good token of the gratitude of Africa, its native soil, to the man who had been under God the African's Emancipator.

We have made great advances in the arts of beautifying our private houses and grounds, but are but beginning to carry the good work into our public life. We are yet to learn that no task is complete, no principle is established, no institution effective until beauty gives the finish and perpetuates the use. What is painted and carved and sung is ever fair and ever young; and the lines of grace are lines of power. The aim should be to make the truths and scenes and characters of religion move in lines of beauty, and so win our private experiences aud personal affections to join in these movements, and so lift our home interests into fellowship with the universal faith and communion. In many ways this good work may go forward; but our present office is not a very ambitious one, and we are only trying to say some of the thoughts that came to us, among the happy children, with the cheerful carols that spoke the great hope, as we looked upon our Easter flowers, and saw Christ's cross and crown set before us in such wealth of bloom and sweetness as to make the very sepulchre a garden, and lift us all up to Him who is the Resurrection and the Life. Every rose and lily, nay, every blade of grass and leaf, means more after the lessons of such a day.

XV.

Toward Sunset.

TOWARD SUNSET.

THOSE of us who live in cities are hardly aware of the changes of the hours as they appear on the dial, and are noted by country people who live in close relation with sunshine. We can readily, indeed, tell what o'clock it is; and the clocks that look upon us, and anon speak to us from so many towers, imply that we have lost the primitive calendar of the hours, and need the cunning hand of art to make up for the loss. In the fields, under the open heavens, among the flowers, and trees, and birds, and beasts, we find constant signals of the passing time; and an expert eye might perhaps tell the hour of the day, not only by the shadows cast by the sun, but by the sights and sounds of the landscape, from the aspect or fragrance of the flowers, or the note of birds and insects, or the turn of the cattle. Each hour has not only its external signs, but also its interior marks, and the mood of the life keeps step with the march of the day. Morning is what it pretends to be in the country, and not a sleepy appendage to the night, as it is apt to be with us in cities. It insists upon opening our eyes, and does not allow us to hide behind brick walls, or forests of chimneys, or close curtains and shutters. It comes upon us in a blaze of glory, and encounters no rivalry from gas-lights in the street or the chamber. Its rays in themselves are highly stimulating, real arrows of Apollo, with points not rusted by city vapors, nor blunted by contact with city brick and stone. The morning light itself in the open country is the best of tonics, and braces the will to its work. Labor begins with its dawning, and continues with its continuance, and closes with its closing. Sunrise and sunset are the natural limits of the farmer's day, and although city habits may urge upon him the need of the ten-hour system with good reason, the result will probably be to deduct the surplus time from the burning mid-day, and to keep the old system of beginning with sunrise and ending with sunset.

The intellectual life in the country shares considerably in the influence of natural conditions. The student there more readily works at his books and pen in the morning, and catches the habit of the early bird. Hard study he does cheerfully before his city friends are stirring, and continues at his task until the sun nears the meridian, and the heat in summer abates his vigor. As evening comes on his mind is moved in a different vein, and tends to such reading and meditation as rather entertains than tasks the faculties, more fond of being the guest than the host, or of yielding to genial companionship than providing for others' nurture by painstaking care. Or, if he is moved to play the host, it is rather to such guests as bring their own welcome than to such as need any anxious attention. We there with him keep open house to the thoughts, fancies, and remembrances that come to us of themselves, and easily make themselves at home. The sunset hour is especially fruitful in such companions, and it is not easy to face the pavilion whose gorgeous curtains are receiving the parting day without feeling our own hearts opening in fellowship to receive and entertain all friends, scenes, and visions that ever passed from our sight.

The old religion made great account of this sunset hour, and the vespers of the ancient church evidently belong to its pensive and solemn inspiration. The vesper hymn ought to be sung while the sun is sinking from sight; and the simple and beautiful prayer of the old English Even Song, beginning, "Lighten our darkness, we beseech thee, O Lord, and by thy great mercy defend us from all perils and dangers of this night!" has great Nature herself for the intoning priest at this mystic time. We, indeed, who live in cities may hardly be able to tell when it is sunset, for we may be wholly in the shadow in our parlor or our pew, while the sunlight may be blazing upon the church-spire or the house-top. In fact, within the city walls the sun rises and sets to most people unannounced, and the day and night fail to utter to our ears their most eloquent speech. We can, indeed, make up for the loss by especial helps of art and companionship. We may have our witching twilight hour of charmed fellowship, and hardly miss the glow of the evening red in the sky, while faces are lit up with hallowed recollections, and friendly eyes shine upon us with the light of other days; or we can rebel against our exile, and, like the Orientals, we can go to the house-top to muse or pray. He is a happy man whose house stands well not only with the social world, where no pests annoy, but also with the elements of nature, so as to give free play to the air and the light. Commend us to a position that allows the evening sunlight to pour into our window, and tell us its witching story of all that we have ever loved, whether lost or kept. We prize a good western exposure more than an eastern, because it is so full of poetry, and because, moreover, we are more sure of being awake to its charms than to the charms of the morning ray. For a man to be sure of seeing the sunset from his own home as long as he lives is happiness rare indeed, and ought to be a great element in his education and comfort. The world in the city is so restless and troubled that we need constant soothing, and if we can not keep a chaplain or poet to cheer or to calm us, we may thus keep the most practiced and efficient of comforters, who has been doing God's blessed work since the first day closed in the bowers of Paradise.

In the city it is not easy, however, to choose our prospect, and a poet or devotee may find himself fixed between inexorable walls that present nothing more varied and animating than rows of windows or stacks of chimneys. In the country we may do very much what we choose with nature, and look to all quarters of the heavens as freely as the weather-cock that follows the veering breezes to all points of the compass. I confess to having paid some attention to the points of the compass in the fitting up as well as the laying out of our small domain; and our little farm makes me fancy sometimes that the whole globe is ours, and north, south, east, and west are waiting our bidding, and a few steps can transport us from the morning land to the evening land, or from the pole to the tropics. The last enlargement of our range of vision is given by clearing up a wild tangle of cat-briar and brush that shut in a charming little grove, which crowns a hillock that looks toward the setting sun. The work was thoroughly done, the ground grubbed and graded to allow sweet honey-suckle and green grass to carpet the earth before covered with weeds. At the foot of the stately cedars the clematis or virgin's bower was freely planted, to furnish an awning fairer than the tent-maker can provide. A belt of evergreens — the Norway spruce, the Scotch fir, and Austrian pine — was set out to encircle the whole as a kind of rural Pantheon. A rustic seat is placed on the tuft of the hillock so as to face the west, and a winding path of some hundred yards connects this pleasant haunt with our cottage. I call the place Sunset, and the seat Vesper Seat. If there seems to be affectation or conceit in this arrangement, so let it be. We all have our hobbies, why should not I have mine? One man fancies horses, another dogs, another yachts, another tends most to wine, or cigars, or to some other or to all forms of dainty living; while the ladies are free to set their affections on all things below, from puppies in pantaloons to poodles in collars, from parrots in caps and curls to parrots in cages. I have a fancy for books and nature, and especially for such combinations of the two as brings the life of literature into play with the life of nature. This pretty evening haunt does this; and all the Muses are generally to be found there about sunset, with their mystic mother Mnemosyne, ready to soothe and cheer you so far as you are willing to open your heart to them at that witching hour. Come and see me sometime, and we will talk over this matter together under influences less prosy than my poor pen can bestow.

But why dwell on individual tastes and especial instances? We all know very well that there is an evening tone that speaks in nature, human life, and in religion. The sounds of nature are then in a sympathetic, plaintive strain, and the minor key prevails in the notes of birds and insects. If there be music in colors, they may be said to speak the same language and sing the same songs with the sparrow, the whippoorwill, and nightingale. Some of the sunset tints are glaring and gorgeous indeed, but the gentler and more pensive shadings prevail, and the violets and kindred hues, that are like the sweet tones of the soprano, are sure to lead on the coming night, and give their pensive cadence to the vesper hymn of nature, as chanted by the notes of her prismatic scale. The rays of the sun themselves seem to have a different quality from that which marks their morning glow. They are less stimulating and more soothing, as if vacated of the electric force that sends them fresh at dawn from Apollo's new-strung bow. We are not sure what the physical fact is, but to us the evening ray has a peculiarly soothing influence, and it seems to stir less the vital powers of plant and animal. It may be, indeed, that the change is in the objects acted upon, not in the agent, and that the weary earth, after yielding for the day to the call of her lord in the sky, no longer heeds the spur as in the morning, and the slanting solar beam abates its noonday directness, and falls upon tired and exhausted nature. The sun himself is apparently never weary and never rests, yet his virtue comes out variously as he is differently touched, and his evening quality to his subjects differs from that of the morning and the noon.

The nervous system of animals and men, and perhaps of plants, if they have any, appear to have its evening mood. It is more sensitive and less active, more ready to be acted upon than to act, more prone to play than work, to muse than to reason. Some of the flowers evidently have their twilight sensibility, and send forth a rare fragrance that made Linnæus call them melancholy flowers. The cattle are in a mild, genial temper, as the poet noted when he said:

"The lowing herd wind slowly o'er the lea."

We of human kind are in the tone of nature, and the more mystical functions of our being come into play. Our senses, sensibilities, thoughts, and fancies seem to move of themselves, and to be possessed by peculiar visitants. The night side of life opens upon us in harmony with the night side of nature. The eye has its visions and the ear its voices without any straining of the powers of attention. The eye, if fixed on vacancy, is not vacant; and the ear, though arrested by no engrossing sound, yet is in a hearing spirit; and the senses wait upon inward powers, ready to serve such spirits as may rise from the deep or come down from the heavens. The memory is wonderfully moved, and opens her great theatre of her own accord, lights her lamps, and passes before us her manifold scenes, and rehearses the life-drama, that she is always working upon and never finishing. She often shows us facts and faces that we had forgotten and could never recall by any act of our own will. This spontaneous function of memory is too little appreciated in our usual estimate of this faculty, and we have absurdly given over to the routine of dunces and book-worms a power that is full of inspiration, and capable of informing past and present with the light of humanity of God. A great artist is this very memory, and in a manner the mother of all arts, reproducing the materials and images of the past with new features, combinations, and powers, and not only recollecting but remembering the rich treasures in her storehouse.

That action or passion of the mind, or both action and passion, that we call Meditation, opens itself to us most readily as the evening draws on, and we find ourselves thinking unawares, and that unconscious movement of the mind from which the best thoughts spring, appears. If we have been thinking all day upon some perplexing subject or knotty problem, without making much progress, we may find, as we sit at sunset, without any effort of forced attention, that the difficulty is cleared away at once, and the subject opens itself to us in full proportion and light. Especially in all subjects of higher interest, or such as call for the affections and fancy, and are capable of inspiration, is this mood of spontaneous meditation effective. Genius — which every soul has undoubtedly to some extent, and enables us all in some way to have inspirations, and to be possessed by superior powers — generally loves the sunset hour, and joins its wizard spell to the witchery of nature. Goethe, as quoted by Eckermann, spoke profoundly of this experience when he said, "Every production of highest art, every significant insight, every invention, every great thought, which bears fruits and has consequences, stands in no man's power, and is raised above all earthly might. Such things man has to regard as unlooked-for gifts from above, as pure children of God, which he is to receive and honor with grateful joy. In such cases man is to be considered as the instrument of a higher Providence — as a fitting vessel for the reception of divine influence."

We believe that we all have something of this receptive power, that is open to Heaven's best gifts. Yet our habits of life and methods of culture make too little of it, and spur us on to too much mere will-work, as if we were forced to do every thing, or almost every thing, for ourselves, and as if God and Nature would do little or nothing for us. It may be that the human will tends westward, and we who live on this side of the Atlantic lack the receptive spirit that so marks the Orientals, and that having all the world before us, a new country to make, we bear ourselves as if nothing were finished and to be enjoyed, and every thing were still to be done. The evening hour, fitly used, helps us correct this folly, and gives us something of the Oriental's quiet contemplation and receptive sentiment. The sunset tells us that the day is done, and the solemn light of history looks upon us from its parting rays, and shows us an image of the great past in this one passing day as emphatically as if it were a thousand years. We find our impatience checked, our feverish haste soothed, as we behold the earth sinking into her repose after toil; and nature, before so anxious and striving, is now peaceful, and moves retrospection instead of care. It is well to keep open soul to this tranquil vision, and let it do as it will with us. We find then that we are prepared to receive that majestic guest, and that we are born of Him who made the universe, and our better acquaintance is constantly bringing out the closeness of the relation. All the senses, especially the master-senses, the eye and ear, unveil their curtains to welcome the visitation. The breeze, the ripple or dash of the waters, the insects, the birds, the cattle, the evening tones of home and village, the shadows of the earth, the colors of the sky, the light of the stars — all touch answering chords within us, and the harmony is greater the less we try to force it, and the more we leave the elements within and without to their own free communion. Each sense is a mystic under such inspiration, and even the palate and the nostrils rise into priestly dignity, as some stray fragrance of a flower seems a delicious dream, and each sip of the cheering cup or taste of luscious fruit interprets the dogma of transubstantiation, and tells us that it is not wholly absurd to believe that matter may rise into spirit, or spirit may descend into matter.

We are yet to learn how great a grace and indeed a virtue is geniality, or openness to all good influences and true fellowship, and that life would not be nearly as poor and hard as it is if we would only take the gifts that God and Nature are so ready to give us. If we were more genial we must be not only more cheerful and calm, but also more earnest and original; and nothing more saddens and impoverishes us than the idea that we must be always exhausting ourselves, and never filling up — always on the go, and never in perfect rest. We are nearly all overworked, and what we call our pleasure is often our hardest work, and keeps us forever on the drive. Society goes with a rush as much as business, and tongues and plates clatter at night after the clink of dollars and the din of hammers cease with the going down of the sun. As soon as day ends we try to quarrel with God's law, and force night into an unnatural day at our presumptuous bidding, reversing instead of perfecting the true economy of the hours. We will not quarrel with art for trying to seize and continue the spell of nature, and prolong the witchery of twilight by music and conversation, paintings and the drama, and the other devices that refresh the genial soul, and entertain without exhausting the waiting intellect, sensibility, and fancy. The longer we live in the great city the more are we convinced that art is one of the most rational and healthful of influences among us, and is doing much to carry out the work of nature, and save us from the follies of artificial society. An evening hour or two in a picture-gallery or at the opera prolongs the charm of sunset, and deepens its delight without of necessity destroying its tranquillity. There is something in all true art that is in the evening tone, and suggests the finished day, and knocks at the door of the genial soul. Each picture or song is, in its way, a rounded whole, and asks to be taken into our hospitality as a ready guest to soothe and cheer, not to fret and fever us. The work of art is of itself something done already, and even a picture of sunrise or the morning chorus of the hunters is a finished composition, and thus bears with it something of the expression of the parting day. But society, as it generally prevails, is unfinished, restless, striving, uncomfortable, and adds the glare and hurry of the morning to the borrowed vexations, the chills and heats, the crowds and blaze of the artificial evening. We would give more for an hour at sunset with a friend or two, under genial sky, than for all the midnight magnificence of our crowded and heated drawing-rooms. It is one of the growing charms of our city life that we are not forced to go far from home to enjoy this solace, and nature is now opening her Eden in the very midst of our rising homes. Our great Park is reclaiming the very hour by many most of all neglected; and the jeweled clasp that binds the mantle of night upon the bosom of day, that sunset hour which is so often lost at the dinner-table or in the after-dinner nap, is becoming a favorite hour with multitudes to revel in the charms of our public gardens, groves, and waters. Art, too, is helping out the spell, and combining her voices and visions with the concerts and galleries of nature. God crown the union until the whole city enjoys the delight, and pleasure rises into refinement, and society becomes a school of education.

We remarked lately in an essay that the Christian church has reversed the order of the natural year, and made the autumn and winter of nature the spring and summer of the soul, beginning her spring-time at Advent, which generally opens with December, and fixing the two great festivals of Christmas and Easter at seasons when among us the earth withholds her bloom. We do not quarrel at this arrangement, and are glad to have the inward life genial as the outward world is cold and dreary. The heart, too, enjoys the contrast, and the Christmas carol and Yule-tide log meet the craving for social joy and godly mirth when snow and ices bind the landscape. It is wise to follow the same principle in the order of the day, and not reverse, but rather interpret and complete the meaning of the hours by a just method. Night is the winter of the day in its darkness and coldness, and we need therefore do what we can to cheer it into a summer of the soul, instead of yielding passively to its humors. Probably, if left to ourselves, we would go to sleep soon after sundown with the beasts and birds; and not so much our individual inclinations as the habits of society keep us awake, and secure to us our round of pleasures and occupations. What we ought to seek in the round of the day, as of the year, is such adaptations as carry out instead of annulling the laws of God and nature. In winter we wisely follow the reaction of the heart from the chill of nature, and try to make life genial and spiritual without vainly forcing the season into an unnatural summer; so we should make the evening social and thoughtful, without trying to bring back the cares and worry and glare of the day. The true evening tone of life is a matter that we are to study as never before — to make it genial without dissipation, intellectual without straining, refining without affectation, and devout without pretention.

It would be well if our higher education as well as our social accomplishments paid more regard to what may be called the evening tone of thought and fellowship. Surely as a people we greatly need geniality; and as we put away convival excesses we ought to cherish the convivial virtues, and have hearty companionship without relying upon the decanter or the beer-mug. Our leading men ought to help us, and we ought to help them to live more at ease and on terms of greater social simplicity, and look upon communion as quite as essential as originality. We ought to be willing to come together more quietly and happily, without demanding the zest of some great excitement or the novelty of some great demonstration, whether of numbers or talent. In our homes, schools, conventions, churches, we should have calm fellowship, allow an hour at least for quiet communion, as under the setting sun or the evening star, and not insist upon being forever under the spur of some peculiar agitation or impassioned appeal, or even original thought. We exhaust ourselves and our leaders by the constant demand for excitement, and err as much as if we insisted that the sun should never set, and life should always be in the noonday blaze.

If we have a brilliant man, we insist upon his always shining, without remembering that his lamp must rest and be filled that it may duly shine, and that even genius keeps its original force only by due fellowship with other minds; and geniality is the receptive side of originality, the mother heart of that masculine head. We ask the day always to continue, the flower always to bloom, the vine always to bear. In fact, there is something tragic in the possession of genius, as of beauty, and they who worship it cruelly insist upon having its light and joy always. Few brilliant men live long and bear constant fruit, partly, perhaps, because such rare gifts are too costly and exhaustive to last long, but frequently because they are not allowed to rest and lie fallow. In no one respect is the prevailing error more conspicuously shown than in our church methods. We generally exhaust or kill our best preachers by insisting that they shall shine always and be one perpetual day. We ask them to shine not a few times in the year, but every week, if not every day; and not once, but twice or three times the same day we exact of them the rare and costly fruits of original thought and composition. Our people do this, not meaning any harm, but ignorant of the first principles of mental economy; and they often quietly set down the original gifts of their minister as part of the fixed social and spiritual capital upon which they and their children are to live and make a figure in this world and in the next. The result is that our ablest preachers die young, or are driven from the pulpit hopeless invalids before the time when men of other professions have matured their gifts and fame. The secret of this appalling fact lies in the exhausting nature of original thinking and composition, and in the incessant call for brilliancy and fire, and the refusal of ample quiet and communion.

The whole country has lately rung with the name of one of our most gifted orators and writers, who died before completing his fortieth year. We will not undertake to fathom the secret purpose of Divine Providence in removing from the world so soon a mind so rare and a temper so genial and fascinating. But it seems to us rather a marvel that he lived so long than that he lives no longer. We hear of monthly, and even perpetual roses, and ever-bearing berries, that keep their promise for a few years during the summer-time; but who has heard of a vine or tree in perpetual bloom, or fruitage without respite? As well ask the vine or apple to put forth fresh leaves and fruit forever, as expect the human brain to be forever originating thought. Starr King died from the effect of disease upon a constitution overwrought by the work of original composition and exciting utterance. In his case this may have been, and probably was, well, for the especial need demanded especial effort, and the pen and voice call for heroes and martyrs as well as the sword. He evidently was aware of the excessive demands made upon his strength in the pulpit, and in the arrangements for his new church in California he expressly guarded against the prevailing error of making the preacher's brain the principal and almost the soul fountain of light and life, and he introduced an order of devotional service that secures communion, instead of depending always upon originality. He read wisely the lesson of the evening hour far away on that pacific shore, and instituted a form of vespers very much upon the idea of the ancient church, with modifications suited to our own age and country. The progress of a similar service among our people so generally is one of the noteworthy signs of the times; and it is a remarkable fact that its calming influence is more craved by the popular taste than the old sensation preaching; and crowds throng to church to hear the old hymn and chants and scriptures, more comforted by the brief exhortation or exposition than by the usual elaborate and lengthy sermon.

Without going into any ecclesiastic antiquities, it might interest readers to know the temper and usage of the ancient church as to the evening hours, and have a glimpse of the forms of devotion and treasures of literature that have gathered around the vésper service. The tone of the service is eminently affectionate and homelike. The Magnificat, or Hymn of Mary of Nazareth, is the favorite melody that has been sung for ages immemorial, even in protestant England, as evening comes on and the lengthening shadows move thoughts of home on earth or heavenward. As the cultus of the Virgin Mother grew into the creed of Christendom the Catholic vespers were more given to Mariolatry, and probably most of the hymns of this class were inspired by the romance of this season. It is hard to believe that this feeling has prompted so much of the lyrical literature of Catholicism. The modern reader is astounded in looking over the grand collection of Latin hymns issued in Germany to find that so many of them are in honor of Mary. Of the three volumes of hymns, the second is wholly filled with lyrics of this class, and is larger than the first volume, that is devoted to the hymns in praise of God and his angels. If there is sad superstition in this, there is also something of our better nature; and we will not wholly scorn the human heart for seeking refuge from a hard and monkish theology at the feet of that lovely vision of faith, the Blessed Mother, who was thought to be first of God's creatures and Queen of Heaven. The new Catholic poet Aubrey de Vere has given new life and beauty to that old faith by presenting it with the refinement and philosophy of the 19th century, and one can admire the poetry of the May carols without accepting the theology.

Even our great iconoclast, Theodore Parker, does not escape this tendency to run for shelter to a divine Mother's arms; and he constantly preached of and prayed to the mother God, whom he regarded as coeternal and coessential with the Eternal Father. To him God was both Mother and Father; and his life would have been longer, and his ministry more edifying, if he had held more of his service in the motherly key, and spared the public much of his self-will and antagonism. He had a kind heart in private relations; but his ministry was not always kind, but struck rudely at the Mother Church, and mother faith and love of the greater part even of tolerant Christians. His voice sometimes, indeed, calls us home to God, but deals more with battle-cries than household words. His divine Mother is presented more as an idea than as a power, and he had little love for the great house, the Church Universal, where maternal love for ages has nursed her children and guarded them from harm, and to which she calls all poor prodigals back as to their native home. He held no evening service generally, and his morning utterances were more frequently a war-cry than a homily, and not even his devout prayer could always secure the hearer's edification. The gentler spirit was in him, and few felt more than he the spell of the evening, or could have given in his better hours a richer book of vesper meditations to the world. He felt the maternal pulses in the heart of nature and humanity, and undoubtedly a considerable part of his evident worry and dissatisfaction with himself came from the conviction that he was often at sword's points with himself; and his sharp invective belied the tenderness of his affections, and his hand brandished the sword and his head planned the campaign, while the dove of peace was nestling in his heart.

The day must come when such unquiet spirits find rest, and cease to make us restless. Why should not the large humanity, and bold convictions, and progressive faith of our advanced thinkers conquer for us and for them a peace, and give us peaceful evening contemplations after their day of toil, and storm, and strife is over? They ought to help us to a home affection deeper and broader than that which seeks the family hearth-stone; they ought to make us feel at home with the master-minds of our race, or domesticate us in the great family of human kind. They should help us, as the day wanes and the night comes, to see in majestic vision the great day's work of the children of God through continuous ages, and hear the ascription that rises from them all as they salute each other before the eternal throne. Something of this great brotherhood we are already feeling, and at twilight not only do the faces of lost kindred and friends come back to us, but the forms of the great thinkers, heroes, and saints, who have made us all brothers, come to mind, and we are no longer alone, but with the great family that the Eternal Father has been gathering together throughout the ages. Every book, picture, wall, garden, house, church, then, has a monumental character, and opens to us the things that have been, and makes the mighty past smile upon us and speak to us as a familiar friend. Looking out from our quiet vesper seat, I see the spire on the western hills, and the stones in the grave-yard near looming up in the evening shadows, and with the setting sun come thoughts of home that do not end with earthly habitations, nor merely dream of some bower of bliss within those gorgeous curtains that veil that pavilion of gold that seems to welcome the vanishing day. It is good at such times to muse and chat, as mind and tongue will have it, and we have taken you, kind reader, into our confidence, and seated you by our side. Good-evening, and then good-night!

THE END.